ADVOCATING FOR THE ENVIRONMENT

Praise for
Advocating for the Environment

"This book arrives at the perfect moment. Many of us, especially those most affected by climate change, feel powerless against big corporations and the government. This inspiring and practical text by Sue Inches shows how ordinary citizens *do* have the power to change the world. In *Advocating for the Environment*, you'll find the courage and the tools you need to join the movement for a clean, healthy, and equitable future."

> —MAY BOEVE, cofounder and executive
> director at 350.org

"Sue Inches is a deep thinker of the best sort. With a wealth of experience in policy, education, and advocacy, she gives terrific advice for all who seek to give voice to nature and inspire both individual and collective action."

> —SETH BERRY, chair of the Energy, Utilities,
> and Technology Committee, House of
> Representatives, Maine Legislature

"This book expands an environmental policy class from theory to action. Drawn from a wealth of practical experience, Sue Inches's insights and advice, from framing a vision to writing a letter to your senator, are credible and valuable to my students. The wisdom in this book is just what student and community advocates need to meet our current environmental challenges."

> —DR. RICHARD PETERSON,
> professor of environmental studies,
> University of New England

"This is that rare book that speaks not only to environment students but to all people who care about their future. At once both holistic and practical, nuanced and vivid, *Advocating for the Environment* gives us the guidance we need to take action for a vibrant and healthy future."

> —GEORGE LAKEY, professor, activist, and
> author of *How We Win*

"Sue Inches turns what could have been a straightforward how-to book into something much more. She crafts a riveting narrative drawing on her personal experiences, tantalizing us with tricks of the trade garnered through a broad and successful career in both the public and private sectors. The reader will finish with a clear understanding of why advocacy matters."

—MARIANNE HILL, senior economist
emerita, Mississippi Research Center

"Demanding change is not enough! We need more effective campaigns, and more organizers, storytellers, and advocates to persuade those with power to do the right thing. Sue Inches breaks down the change process step by step in her book. If you're concerned about the environment and want justice for all, this book will help you craft a winning approach and engage others in making the world a better place."

—MICHAEL BELLIVEAU, founder and
executive director, Defend Our Health

"Sue Inches makes a strong case for grounding advocacy in one's personal experience and describes the importance of understanding the variety of scientific and human factors that will persuade decision makers to act to protect the planet. Her book is a valuable resource for anyone who seeks to influence public policy."

—EVERETT CARSON, chair emeritus of the
Environment and Natural Resources Committee, Senate, Maine Legislature

"Sue Inches has an amazing way of bringing people along the learning curve of effective advocacy. Whether you are a newcomer to environmental advocacy or a longtime advocate like me, there are powerful lessons to be learned from her.

—MAYA K. VAN ROSSUM, founder of the
Green Amendment for the Generations movement, author of *The Green Amendment*, and
leader of the Delaware Riverkeeper Network

We're all in this together!

ADVOCATING FOR THE ENVIRONMENT

How to Gather Your Power and Take Action

Susan B. Inches

SUSAN B. INCHES

Together, we can make the world go 'round!

Onwards —
Andrea
or - Kimmide

North Atlantic Books
Berkeley, California

PLANETEERS of Southern Maine

Published by
North Atlantic Books
Berkeley, California

Cover art © gettyimages.com/keiko takamatsu
Cover design by Rob Johnson
Book design by Happenstance Type-O-Rama

Printed in the United States of America

Advocating for the Environment: How to Gather Your Power and Take Action is sponsored and published by North Atlantic Books, an educational nonprofit based in Berkeley, California, that collaborates with partners to develop cross-cultural perspectives, nurture holistic views of art, science, the humanities, and healing, and seed personal and global transformation by publishing work on the relationship of body, spirit, and nature.

North Atlantic Books' publications are distributed to the US trade and internationally by Penguin Random House Publishers Services. For further information, visit our website at www.northatlanticbooks.com.

Library of Congress Cataloging-in-Publication Data

Names: Inches, Susan B., 1954– author.
Title: Advocating for the environment : how to gather your power and take action / Susan B. Inches.
Description: First. | Berkeley : North Atlantic Books, 2021. | Includes bibliographical references and index.
Identifiers: LCCN 2020052584 (print) | LCCN 2020052585 (ebook) | ISBN 9781623176174 (trade paperback) | ISBN 9781623176181 (ebook)
Subjects: LCSH: Environmental degradation—Prevention. | Environmental protection—Political aspects.
Classification: LCC GE140 .I53 2021 (print) | LCC GE140 (ebook) | DDC 363.7/052—dc23

LC record available at https://lccn.loc.gov/2020052584
LC ebook record available at https://lccn.loc.gov/2020052585

1 2 3 4 5 6 7 8 9 KPC 26 25 24 23 22 21

Author's Note

Every effort has been made to refer to ethnicity, race, and gender in an inclusive and fair way in this book. We have chosen to capitalize the word White when referring to race, in order to avoid framing Whiteness as the standard, and to recognize how Whiteness functions in our institutions and communities. My publisher, North Atlantic Books, also chooses to capitalize the terms Black and Indigenous, as these are used as proper names and not just as adjectives. They are used as ethnicity or nationality markers, signifying identity and importance. Capitalizing the word Black conveys a shared history, identity, and community among people who identify as Black or have African heritage. Capitalizing the word Indigenous references the original inhabitants of a place along with their history and culture.

Contents

Introduction

Imagine how the world would look and feel if we made a healthy, joyous, safe, and equitable planet a reality. Now imagine that it would only take 3.5% of us to bring this about. Research has shown that this can happen.[1] But in order for it to happen, we have to imagine it, we have to feel it, we have to believe it, and we have to take action. That is what this book is about.

Humanity is expanding its understanding of who we are and where we fit with the rest of life on the planet. I'm writing this as we're experiencing the COVID-19 pandemic, a renewed movement to lift up Black lives, a serious economic downturn, and a dangerously warming atmosphere. These events are awakening us to the idea that no one's life, race, gender, country, or occupation is more important than another's, and the earth itself matters. A major shift in consciousness has begun.

Scientific studies show how forests are a single living system with many connected parts. The ocean is also a living system, interacting with the atmosphere and the water cycle to create the weather. We are learning that our bodies are a living system too, composed of microorganisms and human cells that continuously interact. Estimates of the ratio of nonhuman to human cells in our bodies range from 1:1 to 10:1.

Similarly, humanity is a part of a large, interconnected ecosystem. We depend on air, water, and food to survive. Industrialized nations are just beginning to understand the connection between human beliefs, behavior, policies, and practices on the one hand; and our life experience on the other. We are beginning to talk about people as a part of nature instead of the managers of it. As we come to understand our place in a complex natural system, I believe we will choose a sustainable path.

There is also a chance—a smaller chance, I believe—that we will choose a different path, a path where we would be at war over diminishing resources. We would hunker down within our tribes and fight off those who threaten to take our resources away. In this scenario, many more would be without clean air, water, and food. Our health and life expectancy would decline. Fear for survival would reign, and the lives of people, plants, and animals would be in danger. Violence would erupt around the globe. We are seeing signs of this second scenario with the warming atmosphere, acidifying oceans, intensifying storms and fires, concentration of power among a few, and increasing inequality.

My purpose in writing is to illuminate the life-affirming path forward. There's a prophecy in the Bible that says, "I will put my law in their minds and write it in their hearts. I will be their God, and they will be my people. No longer will a man teach his neighbor, or a man his brother, saying know the Lord, because they will all know me, from the least of them to the greatest."[2]

Another way to express this prophecy is to say that there is great wisdom in our hearts, and as we grow and expand, humanity will be able to touch and eventually live from this wisdom. I believe we are at the threshold of the time described by this prophecy, and now have the opportunity to bring it into being.

In order to sustain human life, we have to awaken to the truth of who we really are, and we have to relate to each other and the earth in a more just, loving, and equitable way. We must wake up to the stories we tell ourselves—stories that rationalize policies and behaviors that destroy life. Then we must create and tell new stories that allow our lives to fully bloom and glorify life on earth.

You don't have to agree. In fact, writing this book has been humbling. None of us can see exactly what the future looks like. However, there's one thing I'm absolutely sure of: *If humanity focuses on a vision of the world as we truly want it, our chances of getting there are greatly enhanced.*

This book focuses on advocacy, which is defined as asking decision makers—corporate CEOs, politicians, and community leaders—to do what you want them to do. The main focus of the book is on shifting power from the elite to the people, and how to do that. It shows how to work with stakeholders and decision makers to plot a course for positive social change.

This book also touches on direct action, which is political action outside the policy-making process. It shows how direct action can be effectively used to wake people up and demand change. Direct action and advocacy can (and should) work together to achieve a new vision for life on the planet.

If the last several paragraphs seemed lofty to you, do not despair. In order to meet the challenges of climate change, inequality, and a poisoned planet, we need everyone. Actions as small as bringing cloth shopping bags to the store count. So does an email to your city councilor or state legislator. Small actions can connect you to a sense of hope and purpose, a first step for every advocate. I urge you to begin right where you are.

The shift we need to make is not about giving things up. It is about expanding our concept of love. If we are living a life founded on *love, purpose, and community,* our need to despoil the planet, consume more and more, and extract resources without giving back will subside.

If we want to leave a positive, healthy, and joyful future for our children and grandchildren, we must change our thinking and act differently, beginning now. The situation is urgent. Science tells us we have until 2030 to reduce our carbon emissions before the warming atmosphere plays havoc with our weather and increases extinctions, fires, drought, floods, and famine.

Before taking action, it helps to be clear on what we are trying to do. That's why part I of this book is titled "Learn to Think Differently." It describes the profound shift in consciousness that is a prerequisite to affirming and sustaining life on the planet. If you're interested in the mental models that undergird environmental advocacy, part I is for you.

Chapter 1 shows how to connect with the personal power that is deep within you. Your personal experience and story can touch the most jaded decision makers and stand out like a shining star among highly paid lobbyists. Citizens, students, and community organizers have great power to change things, and this book shows how.

Chapter 2 explains advocacy and shows the many different ways ordinary people can make a difference. It describes the range of actions citizens can take, from short and simple actions to complex campaigns and litigation.

Chapter 3 examines the beliefs we hold—our "earth stories"—both conscious and unconscious. Our underlying stories will hold us back or propel us forward, depending on what we accept as "reality." This chapter shows how questioning and challenging assumptions, beliefs, and stories is the first step toward social change.

Chapters 4 and 5 build on chapter 3 and describe some of the specific constellations of beliefs that hold us back. The opposing worldviews of the left and the right keep us politically stuck at a time when we need policies that protect and support human progress and the natural environment. These chapters show how to bridge these differences.

Chapter 6 is about vision. It's based on the fact that in order to create a changed world, we must first be able to envision it. A positive vision is especially important in sustaining us through troubled times. This chapter shows how we can move from a place of despair to a place of vision and hope.

Part II of this book, titled "Gather Your Power and Take Action," is focused on the practical skills and tools needed to advocate with impact. Part II is all about action. If you are one of those people who acts first and reflects later, part II is where you should start. It shows how to research and analyze your issue, work with those who are for and against your cause, and understand and influence decision makers. The how-tos of organizing a coalition and developing a strategy are here. Although every issue has its own set of variables, the ideas presented in this part can be applied to most any issue.

Chapters 7, 8, 9, and 10 give a candid, inside look at power, strategy, and working with decision makers, based on my personal experience.

Later chapters in part II provide guidance on how to communicate. These chapters cover framing your issue, working with the media, and writing impactful letters to the editor, emails, press releases, and legislative testimony. Real examples that you can use as templates are provided in the text and in the appendices.

The final chapter sketches out my vision for the planet and gives eight specific reasons to be optimistic. If you need inspiration, I suggest you skip to the back of the book and read the last chapter first.

The laboratory for my experiments in advocacy has been the state of Maine, where I've been an environmental advocate and organizer for many years, including fourteen years serving at the senior level in state government. The principles and methods I describe can be applied in any town, city, county, or state in the country. The opportunities to participate in change are numerous and occur at every level!

In order to realize a new, healthy vision for humanity and the earth, your help is needed. During the Second World War, every person in the United States worked in some way to support the war effort. Grandmothers rolled bandages and wrote Christmas cards to soldiers. Young men served in the military, and young women took jobs to keep the economy running. The spirit, commitment, and productive output that won that war was tremendous—unlike anything we had done before. It showed that Americans are capable of great things.

The movement to achieve drawdown, where we stop global warming and reach a point where carbon emissions are declining, could be similar. If a majority is committed and makes a contribution, we can have a healthy planet. Whether it's recycling at home or making national policy, it counts.

Small groups tackling environmental issues are springing up around the country. They are building solar farms, starting community gardens, recycling waste, enacting sustainable land-use ordinances, addressing sea-level rise, holding corporations accountable, and banning toxins. I invite you to join in! Try starting with one thing, and see where it leads. Whether you are a seasoned advocate or just beginning, I wish you good luck, and I offer this book as a field guide to help you on your way.

PART I

LEARN TO
THINK DIFFERENTLY

1

What's Your Advocacy Story?

The most powerful form of influence is always personal.

—ANNETTE SIMMONS, *The Story Factor*

What's Your Story?

Advocacy starts with your story. Your story, my story, and everyone else's stories add up to the Big Story we are telling ourselves about the earth. Over time, our collective stories will guide us to sustainable prosperity and well-being, or to total destruction. But let's not get ahead of ourselves. Let's start with *your* personal story about the earth *you* live on.

What events have touched your heart? Was it a brilliant sunset over the ocean? The birth of an animal or child? Do you have a favorite place outdoors? Where do you spend your free time? Is there a place in nature where you go to connect with your soul? Have you felt the loss of a favorite place? Or the loss of something you loved to do, like swimming in a lake that's now too polluted for swimming, or the loss of something that sustained you, like fishing for a living? Your personal story about connecting with the earth—whether that story is about love or loss—is the starting place for advocacy.

You may think stories are too touchy-feely, less important than facts, or weaker than your carefully crafted argument about your issue. This chapter will show you the opposite is true. It will show you how a well-crafted story is one of the most powerful tools in the advocate's toolbox. Let's start with my story:

There was a sixty-acre farm in back of my house where I loved to play as a child. There were woods filled with giant oaks, fields of hay, and a tiny pond with a stream that ran in at one end and out the other. We named the stream Rushing Water Brook and made T-shirts with the name written on them with Magic Markers. It was a child's paradise. My best friend, Faith, and I played there every afternoon after school.

One day when I was about ten, Faith and I went out to play and found the once-clear stream had turned a menacing shade of opaque, milky orange. You could no longer see the bottom of the foot-deep stream. The pond had a plume of ugly orange where the stream flowed in. Just up the hill from the pond was a construction site. An enormous six-story building was being constructed on one of the farm fields, and the stream was polluted by the construction.

My friend and I felt betrayal, anger, and sadness. We were horrified! How could the grown-ups do something so destructive? Would there be any fish left in our little pond this summer? Would everything we loved about our playing place be destroyed? We were scared and outraged. We told our parents. They gave no answers.

And it just got worse. The pond we loved was turned into a swimming pool with a bright turquoise bottom. The stream was bulldozed into an unnatural ditch beside the pool. The frogs we used to scare disappeared. We stopped playing there.

This experience left me with an indelible memory and a powerful story about the careless pursuit of human goals. It stole my innocence. I'd seen firsthand how carelessness can kill wildlife and exterminate the beauty and bounty of nature. In my parents' lack of response, I could also see that people allowed this without fighting back.

What is your story? How might it connect with your views of the earth today? Your authentic story that shares the details of your human experience—complete with feelings, thoughts, sights, sounds, and dialogue—can touch the heart of a decision maker and be a powerful influence.

I teach college courses in environmental advocacy. At the beginning of each course, I ask students to write a love letter to the earth. You might try this yourself. I ask them to go to a natural area and take off their shoes, turn off all electronic devices, and listen. I ask them to listen for what is near and what is far, and try to describe what they hear in words. I ask them to breathe deeply and focus on what they smell. I ask them to touch the trunk of a tree and the grass under their feet, and then to describe what touching a living thing feels like and what thoughts this brings to mind. I'll ask if they heard any messages from the earth.

Your advocacy is rooted in your relationship with the earth. If you're not sure what that is, a good place to start is by going outdoors and asking the earth to tell you.

The Power of Story

Personal stories are particularly important when confronting people who do not share your beliefs. A person may believe that poor people are poor because they are not working hard enough, for example. A personal story told by a single mother who works three jobs in order to feed her children is a powerful way to cut through a belief that all poor people are lazy.

A multinational corporation owns the electric power company in my area. They installed new billing software, and immediately monthly electric bills for some customers increased by 100%, 200%, and in some cases 1,000%. People called to complain, but neither company managers nor government regulators did much. It wasn't until public hearings were held and people told personal stories of electric bills increasing overnight from $150 a month to $1,500 a month that a response began. People told stories of having to close their businesses, or not refill a prescription, on account of the high electricity rates. Real people with real stories made the problem tangible and opened the way to solutions.

What about the Facts?

People have a hard time relating to facts because they are hard to put into a meaningful context. What does a one-degree increase in our atmosphere's temperature actually mean? If four hundred species become extinct this year, what does that mean? How many species usually go extinct in a year? Should we be worried? Facts by themselves, without stories or narratives to illuminate them, have little meaning. People tend to interpret facts to fit their existing story, values, or view of the world. This means that even clearly presented facts may be ignored or denied, if they don't fit with a person's beliefs.

A good example is recent scientific research showing that codfish stocks off the US East Coast were in serious decline. Federal scientists reported their findings, based on numerous fish samples taken along the coast from New York to Canada. Despite the decline, a robust school of cod still existed just offshore from Gloucester, Massachusetts. Gloucester fishermen, seeing the abundance nearby, denied the science. "There are plenty of fish, we see them and catch them every day," they said, based on their experience. Because of their experience, they continued to deny the science and vote against fishing regulations. In a few years' time, the entire cod population was reduced to very low numbers, and commercial fishing was severely limited.

Environmental advocates need to use facts as an important tool in their toolbox. I highly recommend using facts strategically, to support a story or narrative. But people will believe what they see and experience rather than facts, as in the above example.

Stories, in contrast, take problems out of the conceptual realm and into a human reality that people can relate to. It is hard to argue against a well-articulated story of human experience. Stories that anchor complex issues in the lives of individuals are more likely than facts to change public policy. Even the best factual arguments can rarely stand on their own.

People relate to stories—both the storytellers and the characters in a story—in a variety of ways. People might connect with a storyteller's physical appearance, accent, social identity, geographic location, or life experience. Have you ever met a stranger and found a way to connect through the place or activity at hand? It could be that you both enjoy the same music, TV shows, or craft beer. It could be that you both love vacationing in the same area or that you have children of the same age or a similar breed of dog. This is how people get to know each other and build trust: through finding a common experience.

The same is true in advocacy. If you can find a shared experience related to the change you want to make, it can be powerful. The electric rate payers in the example above shared their experiences and created a coalition that is suing the power company to compensate them for damage caused by the faulty billing system.

Climate change is a topic where stories are especially important. Climate change and its causes are abstract concepts. The effects of climate change are different, depending on where you live. People who are not experiencing direct effects, or who don't understand connections such as how warming oceans can cause increased storms, may deny climate change based on their experience or understanding. The Gloucester fishermen provide a clear example of how personal experience informs political views.

Your "Who Are You and Why Are You Here?" Story

One of the most important stories used in advocacy is what I call your "Who Are You and Why Are You Here?" story. All public testimony starts with this. Incidentally, most job interviews start with this, too. After all, you are advocating for yourself in a job interview.

Your "Who Are You and Why Are You Here?" story should be clearly and firmly in your mind when doing advocacy work—whether advocating for yourself in a job interview, advocating to stop a harmful development, or advocating for some other cause you support.

As an advocate, you might find yourself testifying (in person or in writing) before a planning board, city council, legislative committee, or public utilities commission. If you are testifying before a governing body, your testimony is part of the public record. The minimum required "Who Are You and Why Are You Here?" story for the public record is your name, who you represent, and whether you support or oppose the issue at hand.

But your "Who Are You and Why Are You Here?" story can be much more than that. It can describe your personal connection to the issue and go into detail about why you care about it. It can describe personal experiences you've had related to the issue. Your "Who Are You and Why Are You Here?" story can be a powerful tool that connects decision makers to the heart and human side of the issue being discussed. Here's an example of a public testimony that used the "Who Are You and Why Are You Here?" story in a powerful way:

TESTIMONY OF SETH YENTES

Senators and Representatives of the
Energy, Utilities, and Technology Committee:

My name is Seth Yentes and I am here in strong support of LD 1646, An Act to Restore Local Ownership and Control of Maine's Power Delivery Systems.

I live in Monroe, a small, rural town in Waldo County, with fewer than nine hundred residents. I am a farmer, volunteer firefighter, chair of the planning board, and a father.

With deep roots in my community, I see the hardships and successes of rural Maine. I have talked to many neighbors and friends that are completely fed up with CMP [the electric power company]. Their poor billing systems, losing power after storms, and lack of support for residential solar installation has made it clear that they don't care about Maine people. CMP is a foreign corporation that prioritizes its shareholders and profits.

As a small-business owner, I know the effects that losing electricity has. A couple years back we were in the midst of our busiest season on the farm. In late October, we lost power for three days. We were milking cows, trying to keep the water pump running, keeping our milk tank cool, digging nursery trees to bring to our wholesale buyers, and cleaning up fallen trees on the town roads. Our generator fried over five hundred dollars' worth of electric controls. Now, I know that there are always going to be power outages, but I believe that more could have been done. If we had a consumer-owned grid run by Mainers, we would know that all the money going to pay for electricity would be going back into our infrastructure. We would know that we were not paying some shareholder's dividends. We would know that Mainers come first.

This is a bipartisan issue. We all use electricity. We all want a reliable grid. This bill will save Maine people and businesses money and in turn strengthen our economy.

Thank you.

Messengers and Their Stories

The most effective advocates are credible messengers, like the farmer who wrote the testimony above. They are authentic and believable. Imagine a public hearing in front of a state legislative committee. There are thirteen legislators seated behind a long wooden table listening to perhaps the fourth or fifth issue to come up that day. There will be lobbyists there wearing expensive suits, pricey watches, and cologne. There will also be citizen activists dressed casually, in a clean T-shirt and jeans or maybe a pair of work pants. The decision makers know who the lobbyists are and who the citizen activists are—not just by their clothes, but by what they have to say. Whether you're a citizen or paid lobbyist, *your power is in the authenticity of your story.* Chances are, the legislators will be more interested in your story than in what's said by the professional lobbyists, whose opinions they probably know in advance.

When I was working for Maine's fisheries, I provided fisheries data to decision makers. For instance, I once had a professional survey done for one of our fishing industries. As a result of the survey I could say how many fishing families had health insurance and how many did not. I could say how many fished part time and how many fished full time. This was my role as a government advocate: to provide important facts upon which good public policy could be based.

But I could not effectively substitute or stand in for the fishermen who came to testify about their personal experience in the industry. A fisherman might say that the rising price of diesel fuel was impacting his ability to make ends meet. Or he might say that his son had a lifelong dream to fish but was denied a license because of the limited number of permits being issued. This was powerful testimony that I could not credibly provide.

Good advocates are usually good organizers. They find people who can present firsthand stories to decision makers on their issue. The farmer who testified above might have been invited to the hearing by an advocate or organizer. Anyone can attend and testify at a public meeting or hearing. But it can strengthen your case if you organize and invite people with authentic and relevant experience to come and tell their stories.

One recent example of the effective use of this tactic was when our state considered a proposal to establish the Maine Climate Council. Environmental advocates lined up farmers, fishermen, and owners of small businesses to give testimony to a legislative committee about how their businesses could benefit from renewable energy. Industrial energy users presented their concerns. Expert analysts presented data on the impacts of the proposal. Ultimately, more than ninety individuals and organizations testified on this issue. The Climate Council was established, in part due to advocates organizing to bring credible messengers to speak to decision makers.

Stories That Overwhelm

Sometimes an issue becomes so large and overwhelming that people lose their ability to focus on it or empathize with the people involved. The exodus from Syria a few years ago, which involved thousands of people fleeing that country to escape civil war, illustrates this. TV news reported on the Syrian crisis daily. After a while it became too much to bear. My own thoughts went like this: *It's terrible, we know about it, we can't do much about it. I need to get on with my day.*

Then one day a four-year-old boy's body washed up on a sandy shore. He'd been in a boat trying to cross the Mediterranean. A photo showed the boy's fully clothed body face down on the sand. The visual image was powerful: an innocent child dead as a result of politics and war. We often need to relate to an individual in order to awaken from our numbness. Following the published photo of the boy, donations poured in to help the Syrians.

Climate change and environmental degradation are such large, global issues that it's easy to become numb to them. Photos of polar bears with ice melting around them or movies about great coral reefs bleaching and dying are important, but they can seem abstract and overwhelming. Many of the decisions made about these issues seem far away, in a government chamber or corporate boardroom somewhere. It's hard to connect distant, dying coral reefs to specific actions we might take at home. This can make us feel powerless. Then we become numb to the issue.

A common activity where I live is community movie nights (both virtual and live) where a hard-hitting documentary about climate change or environmental degradation is shown. While these films can be a wake-up call, they can also have the opposite of the intended effect: people can end up thinking the situation is hopeless and there's little they can do about it.

A more effective approach is to offer solutions—things people can do that will make a difference. *Chasing Coral,* a documentary about the Great Barrier Reef in the Pacific Ocean, features a young photographer on assignment to capture time-lapse images of the bleaching and dying reef. Seeing the catastrophe through his eyes humanizes the story and allows us to feel grief along with him. The movie concludes with this photographer speaking to large audiences and teaching children about climate change and the ocean. This approach connects us personally with the reef and shows what we might do to help.

I try to leave people feeling energized when I lecture or teach. I make an effort to present materials showing people making a positive difference in their communities and providing ways for people to make a positive contribution. This helps inspire people to take action, instead of becoming overwhelmed. I recommend you do this, too.

The 80-10-10 Rule

Where is the balance between fighting what is wrong and working to create a more compassionate and healthy world? I have many friends and colleagues, plus the media, who want to talk about problems all the time. Problem-talk all the time can be exhausting! At the outset of the coronavirus pandemic in early 2020, it was hard to find news about much else. This much negativity can put a dent in my resolve to stay positive and focused on the insights I can bring to the world. I imagine it works this way for you, too.

As you know from the introduction to this book, I'm a proponent of focusing on solutions and creating a world that is kind, compassionate, and healthy for all life. But I also know we can't totally ignore the problems we face.

Sherri Mitchell (Penobscot), an Indigenous rights attorney, author, and activist, uses what she calls the 80-10-10 rule. It goes like this: Spend 10% of your time looking at what needs to be changed. Spend 10% of your time repairing the damage done. Spend 80% of your time working to create the world you want, one that offers "compassion, safety, equality, justice and sustainability for all life," she says. I think Mitchell has it right. Working to implement a vision you care about summons new energy, instead of draining you. Spending 80% of your time on creating the world you want also gives you the energy you need to work on the injustices and repair the harm done.[1]

The size of your issue matters, too. You can't create the entire world you want in just one lifetime. In a later chapter, we'll talk about how to define the scope of your advocacy work so you can have an impact and make tangible progress. Making a difference—working on creating the world you want—is energizing!

The Most Powerful Form of Influence

Trust in governments at all levels is very low. This is particularly true in settings where public decisions are being discussed. Decision makers are on guard in these situations and are looking for the motive behind your words. They know you are there to try to influence them. They are wary of being manipulated.

An authentic, true story that shares the details of a real human experience—complete with feelings, thoughts, sights, sounds, and dialogue—can cut through the wariness of your listeners. By telling a good story, you can build a human connection and touch the heart of even the most hard-hearted politician.

Everyone, including politicians and CEOs, wants to feel that they are a good person, doing the right thing. Your job as a storyteller/advocate is to create a scenario where the decision makers can relate to your point of view, integrate the facts to support it, and be persuaded that by supporting your view, they are doing the right thing.

Authenticity is key. You need to be who you are, grounded in your personal story. Twisting facts, lying, or directly challenging your listeners' values is the kiss of death, because it can permanently destroy their trust in what you have to say. But if you are well prepared and authentic, your personal story will have power and influence.

As an advocate, you need to think about how you can keep your issue fresh and alive as you work for change. Personal stories and visual images, like the photo of the Syrian boy, can do this. Being a messenger yourself and telling a compelling "Who Are You and Why Are You Here?" story can make an issue come alive.

You are more powerful than you think. Your story and the stories of others who support what you want can shift the energy of a discussion, change the decision on the table, and bring forward a different way of being.

The West End Revitalization Association (WERA) is a community development corporation in Mebane, North Carolina. When the state secretary of transportation came to town to promote the construction of a four-lane highway that would pass through two low-income majority-Black neighborhoods, the residents spoke up. They organized and presented concerns to the city council. They formed the WERA, and they applied for and received a grant to hire an executive director. Next they filed complaints with the Civil Rights Office of the Federal Highway Administration, and then they filed a complaint with the US Department of Justice for violation of the Civil Rights Act. Through these actions they were able to stop the highway project from destroying seventy-seven houses, several churches, and a Masonic temple. The WERA is alive and well today, providing affordable housing, assuring safe water and sewer services, and working on community-based environmental protection.[2]

The earth needs you to advocate for the health and safety of every living thing—plants, animals, air, water, and people. You could plant trees in your neighborhood. You could write an email to your congressperson about an issue you care about. You could organize a group to protest a harmful development, like they did in Mebane. Or you could join a larger group or movement, following the lead of those who are most impacted by climate change or harmful development. Opportunities to advocate for a better world are right in front of you. All you need to do is act. And that begins with telling your story.

2

What Advocates Do

*Slowing the rapid warming of the planet will require a
unified global effort.*

—AL GORE

Who Decides?

I was sitting nervously at a large wooden conference table. It was my first
day of work at Maine's Department of Marine Resources, and I was having
my first one-on-one meeting with my new boss. He opened the meeting
by saying, "The first thing you need to know is there are federal fish and
there are state fish."

This sounded like a joke, so I quipped, "Do the fish know that?" But
my boss was getting at a fundamental concept of advocacy: who decides?

The word "jurisdiction" literally means "that which you have a legal say over."
In other words, jurisdiction is the extent of an entity's or person's decision-
making authority. In US fisheries, coastal states have authority over waters
extending from the shore to three miles offshore. The federal government has

authority over waters from three miles to two hundred miles offshore. This is important to know if you are working in fisheries. No matter what issue you are working on, you need to know the answer to the question: who decides?

Advocacy, at its root, is asking those in authority to do what you want them to do. Do you want the parking on your street changed? You would ask your city or town council to change it. Do you want to renegotiate your mortgage interest rate? You would ask your banker to do that. Do you want the air to be cleaner? You would ask your elected officials to pass an ordinance or a law to do that. To be an effective advocate, you need to clearly understand who has the authority to do what you are asking them to do. Simple. Except when it's not.

A group in Maine wanted the electric power company to purchase more solar energy. They planned a sit-in at the Central Maine Power (CMP) state headquarters. But CMP is owned by Avangrid, based in Connecticut. And Avangrid is owned by Iberdrola, a conglomerate based in Spain. And Iberdrola is publicly owned by shareholders from all over the world. A state agency, the Public Utilities Commission, regulates how much solar power the electric company is required to buy. Hmmm. Where is the decision made? Who decides? Does it make sense to pressure the company's state office? The regional office? Shareholders? State regulators? Research is required to answer these questions. Better to do the research first than to spend time sitting in the wrong office.

Some of my college students wanted the state to divest its funds from fossil fuel investments. They wanted to present their request to a state legislative committee. I asked them, "Can a legislative committee tell investors how to invest?" They hesitated, confused. I explained, "The authority for making investment decisions lies with the state pension fund or the university Board of Trustees, depending on which bucket of funds you want to divest." Once the students understood this, they decided to start with asking their college's Board of Trustees to divest the college endowment fund from fossil fuels. Once this was clear, they knew exactly who to approach. They knew the answer to the question: who decides?

Decision Makers Need You

Have you ever felt discouraged about politics? Thought your vote doesn't count? Or maybe you're sick of nonstop negative news stories, and you feel there's little you can do to create the changes you want. Many of us, including myself, have felt this way.

But consider this: *politicians and decision makers need you.* Without your support, decision makers can't take a stand for change. Think about it: no one is going to step up and advocate for change without a base of support. Nor will they act on issues they haven't heard of, don't understand, or don't think have a chance of moving forward. On the other hand, if a decision maker sees a well-organized and informed group that's willing to advocate publicly, this gives them cover and support.

Trust in the federal government has been at an all-time low in recent years. It takes a great deal of money to win elections. Elected officials must campaign continuously and weigh every decision against its potential effect on the next election. They need to keep large donors happy can make it difficult to take a moral stand. There are other factors that have eroded trust, like the fact that Congress is allowed to attach unrelated items to bills. This creates conflicts in which a congressperson may support one part of a bill and oppose another part. Because of this, no matter how they vote, some constituents will feel betrayed. The senate majority leader has the power to decide which bills will reach the floor. If your bill is not supported by this one person, it has little to no chance of getting heard. Then there is the filibuster, a procedure to delay or block legislation. Sixty votes in the Senate are needed to end the filibuster, resulting in most major legislation needing a super majority of sixty votes to pass. Because of the difficulties with congressional rules and politics, it's often a better bet for environmental advocates to work with state, city, or other local decision makers.

Many town, city, and county politicians serve without pay. In my state, legislators receive a small stipend—about enough to cover their gas mileage. In more populated states, legislators do make a salary, but the vast majority of local and regional politicians do not. So why would they serve?

Usually it's because they want to serve the people, and they want to make a difference. This is especially true in city, county, and state governments. Politicians generally want to do good and want to be perceived as supporting the people they represent. You can help them achieve this.

You're More Powerful Than You Think

Americans feel less control over their lives than ever before. Fear reigns. We fear gun violence. Massive storms and floods. Wildfires. Political turmoil in Washington. Pandemics. Discrimination. *The Week,* a national news magazine, carries a regular column called "Health Care Scare of the Week." It's one small example of how the media promotes fear.

On top of this is the ever-growing concentration of wealth. Your income level has tremendous implications for your health, the future prospects of your children, and your life expectancy. As wealth concentrates in the hands of a few, others are falling behind. Politics seems rigged, and to a large extent it is. Wealthy elites fund the candidates and lobbyists who represent their views. Daily news stories reinforce our fears and sense of inequality. This tends to disempower people. Many feel they don't have a voice.

But remember, decision makers—especially those at the local, regional, and state levels—need you in order to do their job. Many Maine lawmakers have told me that a total of *ten personal emails or phone calls* is all they need to persuade them that an issue is important. In a large city or state, thirty to fifty emails or calls will be needed to have a similar influence.

Imagine if these same legislators were to get twenty to fifty calls every week for a month! This would be a groundswell of support or opposition. Now imagine if a small group got together, did a little research, and presented their legislator with an idea that *solved a problem,* in addition to letting them know that the problem existed. If you do this, it's a gift to a decision maker. And you can make this kind of gift even if you don't have a penny to spare.

If all you can do is send an email to your town or city council saying you want your road cleaned up, you will make a difference. If you get three neighbors to join you on your email or letter, even better. Or if you ask your city council to implement a citywide cleanup, you'll make an even bigger difference. You're more powerful than you think.

Three Ways to Get Involved

There are three ways to work for change, all of which provide avenues for student and community advocates to get involved. One is to organize locally or regionally on issues that directly affect you and your community. You might initiate an action yourself or join a group that is working on an issue you care about.

A second way is to work with a nonprofit advocacy organization that works on local, regional, state, or national issues. Advocacy groups work on a host of environmental issues, such as combating climate change, opposing harmful developments, and cleaning up toxic pollution. These organizations have paid staff, but they depend on volunteers to be effective. Volunteers support campaigns organized by nonprofit leaders with their personal experiences, connections, and stories. Volunteers also provide hours of labor getting the word out, recruiting other volunteers, speaking with decision makers, and so on.

A third way to work for change is to join a campaign or movement where you may not be directly affected, but you want to provide support to those who are. White people who march in support of the Black Lives Matter movement are an example. The appropriate leaders of this movement are those who come from frontline communities that are deeply and directly affected by the issues they are protesting. They are the ones who should lead. But when other individuals or groups join them in support, that sends a powerful message.

The Importance of Grassroots Participation

Research has proven that winning movements are fueled by local grassroots action. Author Leslie Crutchfield wrote a well-researched book titled *How Change Happens: Why Some Social Movements Succeed While Others Don't,* in which she found that seeding and growing networks of citizen activists was a critical factor in every successful movement she studied. She cites the National Rifle Association's success in blocking gun control legislation as the direct result of passionate and active local groups. Each time a local gun control or gun safety proposal comes up, local activists immediately contact their decision makers and persuade them to vote it down. Local gun ownership groups are organized and ready to respond. Gun safety groups have not yet matched the scale and intensity of the local gun ownership groups. Gun safety will not prevail until stronger local activist networks are in place.

Imagine if the same local intensity could be organized for addressing climate change, toxic pollution, or confronting the fossil fuel industry. The success of local advocates in other movements should give hope to concerned citizens who are meeting about climate change in virtual and actual living rooms across the country. The active support and responsiveness of multiple local groups is needed to solve our environmental problems.

Your Participation Is Urgently Needed

Scientists have given us until 2030 to reduce climate emissions by half and until 2050 to achieve net zero emissions. If we don't do this, we will face catastrophic changes: ecosystem collapse, famine, permanent flooding of coastal cities, mass extinctions, collapse of the food supply from drought, and more.

It's urgent that each and every one of us figure out a way to be an advocate for change. Fortunately, there are as many ways to advocate as there are people. You can find a way to address climate change and environmental degradation that fits for you. You can take individual action, you can organize or join a local group or campaign, or you can join a larger campaign or movement led by those who are most impacted. The rest of this chapter outlines the different categories of activity that fall under the "advocacy" umbrella. From this, I hope you will find your own advocacy path.

Advocacy and Lobbying:
What You Can and Cannot Do

Advocacy is defined as any action that speaks in favor of, recommends, argues, supports, or defends a cause. Advocacy can also mean to plead on behalf of others. The purpose of advocacy is to bring about change. Advocacy is usually thought of as working within the system for change. Things advocates do include:

Talking with and persuading decision makers	Reporting on findings
	Generating publicity
Fact and story finding	Organizing
Educating	Campaigning
Writing	Negotiating
Speaking	Litigating
Researching an issue	Lobbying

Lobbying is just one of the things advocates do (other activities on the above list are addressed later in this book). Traditionally, lobbyists waited outside the legislative chambers in the lobby and approached legislators as they exited the chamber. This is the origin of the verb "to lobby."

When I'm lobbying, I wait in the State House lobby, and when the legislator I need to speak with appears, I take one step forward and say, "Can I have a word with you?" A legislator might say, "Yes, how can I help?" or they might say, "Can you call me later?" It would be very unusual for them to look away and not make personal contact. But occasionally this happens.

This is how lobbying is done today in Maine. In other places, security may not allow you to stand outside legislative chambers. Following the 9/11 attacks, most statehouses introduced security checkpoints at entrances. Some require photo IDs, and others, such as Indiana, have a limit on how many visitors are allowed in the building at one time. But even with restrictions and the introduction of online meetings, lobbying remains a person-to-person conversation about a specific piece of legislation. Lobbying consists of influencing and persuading decision makers to make decisions that support your point of view. Town councilors, county commissioners, city councilors, and legislators can all be lobbied.

Lobbyists usually represent organized groups, ranging from small non-profits to large corporations. Despite the negative press, most lobbyists provide useful information to decision makers. When I worked in the state executive branch, I lobbied on behalf of the governor. My job was to present facts and research results, as well as to communicate the governor's point of view on issues assigned to me.

Legally, lobbying is defined as attempting to influence a decision maker on a specific piece of legislation. Lobbying is regulated by federal and state law. For instance, most nonprofit organizations are organized as 501I(3) organizations under the US tax code, which means they can spend no more than 10% of their annual budget on lobbying. (Sometimes nonprofit groups will organize under 501I(4) or 501I(6) tax designations, which allow unlimited lobbying, but such organizations cannot accept tax-exempt donations.) But producing educational brochures, holding an informational seminar, or inviting legislators to your facility would not legally be considered lobbying, as long as there is no attempt to influence a legislator on a particular piece of legislation.

Volunteers who lobby but are not paid are not regulated by law. Any citizen or community member has the right to speak with decision makers about a bill, testify in hearings, make public comments, or submit written comments or testimony. If you decide to engage in lobbying by writing, calling, or emailing your legislator, city councilor, or any other decision maker, you are free to do so. As long as you are not being paid to lobby, you are not restricted by law.

Working with decision makers is *relationship-based*. Despite the rise of social media, most lobbying takes place in person, on the fly. More person-to-person lobbying does take place online and on the phone nowadays, but my college students are still surprised when I take them to our State House and they see crowds of people talking to each other in the halls. Decisions to support or oppose an issue are made in these hallway conversations. Hallway decisions can happen so fast that websites and social media cannot keep up. To have up-to-the-minute information on an issue, you or someone working with you needs to be there in person.

Because most of us can't be present in the statehouse for hours at a time, or we can't take the time to make numerous calls about an issue, we will instead support an organization that can represent our views. As an environmental advocate, it makes sense to find out what organizations in your area are active on the issues you care about. You can also look for and join organizations and groups led by communities most impacted by climate change and environmental destruction. You can then make a donation to support them and get on an email list so they can alert you when they need you to email, call, testify, or attend a meeting.

Alternatively, your group might hire a lobbyist for your city council or state legislature. You don't need to have power, influence, or a large budget to hire a lobbyist. Many lobbyists work part time, have a portfolio of small environmental groups they work for, and are reasonably priced. In Maine, the local Sierra Club chapter and a state housing coalition each have a part-time lobbyist. If your group decides to do this, you'll want to find someone who is familiar with your issue and has a personal relationship with the decision makers. The advantage of hiring a lobbyist is that you'll have someone who can monitor your issue, speak on your organization's behalf, and be present when decisions are being made.

Nonviolent Direct Action

"Nonviolent direct action is a set of tactics that go outside the conventional means of advocacy," says George Lakey, a longtime activist, author, and trainer. Most people think of direct action as disruptive activities, like blocking entrances, boycotting, marching, fasting, and occupying. Generally speaking, nonviolent direct action is used when traditional advocacy methods and tools are not working or will not work. Nonviolent direct action is used to:

- Raise awareness of an issue
- Disrupt the status quo, especially when conventional advocacy is not working
- Gather and build support for an issue
- Generate media coverage
- Influence decision makers who are outside the public policy arena, such as corporate CEOs
- Influence decision makers when there is no direct access to them, e.g., protests outside the White House
- Link people, coalitions, and campaigns in multiple locations through coordinated action, like the climate strikes

Direct action can and should work hand in hand with traditional advocacy. Direct action groups who were both in favor of and opposed to requiring vaccines for public school students demonstrated in our state legislature last year. They filled the hallways of the State House. Walking through those hallways meant being touched by babies, having leaflets pressed into your hands, and seeing hundreds of people with banners and signs. The presence of protesters on both sides of the hallways meant there was no way for decision makers to avoid the people or the issue.

With activists both for and against vaccines protesting, you might ask: What good did this do? Didn't they cancel each other out? No, it resulted in the issue being seen for what it was—a question of freedoms: the freedom to choose what substances enter the body versus the freedom to attend school without risk of disease. The legislative debate went hours into overtime, and a series of very close votes and revotes were held. The importance of the issue was understood, and it was given the time it deserved.

At the same time that protesters were lining the State House hallways, lobbyists for and against vaccines were negotiating in person with the decision makers, which shows how direct action and advocacy can reinforce each other. Later the issue went to public referendum, and the pro-vaccine side won.

Typically, direct action takes place at the beginning of an initiative for change, serving to build awareness of and support for an issue. Over time, issues tend to move from direct action to being lobbied and then to being encoded in policies or law. The process from initiating action to passing laws can take time; three to ten years is typical.

As George Lakey describes in his book *How We Win,* direct action events can be the match that lights a local campaign, the spark that ignites campaigns in other jurisdictions, and the flame that turns multiple campaigns into a movement, which then can lead to major social change.

The controversy surrounding the Dakota Access Pipeline (also known as the Bakken pipeline) is a good example of an effective use of direct action. The $3.7 billion pipeline carries crude oil from shale oil fields in North Dakota to an oil terminal 1,172 miles away in Patoka, Illinois, near Chicago. The pipeline was routed through sacred sites and Indigenous lands of the Sioux tribal nations. Of particular concern was the fact that the pipeline company, Dakota Access LLC (controlled by Energy Transfer Partners), was determined to build the pipeline under Lake Oahe, the sole source of drinking water of the Standing Rock Sioux. If the pipeline were to leak or rupture, tribal leaders argued, sacred sites and the health of tribal members would be harmed.[1]

Over the course of several years, numerous actions were taken to protest the pipeline, both before construction and as it was being built. Direct action was conducted under the leadership of tribal elder LaDonna Brave Bull Allard, who established Sacred Stone Camp as a center for cultural preservation and spiritual resistance to the pipeline. Over time, people from three hundred federally recognized tribes and as many as five thousand supporters were camped there or nearby. Joining the Indigenous protesters was a delegation of more than two thousand US military veterans and numerous White activists. Police responded by making more than four hundred arrests and using tanks, riot gear, mace, pepper spray, rubber bullets, and dogs to disperse protesters. North Dakota's governor called in the National Guard.

Direct action against the pipeline continued for months, including a National Day of Action when protests were held in hundreds of cities across the United States, Thanksgiving Day protests in which several thousand joined the protest at Standing Rock, and a four-day protest in Washington, DC. Numerous politicians and celebrities publicly supported the protesters.

On December 4, 2016, the US Army Corps of Engineers under President Obama denied an easement under Lake Oahe for the pipeline, a major victory for the Sioux and those who stood with them. Unfortunately the victory was short-lived. In his first week in office in January 2017, President Trump signed an executive order to reverse the earlier decision and terminate the environmental review that was underway.[2]

Earthjustice, a nonprofit environmental advocacy group, then filed a motion in court against the Corps of Engineers. In July 2020, a federal judge found that the pipeline violated federal law and ordered it shut down. An environmental impact statement examining the effects of the pipeline on the Sioux is now required before a permit can be reissued. As of this writing the case is on appeal, with twenty-four members of Congress, twenty-seven tribes, and nineteen state governments submitting supporting briefs.[3]

This story illustrates how campaigns must keep the pressure on *continuously over time* to be effective. After six years of direct action, the Dakota Access Pipeline is now under legal review. Single direct actions by themselves have little effect. Continuous activity for an extended period is often necessary to make the changes you want.

Challenging Corporations to Change

Sometimes direct action is needed to directly challenge a corporation to change its policies. This was the case when the Earth Quaker Action Team (EQAT) took on PNC Bank, demanding that it stop financing mountaintop removal coal mining, which has destroyed five hundred mountains and two thousand miles of river and stream beds in Appalachia.[4]

Their campaign included protests at hundreds of bank branches in thirteen states, a march across Pennsylvania, and direct confrontation of bank executives during a board meeting. After five years of action, EQAT was successful; PNC stopped investing in mountaintop removal projects.

EQAT is now engaged in another campaign, demanding that Pennsylvania's largest utility, PECO Energy, purchase locally generated solar energy and pay workers a livable wage to produce it. EQAT has presented four clear demands to PECO:

1. Dramatically increase the purchase of solar power so that 20% of PECO's electricity comes from solar by 2025.

2. Ensure that all 20% of PECO's solar power is produced locally, with a priority on both community-owned distributed solar and ownership by low-income communities in PECO's service area.

3. Prioritize installation by local workers paid livable wages, especially from high-unemployment areas in PECO's service area.

4. Push for community solar in Pennsylvania, as well as any other legislation and regulation that ease the way to a solar transition.

In corporate campaigns, the pathway to change is less clear than it is in political campaigns. More creativity is needed to capture the attention of decision makers and articulate demands. EQAT is particularly good at this. A few examples of their creative actions include having 150 people singing gospel songs outside PECO's corporate headquarters, holding Quaker worship services in the PECO corporate lobby, conducting a hundred-mile walk ending at PECO headquarters, and sending flowers and cards with their list of demands to corporate board members.

Keeping the pressure on for a long period of time is as important as the creativity and visibility of these actions. EQAT is now in its sixth year of continuous action against PECO. Media attention is an important component of these actions. TV, newspaper, and social media coverage are essential to put pressure on decision makers to change their policies. More on working with the media can be found in Chapter 13.

The Four Roles in Successful Campaigns

Many people shy away from advocacy work because they don't feel comfortable in public roles. But the truth behind every successful campaign is that there are many kinds of people and many different roles to play. Some people prefer being on stage, while others prefer working behind the scenes. Handing flyers to the right people at the right time can be as important as delivering a compelling speech. Different personal styles can be effective, too. I am always amazed how a soft, quiet voice can be as effective as—or even more effective than—louder, more assertive voices.

Bill Moyer, a longtime activist and observer of social movements (not to be confused with TV journalist Bill Moyers), came up with a model of four essential roles at work in every successful campaign. Of course, people can do more than just one thing; but according to Moyer, people are generally attracted to and more skilled at one of the following four roles:

1. **Organizers** who bring people together and take the lead in charting a course forward.

2. **Advocates** who work to present the issue and persuade decision makers.

3. **Direct support people** who take concrete actions to support the cause. Examples include cleaning the river, building homes in poor communities, stuffing envelopes, making signs, and providing logistical support at events.

4. **Rebels/disruptors** who take disruptive action. Examples include NFL quarterback Colin Kaepernick kneeling during the national anthem at football games to protest police brutality against Black people, and Greta Thunberg spending Fridays out of school, sitting outside the Swedish parliament and protesting climate change.

The key is that every campaign needs a variety of players, and those players need to be able to work together. Rebels who parachute in to a meeting or a community and favor spontaneous action sometimes get in the way of organizers who want every action planned out ahead of time. On the other hand, advocates may dismiss direct action events as silly or ineffective, thereby overlooking the potential of group actions and diminishing the effectiveness of their campaign. And so on. The best way to move forward is to value and respect the variety of skills and perspectives each person brings.

The Key to Successful Direct Action: Organization and Planning

For most of my career I've worked as an advocate, organizing public engagement and lobbying for bills in the state legislature. Until recently, I didn't understand direct action. I thought direct action was a spontaneous activity where people came together informally to protest something. You could just show up at the appointed time with a sign. This is true for rallies, where the public is invited. But for specific direct action events, I was completely wrong.

Effective direct action is well organized and planned. This is true for both individual events and for campaigns consisting of multiple events. Eileen Flanagan, a direct action trainer, identifies the specific roles people play in a direct action event. People make a serious commitment to take on roles such as action leader, media liaison, health and safety person, police liaison, moderator if there are speakers, audiovisual person, crowd manager, and so on. Many roles are defined and committed to in advance.

To be most effective, every step of a direct action event is planned in advance. Participants are trained on what to do at each moment. If there's a possibility of arrest, extra training is given for how to respond to that. Being bold and taking direct action can be scary and dangerous. Serious direct action is serious business, which calls for serious advance planning and training.

The Clamshell Alliance, a group opposed to nuclear power, organized protests against the construction of a multi-unit nuclear power plant in Seabrook, New Hampshire. Participants from a wide region were required to attend six weekly trainings in nonviolent protest techniques. The

trainings included films, discussions, and role-playing that put participants in the shoes of state police and National Guard troops. Participants
practiced being arrested and allowing their limp bodies to be dragged or
carried away. They also learned not to take it personally when an action
was performed against them, to reduce the risk that they'd respond with
violence. Participants were required to join a self-governed affinity group
of ten to twenty protesters who would become their team, protectors, and
friends during the protest. People with assigned roles, like police liaison,
practiced scenarios for what they might do or say. This thorough training
and planning paid off when 1,414 protesters were arrested at Seabrook
without violence.[5] Although the first Seabrook unit was built, the protests contributed to the scrapping of plans to build a second reactor unit
at the plant.

Sometimes unexpected violence can take place. Event leaders need to
prepare as well as they can in advance to mitigate or de-escalate these
situations. Organizers for both Occupy Wall Street and the Global Climate
Strikes met with local police ahead of time and regularly throughout their
events to tell them what was planned and engage them in keeping out
unwanted people and violence. This is a highly recommended strategy for
reducing the possibility of violence.

Serving on Task Forces, Committees, and Advisory Councils

Serving on a task force, committee, or advisory council is a great way to
learn about an issue, meet others with similar interests, and make your stance
known. Most town and city governments have committees on sustainability,
comprehensive planning, or conservation. These committees usually welcome enthusiastic and committed people of all ages and backgrounds!

There are many opportunities to serve at the county and state level, as
well. Within Maine's Department of Marine Resources (DMR) there are
numerous advisory groups, including the DMR Advisory Council, Lobster
Advisory Council, Shellfish Advisory Council, Scallop Advisory Council,

Aquaculture Advisory Council, and Seaweed Advisory Council. In addition to standing councils, there are often temporary task forces appointed to address specific issues and concerns. The members of these advisory groups are fishermen who are knowledgeable in their industry and who advocate for their interests to regulators. As a result of their work, policies and rules are well thought out, and the Maine fishing community generally believes the rules are created and enforced fairly.

In larger cities and at the state level, people are usually required to have some background in the subject matter in order to serve on an advisory council. There's often a designated number of seats for people representing specific interest groups or perspectives. If you are interested in joining one of these, you will want to find out how the council or task force is structured and whether you fit the profile of any of the designated seats.

If you are interested in serving on a city or state advisory council, you should let environmental and community groups in your area know. These groups will often nominate council members to represent their interests. Your show of interest will be appreciated and may result in a nomination. But it doesn't guarantee you a seat. Organizations are looking for the best representatives they can find as nominees. After nominations are submitted (whether by an individual or an organization), the sponsoring city or state will vet them and decide who will be seated.

Committees and advisory groups can be political in a number of ways. For instance, I chaired the Maine Governor's Council on Solid Waste some years ago. This advisory group was tasked with giving input on a five-year state solid waste plan. Many clamored for a seat at the table, and more than forty people were appointed. Each person represented an element of the solid waste system: trash haulers, landfill and incinerator operators, bottling companies, grocery stores, and so on. Participants joined mostly to preserve the status quo and defend their interests. Citizens who joined because they wanted change would likely have been disappointed. Nothing changed.

If you are looking to join a task force, advisory board, or other group, it's helpful to contact the leader or members you know in advance, to learn about the task force's true mission, goals, and politics. This way you can join a group that is aligned with your interests, and avoid working with people who are looking for different outcomes than you are.

Conversely, you may want to join a group in order to shake it up and create change. If you decide to do this, you will want to call or meet privately with the leaders to find out what level of support they can give you. If you decide to challenge the status quo, you will have a better chance of success if you have obtained the support of leaders in advance.

Litigation

Litigation is a powerful advocacy tool. It bypasses decision makers who have been bought by corporate lobbyists, or opposition groups who are entrenched in the status quo. Corporations in particular have learned how to buy science to build their case, use economic arguments to cover up the damage their operations may cause, and fund lobbying efforts to win over politicians.

Legal action becomes the tool of choice when citizen and legislative campaigns have reached their limit. Even if you are not a lawyer, you can support legal action as a community member or student. There is always a need to provide stories related to the issue being litigated, gather information, and help get the word out.

There's a long history of lawsuits that have led to changes in environmental law. Legal actions specifically to slow climate change have been brought to court systems since the 1980s. Several current cases take a new approach, as they work to establish constitutional rights to clean air and water and a healthy environment. These cases hold great promise as a tool for addressing environmental degradation and climate change.

Juliana v. United States was brought in 2015 by twenty-one youth plaintiffs who claim their right to life and liberty under the Constitution has been harmed by greenhouse gas emissions. This case wasn't taken seriously at first: a bunch of kids are suing the federal government? People laughed. But in

2016, when US District Judge Ann Aiken upheld the idea that access to a clean environment is a fundamental right, people began to pay attention.

In 2019 the case was heard by a panel of three judges from the Ninth Circuit Court. They recognized the seriousness of the charges—that the youth have been injured by climate change, and the government has played a role in causing their injuries. But two of the three judges said the matter should be addressed by the legislative and executive branch, not the courts. Following this, the youth's attorney filed a petition requesting a full court hearing with all eleven judges to review the case. This case is ongoing and may reach the Supreme Court.[6] If it succeeds, it will be groundbreaking, giving new power to individuals and communities to challenge the government on environmental issues based on environmental rights. If it fails, the publicity it has generated—including two feature stories on *60 Minutes*—has helped fuel the emerging national movement to establish environmental rights.

In another case, community activist Maya K. van Rossum and her team won a victory that affirms the right of Pennsylvanians to a clean and healthy environment. They did this by reviving a long-ignored part of the state constitution and empowering it to protect people's right to pure water, clean air, and a healthy environment. They brought their "Environmental Rights Amendment" lawsuit to the Pennsylvania Supreme Court and won. With a state constitutional amendment in place, Pennsylvania's individuals and communities now have a legal basis to protect themselves from frackers and other polluters.

Prior to the amendment, industry lobbyists used arguments about job creation, energy independence, and the fact that burning natural gas emits less carbon dioxide than coal or oil to win over Pennsylvania's politicians. The result was Act 13, a state law that required towns to open every zoning district to drilling and fracking. As a result, schools, residences, protected waterways, public parks, and wildlife sanctuaries were all open for drilling. The law permitted fracking companies to take private land by eminent domain and store vast amounts of polluted water under those lands.

The legislation even included a "medical gag rule" that prohibited doctors from publicly disclosing medical cases resulting from chemical exposure due to fracking. Information about the chemicals deployed in fracking was proprietary, despite the fact that more than 100 studies nationwide have documented the health risks of these chemicals. Despite an active citizen campaign in opposition to this law, the Pennsylvania legislature approved it, and the governor signed it into law.

It was at this point that the Delaware Riverkeeper Network brought legal action. Using a little-known clause in the Pennsylvania Constitution, the organization argued that Act 13 violated Pennsylvanians' rights to "clean air, pure water, and the preservation of the natural, scenic, historic, and aesthetic values of the environment." In a protracted series of court actions and appeals, Act 13 was declared unconstitutional. Municipal zoning rights and private property rights were restored, and eventually the medical gag rule was repealed. As a result of the case, environmental rights were elevated to the level of other human rights and declared to be natural, permanent, and inalienable rights that extend to present and future generations. Pennsylvania communities now have legal standing and constitutional backing to ban fracking or any other harmful industrial activity.[7]

Similarly, the Montana Constitution includes the "right to a clean and healthful environment" in its Declaration of Rights, and a later section states that "the state and each person shall maintain and improve a clean and healthful environment in Montana for present and future generations."[8] When gold-mining operations threatened to level several mountains and discharge millions of gallons of cyanide-laced water into the pristine Blackfoot River, two environmental groups, the Montana Environmental Information Center and Women's Voice for the Earth, filed suit based on the environmental rights in the state constitution. They won, and the proposed gold mine was never built.[9]

Van Rossum is now focused on a Green Amendment Movement, encouraging and working with advocates in other states to litigate for state constitutional amendments that establish environmental rights. A dozen states have joined the effort. If advocates succeed, they will have created a powerful new tool to protect local communities.

Most community and student advocates don't have a legal background. But, like the youth in the *Juliana* case, ordinary people can engage with legal experts who can help. The Oregon nonprofit Our Children's Trust was formed to litigate cases urging states and the federal government to mitigate climate change. They were the ones who contacted the youth plaintiffs and organized the legal challenge in the *Juliana* case. In van Rossum's Green Amendment lawsuit, the Delaware Riverkeeper Network provided the legal and organizational support to move the case forward. Her Green Amendment Movement depends on volunteers to organize and advocate for change in other states.

Many environmental organizations use legal tools to protect the environment, and they need citizen support. The Natural Resources Defense Council has worked since 1970 to defend air, water, communities, and wild places across the country. The Conservation Law Foundation on the East Coast and Earthjustice on the West Coast have pursued legal cases for many years, with strong track records of success. The websites of these and other organizations list ways you can help. All organizations of this type welcome citizen volunteers to help get the word out, organize locally, and join in making calls to their government representatives.

Election Campaigns

Sometimes the best advocacy strategy is to elect politicians who care about the environment. In working to remove obsolete dams from the Royal River in Yarmouth, Maine, the Royal River Alliance sought candidates for the Yarmouth Town Council who were supportive of "freeing the river" and removing the dams. Once candidates were running for office, Alliance members spoke with each of them personally to inform them about the river. Several of them now serve on the town council, and the status of the dams is actively under review.

You, too, can work on election campaigns or even run for office. In supporting a candidate, you want to consider two things. First, are they supportive of cleaning up the environment and everything that entails? Second, do they have the skills to work with others and move issues forward?

Often the second part of this equation is neglected. We need politicians who can do more than speak well to a crowd or a camera. *We need politicians who can bring people together and lead change efforts.*

In Maine, after eight years of political infighting in the state legislature, voters elected Republican, Democratic, and independent candidates who were able to work with others and get things done. Less than two years later, they passed a state climate action plan that will eliminate state greenhouse gas emissions entirely by 2050. Working on campaigns and electing effective and supportive politicians of all parties is a highly effective way to advocate for the environment!

Advocacy Demystified

Advocacy is for everyone. This chapter shows that people can choose a role that fits their unique experience, skill set, and schedule. And we certainly do need everyone to contribute if we are to solve global problems such as climate change, racism, poverty, and toxic pollution. It will take people of all kinds working together to do this.

But advocacy is not enough to solve our global problems. We also have to change ourselves and what we believe about the world. Our perceptions of what is possible must change if we are to have a healthy and peaceful future. In the next several chapters, we'll explore how our views of the earth and humanity have led to climate change, toxic pollution, and inequality, and how we must shift those views in order to fully heal the planet.

3

Earth Stories and Why They Matter

In every outthrust headland, in every curving beach, in every grain of sand there is the story of the earth.

—RACHEL CARSON

Is it right to burn rainforests that provide oxygen for all of us, so local farmers can grow food? Is it right that 85% of the wealth in the world is owned by 10% of the people? Is it right to allow corporations to manufacture toxic chemicals that damage human and environmental health? Is it right to leave global warming for the next generations to solve?

These are just a few of the moral questions humanity faces today. In order to address them, we have to look within, recognize the stories and beliefs that have rationalized our behavior in the past, and begin to tell a new story.

The environmental advocate's job is to tell a "new earth story." This means delving into the conscious and unconscious beliefs that determine our thoughts and actions toward the earth. In Western culture, many of our current earth stories are destructive and outdated. Advocates must shine a light on these and point out how and why our collective thinking and behavior must change. Advocates need to fully embrace a life-affirming concept of how we relate to each other and the earth. This chapter shows us the path forward.

Our Collective Earth Stories

When I was a child, I asked my father what happened to sewage. There were open sewer pipes draining into the ocean near our house at the time. I wanted to know how this worked. His answer reflected the dominant American story about the earth in the early 1960s. He said, "The sewage passes through the sand into the water. The sand filters it and the water neutralizes it."

The mainstream American earth story then was that the ocean and the land were large enough to "self-clean." Waste of all kinds would be absorbed and neutralized by natural elements. To a large extent, this was true. The US population was just over 100 million, and we live in a big country. We could dump old cars in ditches and household wastes in wetlands. Town dumps were located on the edge of town, where few would see them. This sort of worked. Until it didn't.

Now, with a US population of 330 million and growing, we can no longer tell ourselves that "the earth will take care of it" when it comes to human and industrial waste. We are consuming much more per person in fossil fuels, plastics, food, electronics, and dry goods than ever before. We can't dump waste on the edge of town without harming the health of everything and everyone nearby. Our growing awareness of environmental justice tells us that dumping waste at the edge of town negatively affects the marginalized communities and wildlife that live there.

To give this some perspective, ten thousand years ago, before the advent of agriculture, there were five million people on the earth. Today there are

The size of the world population over the last 12,000 years

7 billion

6.5 billion

6 billion

5.5 billion

5 billion

4.5 billion

4 billion

3.5 billion

3 billion

2.5 billion

2 billion

1.5 billion

1 billion

0.5 billion

4 million in 10,000 BCE

10,000 BCE   8,000 BCE   6,000 BCE   4,000 BCE   2,000 BCE   0   2000

The average growth rate from 10,000 BCE to 1700 was just 0.04% per year.

190 million in the year 0

Mid 14th century: The Black Death pandemic in Europe kills 200 million people.

600 million in 1700

990 million in 1800

1.65 billion in 1900

2 billion in 1928

3 billion in 1960

4 billion in 1975

5 billion in 1987

6 billion in 1999

7 billion in 2011

7.7 billion in 2019

Based on estimates by the *History Database of the Global Environment* (HYDE) and the United Nations. On OurWorldinData.org you can download the annual data.

This is a visualization from OurWorldinData.org where you find data and research on how the world is changing.

nearly eight billion. Our population today is more than *one thousand times larger* than it was then. So if New York City, with its present population of 8.6 million, had existed ten thousand years ago it would have had a population of 8,623. Or take a smaller city like Portland, Maine, which has sixty thousand people now; it would have had 60 people then. The following chart shows how the earth's population has grown over time.

The stories we tell ourselves about the earth have not kept up with reality. Western cultures hold an outdated story. The story's theme is that it's our job to tame and subdue the earth—indefinitely. The earth is here for us to consume, providing food and materials for our use. The earth is large and can give us what we need, without limit. This is the story of dominion: the earth, dominated by people.

The word "dominion" has its roots in governing a domain or territory. The Bible refers to this in Genesis where it says: "And God said unto them, Be fruitful and multiply, and replenish the earth and subdue it: and *have dominion* over the fish of the sea and over the fowl of the air, and over every living thing that moveth upon the earth. Rule over the fish of the sea and the birds of the air and over every living creature that moves on the ground"[1] (italics added for emphasis).

Then the question becomes: How best to "have dominion"? Is it to consume and despoil the earth in an effort to achieve the highest economic growth? Some people have interpreted this passage to mean "the earth is wild and is here for humans to tame." For others, it means "the earth provides my livelihood, and I can consume as much as I need and want from it." Commercial logging, fishing, and agriculture have viewed the earth this way. For still others, it means "the earth is my slave and is here to please me." For some, a gigantic oceanfront or mountain home is an example of an unconscious idea that "the earth is here to please me."

Many, including Pope Francis, have made the case for an entirely different interpretation of Genesis. In his words: "We must regain the conviction that we need one another, that we have a shared responsibility for others and the world, and that being good and decent are worth it."[2]

To "have dominion" can mean to take care of, to steward, to share responsibility, and to live in harmony with. An analogy would be to regard and treat the earth like a dog or cat that you truly love. You would feed it, joyfully play with it, provide ongoing love and attention, and provide extra care if it is sick. Imagine if we took care of the earth this way!

Outdated Earth Stories Persist

A term I learned in fisheries is "underutilized species." This term is commonly used without recognizing the *human-centered earth story* at the root of it. An underutilized species is a species of fish that's not being harvested and eaten by humans. If we don't consume enough, we are not meeting our obligation to consume. How much we consume has been a display of status for all of human history. By using this term, fisheries managers—perhaps without realizing it—have accepted a story about the earth that has humans at the center, consuming, harvesting, managing, and dominating.

The Magnuson-Stevens Fisheries Management Act governs US fisheries today. The description of the act in Wikipedia illustrates the language of human supremacy and exploitation: "Passed in 1976, the Magnuson-Stevens Fishery Conservation and Management Act is the legal provision for *promoting optimal exploitation* of coastal fisheries" (italics added for emphasis).

Inherent in the concept of underutilized species is human supremacy. Western societies have come a long way in valuing people who are different from us. Diversity that values ethnic, racial, sexual, and gender differences is a virtue in many of our institutions today. We are getting closer to viewing all human life as sacred. But, as the Black Lives Matter and feminist movements have shown us, we still have a ways to go.

In Western cultures, most everyone hates rats, snakes, spiders, and coyotes. Isn't this also a form of bigotry? You could call it "speciesism." We have picked out certain species and vilified them. Human life may be seen as sacred, but other living things have no rights at all. We have devalued the contributions many species make as a part of the earth's ecosystem, and by vilifying these species, we can justify eradicating them. By eradicating them, we endanger all the other species that depend on them, threatening the entire ecosystem.

We have hunted and consumed species like whales and cod to the point of collapse. We have destroyed the ecosystems that support species like bison and elephants, greatly reducing their numbers. These actions come from a worldview that sees humans as superior to and separate from other species.

Conquest

Our outdated earth stories also include conquest. A common story of the settling of this country is about the courage and stamina it took to carve out a subsistence from the wild, untamed earth. Settlers risked death and worked hard to stay alive. They had to subdue the wilderness, protect themselves from the weather, and cultivate food to eat. Their story is usually told from a perspective of valor, courage, and success. As part of the conquest narrative, species like buffalo, wolves, and carrier pigeons were wiped out. Whales, which were prized for their oil, were hunted furiously in the 1800s and were only saved by the introduction of fossil fuels (kerosene) in the 1880s.

This conquest narrative, which is commonly taught in schools, is not only an outdated earth story; it is also a White narrative, narrowly confined to the White settlers' point of view. Before the arrival of White colonists, there were hundreds of sovereign Indigenous nations in the lands now called the United States. Indigenous people did not view the lands as wild and untamed, but rather as their kin, part of an extended family that they partnered with. Native peoples had built an extensive network of roads and trails across the country; cultivated corn, squash, and beans for food; and used fire to manage fields and forests as habitat for game. They stewarded the land by taking the plants and animals they needed as food, and returning wastes to nurture it. Unfortunately, Native Americans were nearly eradicated by disease, slaughter, and relocation under the conquest story. The story of conquest has been a major theme in US history, and it perpetuates the mindset of domination today.

Embedded in the story of conquest is the concept of hierarchy: men over women, White people over people of color, humans over plant and animal life, "good" plants and animals over "bad" ones, industry over nature, and jobs over community. Making anything "better than" something else is to devalue the other. People everywhere tend to exploit and waste things that are not valued. Industrial cultures have used the concept of hierarchy in making decisions and growing economies, causing great harm to life that falls lower on the hierarchy scale.

Industrial cultures have made progress in their thinking to varying degrees since the days of colonial settlement. But as you will see throughout this book, the underlying story of humans dominating the earth, and of life organized in a hierarchy where some people are valued more than others, is still deep within us today.

Separateness

Our collective earth story is also about a perception of separateness. Ask a typical American child where water comes from, and they are likely to say, "the faucet." They are also likely to tell you that food comes from the grocery store. Many people in the United States rarely spend time outdoors and are afraid of wildlife and insects. Children are more likely these days to spend their after-school time in organized programs instead of playing in the woods. In the twenty-first century, a majority of people in industrialized countries live quite separately from nature.

Many of us live in ways that separate us from other people, too. The number of single and nonfamily households has more than doubled since 1960.[3] A survey of more than twenty thousand Americans showed that 46% "sometimes or always feel alone."[4] Church membership in the United States has declined from 70% in 1998 to 50% in 2019, with a greater number of people with no religious affiliation.[5]

Where I live in Maine, there used to be a grange in every town. Granges functioned as community centers hosting potluck suppers, plays, musicals, and birthday parties. Almost all are now closed, with their buildings torn down or repurposed. Our entertainment has shifted from bowling leagues and card games to cell phones, laptops, TV, and movies—all individual forms of entertainment. It's ironic that as population density has grown, we have become more separate emotionally from others.

We have also become separated from the consequences of our actions. We are not aware of the working conditions where the products we purchase are made. We don't know where fish are caught or chicken is grown. Coffee and chocolate growers are often poorly paid by exporters, with many losing money every year on their crops.[6] Most people don't know where their trash, recyclables, or sewage end up, either.

Separateness in Managing Natural Resources

In managing fisheries, forests, and farms, we are still managing by single species without giving thought to the fact that each species is part of a larger living system. Forests are managed for pine, maple, spruce, or fir. Fisheries are managed for single species such as cod, haddock, crab, or salmon. Farm crops are managed in large acreages of a single species like corn or soybeans.

Cod is a predator on baby lobsters. Since the cod fishery industry collapsed in the late 1990s, the Gulf of Maine has experienced record lobster catches. The collapse of the cod population is thought to be a major factor in the rise of lobsters. But the fact that cod feed on baby lobsters was not considered in making the cod or lobster fishing rules. Fortunately for fishermen, lobsters have been highly valued, partially making up for the loss of cod. The following charts illustrate Maine cod and lobster landings over time. If you look at the most recent years, you'll see they mirror each other almost exactly, showing how interrelated these species are.[7]

A common practice in industrial agriculture is monocropping—extracting the largest possible harvests of a single crop species and selling them at commodity prices that are much lower than smaller farms can afford to charge. This practice comes at great cost to the environment. Large acreages of a single species require pesticides to control pests. Centralized megafarms require a great deal of fossil fuel to produce products and ship them across the country. A one-pound box of lettuce grown in California contains 80 food calories, and it requires 4,600 calories of fossil fuels to grow and ship to the East Coast.[8]

Massive commodity farms grow corn and soybeans to feed cattle and hogs for the meat market. US farmers planted 91.7 million acres of corn in 2019, enough to cover sixty-nine million football fields.[9] We have accomplished much with agricultural technology. We can feed billions, based on fertilizer, irrigation, pesticides, and now computer-managed cultivation.

This works, until it doesn't. Agriculture is one of the leading causes of deforestation, biodiversity loss, soil depletion, and water pollution. Raising livestock for meat, eggs, and milk generates 14.5% of the world's greenhouse gas emissions, and it uses about 70% of the world's agricultural land.[10]

As the above examples illustrate, our agricultural system is based on trying to tame the earth instead of working with it. We bulldoze and burn forests to make way for crops. Then, by continually harvesting without putting nutrients back into the soil, we deplete the land until it can't grow enough to be profitable. When this point is reached, the land is abandoned. The United States lost almost ninety-eight thousand square miles of farmland between 1997 and 2018.[11] China reports losing about 770 square miles of agricultural land each year.[12]

Regenerative agriculture, an umbrella term for many practices that work with the earth's natural cycles to restore and preserve the fertility of the land, is an opposite approach. Through the use of crop rotation, cover crops that add nutrients and aerate the soil, integration of livestock with crops, tree planting, and other techniques, soil fertility can be restored and maintained. Another benefit of regenerative agriculture is that healthy soils capture and store excess carbon from the atmosphere, which directly addresses climate change.

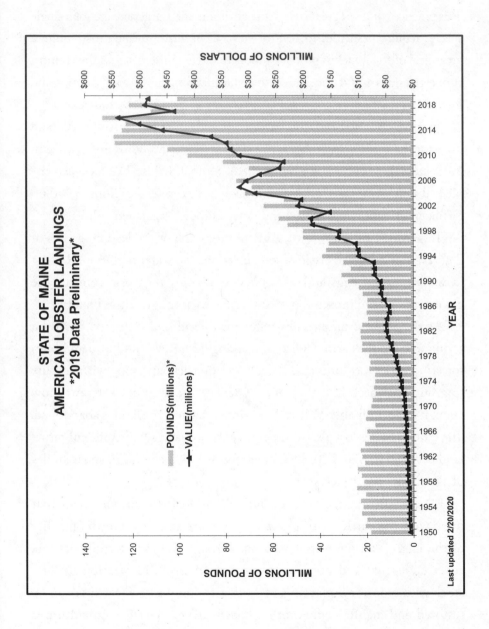

STATE OF MAINE
AMERICAN LOBSTER LANDINGS
2019 Data Preliminary

POUNDS(millions)*
VALUE(millions)

MILLIONS OF DOLLARS

MILLIONS OF POUNDS

YEAR

Last updated 2/20/2020

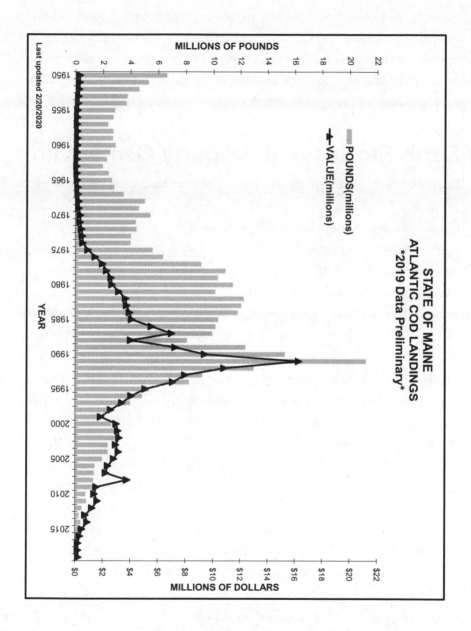
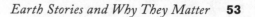

Methods for regenerative agriculture are known, have been practiced for centuries in some cultures, and are being continuously refined. What's needed is a *shift in thinking* from maximizing profits in the short term to restoring and maintaining soil health for the long term. We need to move from a story of separation and conquest of the earth to a story of regeneration and partnership with the earth.

Earth Stories and Property Ownership

Deeply embedded in our current earth story is the concept of property ownership. Land is generally owned by individuals, corporations, governments, churches, or nonprofits. What this means is that "owners" own the rights of use and the natural resources on a defined piece of land. Owners' rights include the right to develop, build, cultivate, mine, log, fill wetlands, dam streams, extract water, and so on.

Variations on land ownership exist in different places. In Maine, the fish in the rivers belong to the state, and the right to pass over land is owned by private landowners. In England and Scotland, the reverse is true: the fish in the rivers are the private property of landowners, and the right to pass over land on foot is public (a great bonus for hikers!). In the United States, passing over private land without permission is called "trespassing," and people can be prosecuted for it.

In recent years, landowners' rights to dump waste or emit toxic gases have been regulated. Before regulation, owners were free to create private landfills on their own land. Farmers, hotels, and other businesses commonly dumped trash, old cars, and used equipment in ditches on their property. This was in accord with the old story that the earth was vast enough to accommodate this practice. When I purchased an old Maine farm, I had a metal recycler haul away old car chassis, rusted metal drums, and other waste from a stream bed on the property.

The oceans, air, and large rivers and lakes are generally held as a public trust, which means they are managed for the public welfare, not for the benefit of private owners or individuals. Should land also be held as a public trust, with the public giving private users specific rights to use it? This is the common practice in allowing logging and grazing on federal lands.

Or, conversely, should oceans, air, and rivers and lakes be privatized? In allocating fishing quotas and allowing private companies to extract and sell bottled water, we have begun to privatize what used to be considered public assets.

Not all cultures view the earth's natural resources as something that can be privately owned and controlled. Many Indigenous cultures regard land as a public commons, with hunting, fishing, passing over, and cultivation held as a public right. While not all Indigenous cultures are the same, they all see themselves as part of nature, not separate from it. They view the use of plants, animals, and land as a privilege to be respected by all, not a private right to extract, harvest, or profit from.[13]

Arguments for and against privatizing the earth are philosophical, dealing with the questions raised by the quote from Genesis cited earlier in this chapter: Are humans to dominate the earth and subdue it? Should we rule over the fish of the sea and birds of the air? Does ownership mean owners can do anything they want to properties they own? Does ownership give people the right to poison and pollute? Is it morally right to allow an owner to use herbicides or pesticides? What if the herbicides and pesticides affect others through water runoff or wind drift? Is it morally right to allow corporations to pollute millions of gallons of fresh water as they frack for natural gas? Where do we draw the lines? These questions arise as more and more people question the domination story, causing this view to crack and weaken.

The earth's resources are finite. There is only so much sunlight coming into the earth's atmosphere. Only so much biomass and animal life can draw energy from that sunlight to grow. Fossil fuels, fresh water, and minerals are finite. Somehow, the earth seems less wild when we think about it this way. Do industrialized cultures want to continue to live a story of human domination until the resources run out?

It is past time to question the underlying stories we tell ourselves about the earth. We can no longer extract materials, eliminate forests, emit toxic gases, and dump waste as though the earth has infinite capacity to support these activities. We need to wake up to our enormous and wasteful consumption, and to the consequences it has for our health and future. We continue to poison and consume the earth's resources at our own peril. The human-centered story of earth as solely our property to consume and control is dangerous and outdated.

A "New" Earth Story

People in Western cultures are beginning to tell and act from a new earth story. This story is about all living things being connected. In *The Hidden Life of Trees,* author and botanist Peter Wohlleben explains how a forest is a single living entity, in which microbial, plant, and animal life communicate with each other to support the whole. When some trees are threatened by disease, nearby trees emit chemicals through their roots to support the infested trees. A vast underground network of roots and friendly fungi supports forest life. When plants need to be pollinated, they emit hormones and scents to attract pollinators. Every year, various plants and trees coordinate their blooming and fruiting, which benefits the entire system. Orchards will fruit heavily one year and lightly the next, as if they need a rest every other year. We are still learning how forest systems work.

In this story of connection, life energy is seen as present in all living things. Changes in any species affect all the others. If the pollinators die, we'll have no fruit. If the trees die, we'll have no oxygen. Seeing life as a connected system is a profound shift. It means that harvesting or extracting anything from the earth has implications for all other life.

The raw sewage flowing into the ocean near my childhood home added nutrients and toxins to the harbor. This affected plants, fish, and shellfish who lived and fed there. It introduced bacteria that may have made the water unsafe for swimming and shellfish unsafe to eat. But under the sway of the old earth story, this was not something we thought about.

The story of the earth as a complex, interconnected web of life is actually not new. As mentioned earlier, Native peoples from around the globe have viewed the earth this way for thousands of years. They regard land and water as sacred. Plants and animals are thought of as kin, by which they mean human relations, relatives, and ancestors. From this comes a sense of responsibility for life, because all life is thought of as part of an extended family. From this standpoint, Indigenous peoples take from the earth only what they need to live, leaving enough for other species to feed and for the ecosystem to thrive.[14]

This "new" earth story focuses on the *interconnection* of all living beings. It puts the earth at the center of life instead of humans. Human beings are neither at the center nor at the top of a hierarchy, but are intimately connected with each other and all life. Pope Francis, in his encyclical pamphlet *Laudato Si'* (subtitled "On Care for Our Common Home") puts it this way: "When we speak of *environment* what we really mean is a relationship existing between nature and society that lives in it. Nature cannot be regarded as something separate from ourselves, or as a mere setting in which we live. We are part of nature, included in it and thus in constant interaction with it."[15]

This story of interconnection also recognizes that everything on earth is composed of energy, vibrating at different speeds. Life energy is inherent in all that is. Some cultures describe this spiritually, saying that everything on the earth—plants, trees, animals, water, rocks, and minerals—has a soul.

This interconnection story appears in the writings of many authors today, from academic scholars to Indigenous authors to fiction writers. Different authors use different metaphors and words but are essentially saying the same thing: we need to view the earth and our place in it in a more balanced, harmonious way. If we don't come around to a more balanced view, we run the risk of degrading and polluting the air, water, and land to the point where we become extinct.

It's exciting to see the story of interconnection entering the mainstream. And it is necessary. In order to address climate change and environmental degradation, Western cultures have to address the entire system of finance, planning, business, government, transportation, energy, land use, and agriculture. Increasing numbers of people in industrialized cultures are seeking Indigenous teachers to learn about their ways.[16] We are only beginning to understand what an earth-centered, life-affirming economy and culture might look like.

The Whanganui River in New Zealand, considered sacred by the Indigenous Whanganui Iwi people, was desecrated for years by hydroelectric dams, gravel mining, and municipal waste. In 2017, New Zealand's parliament passed a law recognizing the river as a legal person, establishing legal standing for the river.[17] In India, the Ganges and Yamuna Rivers have also gained legal rights as a person. These developments provide a legal basis for defending natural resources from harm. Actions like this are a step to restoring a more balanced relationship between human enterprise and the earth.

Change Our Thinking, Change Our Environment

Fifty years ago, stories about drunks were considered humorous, even cute. I remember watching TV skits when I was a child that featured drunken people doing silly things. When a drunk driver killed or injured someone, it was considered an unavoidable tragedy. "It was an accident," we would say. Sad, but unavoidable. We wept.

Mothers Against Drunk Drivers (MADD) campaigned on the idea that driving drunk *is a crime*—a crime that can and must be stopped. Through this reframing and a very effective campaign, they succeeded in changing public thinking. Now, there is a legal limit on the amount of alcohol allowed in one's blood when driving. If a drunk driver causes an accident, we assume they will be held accountable through suspension of their license, a fine, or jail time, and maybe rehab. The term "designated driver" has become a norm. MADD succeeded in radically changing our thinking.

When it comes to climate and the environment, we have to question and change our thinking in a similar way. *People take action only after waking up to an issue, questioning the status quo, and changing how they think about it.*

The moral questions that began this chapter—such as "Is it right that 85% of the wealth is owned by 10% of the people? Is it right to allow corporations to manufacture chemicals that damage human and environmental health? Is it right to leave global warming for the next generations to solve?"—are the kinds of questions we need to ask to challenge the status quo.

But unlike drunk driving, environmental issues are multifaceted. It will take multiple changes in thinking and multiple campaigns to put us on a sustainable path. Our beliefs are changing more quickly on some issues than on others, so progress is uneven. The connection between nutritious, chemical-free food and our health is well understood, for example. But the connection between the artificially bright night sky and the effects it has on humans and wildlife is less well known.

Uneven progress on environmental issues is also caused by the fact that many of the effects of climate change and toxic pollution are concentrated locally. Water pollution caused by fracking is well known in Pennsylvania and Ohio, but people in other parts of the country don't think much about it. Wildfires like those in Australia and California are experienced region-ally, making it difficult for people to connect them to global causes, such as increasing greenhouse gas emissions.

Rivers: A National Success Story

One environmental issue where the United States has succeeded in making a major shift is cleaning up rivers. In the 1800s and 1900s, rivers were thought of as the engines of modern industry and a symbol of progress. The Royal, a small river running through the town where I live, hosted fifty-seven manufacturing plants from 1674 to 1923. Flour, boards, paper, bricks, shoes, textiles, and rope were made there. The river provided water power and later electricity to run the factories. The river also functioned as a drain pipe, carrying industrial wastes like toxic chemicals and dyes used in papermaking, leather tanning, and textiles out to sea.

By the 1950s and 1960s, rivers across the country smelled terrible and were dangerous to wade or swim in due to toxic pollution. The Cuyahoga River near Cleveland, Ohio, caught fire numerous times. In 1969, TV news cameras showed the Cuyahoga burning, with flames leaping into the night sky. These were powerful images—so powerful that people began to question dumping industrial wastes into rivers.

Once the moral question was asked—"Is it right to allow our rivers to be so polluted in the name of progress?"—the way was cleared to introduce the Clean Water Act. It passed in 1970 with bipartisan support, just a year after the Cuyahoga fire appeared on television. It was signed by President Richard Nixon, a Republican. In 1974, the Cuyahoga Valley National Park was established a few miles north of the historic river fire. Swimming, kayaking, and fishing are offered at the park today.

Sometimes there is a longer period of time between changing our thinking and taking action. In 1930, a large paper mill on the Royal River burned down. Twenty acres of burned rubble, rusted metal, and broken glass remained on the site from 1930 to the late 1970s. Parents forbade children from playing there. Finally, eight years after the Clean Water Act passed, the community took action and cleaned up the site. There's an attractive river-walk park there now.

Nationwide, our thinking about rivers has changed. Where we once saw rivers as engines of industry and industrial sewer pipes, now we view them as valuable public and community assets that provide outdoor recreation. The change began when we saw the Cuyahoga burning and questioned the moral wisdom of unregulated dumping into our rivers.

Climate Change: Asking the Moral Question

Industrialized societies are now at a point where we must change our thinking about fossil fuels. We have depended on fossil fuels for energy and to make plastics. Fossil fuels have provided us with cheap transportation and unprecedented mobility. They've provided electricity and powered manufacturing. Fossil fuels have supported agriculture and medicine. Dividends from investments in oil and gas companies have supported the retirement funds of many. We have much to be grateful for when it comes to fossil fuels.

But we are at the end of the fossil fuel era. We know this because emissions from burning fossil fuels are warming the climate and, if unaddressed, will continue to cause sea level rise, ecosystem collapse, hunger, disease, storms, fires, drought, and mass migration. In the United States, many people have changed their thinking from "burning fossil fuels is fueling our economic growth" to "burning fossil fuels may be harmful" to "burning fossil fuels is causing climate change." This is progress.

But as climate activist Greta Thunberg has said, the changes we've made in our thinking have not been enough to bring about the changes we need to sustain life on earth. In fact, fossil fuel use has been steadily *increasing* while we talk about climate change. In 2018, the use of coal, oil, and natural gas increased by 4%, reaching a new all-time high.[18] Exxon's investment strategy shows yearly carbon emissions rising 17% by 2025.[19]

Collectively, we have begun to question burning fossil fuels, but we have not entirely changed our view of them. We have not yet collectively asked the moral question: "Is it right to allow continued burning of fossil fuels?" If we had, we would have banned oil and gas furnaces by now, as they have in Denmark.

Another moral question—"Is it right to leave global warming and climate change for the next generations to solve?"—was publicly raised by young climate activists in late 2018. I was thrilled to hear their message!

The rising of youth around the world to ask this question is the moral pivot point we need to move forward and address climate change. It shows we have finally reached a tipping point in our thinking. Many young leaders from around the world have made addressing climate change and climate justice their central moral issue. They recognize that their future is at stake. I know from history that asking a moral question is the first step to real social change. If humanity is to survive, we must support our youth in questioning what we are doing to the planet.

Why Earth Stories Matter

In order to fully address climate change, those of us in industrialized societies will have to go all the way to the bottom of our thinking and change what we believe. We are talking about *a conceptual revolution* here. We are talking about changing what we call "reality." We are talking about changing the stories we are telling ourselves about the earth and our place in it. We must change these stories in order to clearly perceive the *solutions* to climate change and environmental degradation. We must change our thinking and perceptions before we will act differently. This is why earth stories matter.

Most people know what the solutions to today's problems are. My grandfather died of cancer when he was thirty-nine years old, leaving behind his wife and three young girls. He smoked four packs of cigarettes a day. I asked my mom if people knew that smoking caused cancer in 1935. "Of course we did," she said, "but everybody smoked." They knew about the problem and they knew the solution. But they hadn't shifted their thinking to a place where they questioned tobacco companies who actively promoted products that caused disease and death.

Tobacco is a powerful story of the negative aspects of groupthink and how destructive behavior can so easily be normalized. It shows what happens when we don't question norms, popular opinion, or our own habits. It raises similar questions about climate change and poisoning the planet: Are we going to continue to look the other way when lives end too early or homes, businesses, and forests are destroyed by floods or fires? Is it time to put away politeness and talk about what's really going on, even if it's uncomfortable?

With environmental issues, we have to look at business as usual and question it. We must question the belief that we must sacrifice a clean environment for jobs. We must question the assumption that chemical companies should be free to make any product they want and that regulators will catch any bad products before they cause harm. We must question the priority we put on short-term profits and find new ways to do business. We must question commodity-scale agriculture, fishing, and forestry that puts production and short-term profits ahead of long-term sustainability. We must find ways to produce food and energy that work *with* the earth's natural systems, instead of *against* them.

Natural Climate Solutions

Activist and author Paul Hawken worked with a coalition of seventy academic fellows and 120 advisors from around the world to study one hundred climate-change solutions in an initiative called Project Drawdown. They say that if all of their recommended solutions are implemented, it is possible to create a "climate drawdown" in which greenhouse gases and global temperatures are declining, not rising.[20]

What's most interesting about the drawdown solutions is how many of them—ten of the top twenty—involve agricultural, forestry, and land conservation methods that harness and work with natural systems. Silvopasture, the practice of grazing animals among trees, is a powerful example. Instead of removing trees to create pasture, pastureland is managed as a symbiotic system of trees, plants, and grazing animals. The trees provide shade, hold moisture in the soil allowing grasses to thrive, protect and regenerate the soil, provide protection from wind, absorb carbon from the atmosphere, and emit oxygen through photosynthesis. Animals feed on the grasses and plants between the trees.

Silvopasture has been practiced for 4,500 years in Spain and Portugal. The results are proven: farmers spend less on pesticides and fertilizers, the soil remains healthy, animal health is improved, and production of milk, meat, and offspring rises. Expanding the acreage in silvopasture from the current 351 million acres to 554 million acres worldwide would reduce carbon emissions by 31.2 gigatons over 30 years.[21] A gigaton of greenhouse gases would fill a space larger than 500,000 Olympic-sized swimming pools. The bottom line is that increasing silvopasture acreage would make a significant difference to the health of the animals, land, water, and air. And it would significantly diminish greenhouse gas emissions.

What stands in the way of meeting the silvopasture goal of 554 million acres worldwide? Human belief and investment dollars. Many farmers are wedded to a belief that grazing animals must be done on cleared fields. Farmers who deviate from traditional practice may be ridiculed or even have their trees burned. Even though the return on investment for silvopasture is positive, the $400–$800 cost per acre to convert to silvopasture is financially out of reach for most farmers.

I recently attended a webinar on natural climate solutions. Research and pilot projects are underway across the world to better understand agricultural and forestry practices that improve water and soils and lower greenhouse gas emissions. While practices will vary from region to region, some that I heard about on the webinar include:

No-till farming

Cover crops

Land conservation

Shoreline management

Reforestation

Fire management

Natural forest management with longer rotation times

Plantation forestry

Peatland preservation

Timber stand improvement

Salt marsh preservation

Carbon storage in soils

All of these solutions are regenerative and work with the earth's natural systems instead of dominating them. Many policies and programs to incentivize natural climate solutions are being studied and implemented, which is exciting news. Some of these include tax incentives, grant programs, green investment banks, and conservation easements.

Businesses are working on technology-based solutions, too. One example is the Terraton Initiative, launched by Indigo Agriculture, an early-stage business.[22] This experimental program uses software to create a carbon market that would provide farmers with financial incentives to remove carbon from the atmosphere and sequester it in agricultural soil. Farmers would accomplish this through regenerative agriculture—a combination of minimal tillage, cover crops, crop rotations, using fewer chemicals and fertilizers, and silvopasture. This and other programs like it are what's needed to provide incentives for farmers to rebalance agriculture with the earth's natural systems.

The solutions listed here and outlined in Project Drawdown are measurable ways of implementing the story of interconnection, where humans work in harmony with the earth instead of against it.

Like smoking in the 1930s, both the problems and the solutions are known. But we need to fully shift our thinking about the earth and make different choices in order to save ourselves and the planet. Seeing the earth as a *partner* reveals new ways of being and acting that support our collective health and future.

The Advocate's Role

The role of the environmental advocate is to tell the story of interconnection. Advocates must question assumptions and beliefs, create new ways of seeing and communicating about the environment, and change public thinking, like MADD did for drunk driving.

Some environmental activists don't just tell the story, they act it out. People in cities have planted gardens in empty lots and then defended them with civil disobedience when owners wanted to pave them over for parking lots. Tree-sitter Julia Butterfly Hill lived for two years in a three-thousand-year-old sequoia tree in order to save it from being cut down by loggers. She and her support team succeeded in saving her tree and others nearby. This kind of direct action is story making, an example of what direct action, at its best, does.

Both environmental advocates and activists must tell the story of interconnection to family members, community members, professional colleagues, and decision makers. The environmental advocate must act on the story by showing kindness to the earth, both individually and collectively.

When I pick wildflowers, I always leave some to go to seed and regenerate the patch for next year. When I select a tree to cut for firewood, I consider the surrounding forest and how my cutting can cause the least damage and support the forest's continued growth. When I work with opponents and decision makers on a policy issue, I work to maintain respect for the integrity of others, and I do my best to understand the broader consequences of the proposed policy change. When I work within organizations, I do my best to put myself in others' shoes before responding.

The shift in thinking that industrialized cultures need to make for a healthy environment is profound: We must shift from dominating the earth to valuing it as the system on which our lives and all life depends. We must value every human being, no matter their race, class, gender, background, or education. We must honor every living thing, from a tiny seed to a giant whale, as part of a whole system of life. We must see all life as part of an interconnected system. We must consider everyone and everything that is affected when making public and corporate decisions. We must cultivate and harvest in a way that returns nutrients to the soil. We must value and honor human creativity and productivity, but not at the expense of future generations. We must give resources back to the earth in exchange for the resources we take. We must implement solutions, like those recommended by Project Drawdown, that work with the earth's natural systems instead of against them.

The wonderful thing is that by opening our minds and hearts to a more inclusive, connected, and loving way of being, we will feel healthier and happier. By expanding our love for each other and for all of life, we will have a more joy-filled experience. By creating systems of business, government, agriculture, education, medicine, and community that are integrated with nature, we will feel more connected and more satisfied with our lives. This should motivate environmental advocates everywhere.

In addition to hope, advocates also need courage. Many in society will push back against advocates' proposals to support the environment. Many will defend their interests against environmentalists, especially those who are heavily invested in the status quo. Advocates must do the hard work of listening to opponents and finding possible ways to accommodate their needs.

Others will attack advocates, calling them ignorant, uninformed, and worse. This is why advocates need to be grounded in their own hearts, their own truth, and their own personal stories. Being grounded and holding a vision of a healthier, more peaceful planet will bring advocates through the difficult times.

4

Bridging the Left and the Right

Now we must move towards understanding our shared existence on the planet, not because it is a nice addition to what we do, but because it is a matter of survival.

—CHRISTIANA FIGUERES and TOM RIVETT-CARNAC,
architects of the 2015 Paris Agreement

This chapter will shine a light on the different ways in which people on the right and the left think, based on the unconscious worldview a person has accepted as reality. It will deepen your understanding of the earth stories discussed in chapter 3. It will help you have persuasive conversations with decision makers and stakeholders who see the world in different ways. Bridging the gap between how the right and the left think is key to crafting viable policy solutions and getting the results you want.

Beginnings of the Environmental Movement

Protecting the environment didn't use to be partisan. The US Congress passed twenty-eight major environmental laws between 1970 and 1980. These foundational pieces of legislation were sponsored by prominent Republicans in Congress and were supported by Democrats, and most were signed by President Nixon, a Republican. The box below presents some highlights of environmental legislation enacted during this period.

1970–1980: THE GOLDEN AGE OF ENVIRONMENTAL LEGISLATION

Clean Air Act: enacted 1963; amended 1970, 1977, 1990

National Environmental Policy Act: enacted 1970

First Earth Day: April 22, 1970

Environmental Protection Agency: created 1970

Clean Water Act: enacted 1972

Ban on DDT: enacted 1972

Coastal Zone Management Act: enacted 1972

Endangered Species Act: enacted 1973

Toxic Substances Control Act: enacted 1976

Resource Conservation and Recovery Act (solid waste): enacted 1976

Comprehensive Environmental Response, Compensation, and Liability Act (Superfund): enacted 1980

What caused this groundswell of environmental law in the 1970s? Many say it was the visible mess this country had made of waterways and air due to industrial pollution. By the 1960s the nation was deeply engaged with an old earth story that said the stench in the air near paper plants and the oil slicks on rivers were signs of progress, jobs, and money. We accepted these conditions on the basis of industrial progress. In the 1970s, that earth story started to change.

How did Americans shift away from thinking of pollution as an unavoidable side effect of industry and toward thinking of it as something we needed to change? Television news was an important factor. By the late 1960s a majority of US households had a television, and national news programs were broadcast on three networks every evening. Entire families would sit and watch the news together.

In 1969, an oil well off Santa Barbara, California, blew up, spewing a thousand gallons of oil per hour for a month before it could be stopped. Television news showed a growing thirty-five-mile oil slick along California's coast. Images of birds soaked in thick black oil and dead seals washing up in tar-blackened waves were startling.

Later the same year, TV cameras caught images of burning oil slicks on the Cuyahoga River near Cleveland. The Cuyahoga had caught fire before, but when TV footage showed flames leaping into the night sky with the city in the background, people began to wake up. TV news also showed dark clouds of smog in the sky over Los Angeles. These images were presented night after night.[1] They became a flashpoint for the founding of the environmental movement, leading to a flurry of advocacy for new laws and regulations.

The very first Earth Day was celebrated on April 22, 1970. Twenty million people turned out for Earth Day events across the country that day, representing almost 10% of the US population at the time. There was a growing consensus that protecting our environment was the right thing to do. With this level of support, passing environmental legislation was not difficult. What has happened since then? A look at prevailing worldviews and the morals behind them will provide some clues.

LOVE CANAL

A neighborhood of about one thousand working-class homes in the town of Niagara Falls, New York, made headlines in 1978. Back in the 1890s, entrepreneur William Love had founded a town named Model City on the banks of Lake Ontario. As part of the project, he started digging a canal that would bypass the Niagara River as a shipping lane while providing power to the town. Love's Model City project failed, and the property was acquired by the Hooker Chemical Company in the 1940s. Hooker dumped a large quantity of chemical waste there from the 1940s until the early 1950s, a total of about twenty thousand tons of caustics, alkalines, fatty acids, and chlorinated hydrocarbons over a seventy-acre burial site.

In the early 1950s the Niagara Falls City School District acquired the site, built two schools there, and sold the rest of the land for housing development. The new construction breached the clay walls of the underground dump, and subsequent wet weather washed black fluids into backyards and public playgrounds. In 1978 a harsh winter storm dumped three feet of snow, raising the water table and flooding basements nearby with chemical waste. At this time local journalists began reporting the story, and the city's consultants found two hundred organic chemical compounds present in the neighborhood, including many known carcinogens.

In response, community residents organized protests and rallies, including holding several employees of the US Environmental Protection Agency (EPA) hostage, in order to bring attention to their demands. Seven or eight organizations participated in the protests. In 1978, President Carter announced a federal emergency at Love Canal, the first time federal emergency funds had been used for a situation other than a natural disaster. In 1980, largely in response to Love Canal, Congress passed the Comprehensive Environmental Response, Compensation, and Liability Act, and Love Canal was put first on the list of so-called Superfund sites to be cleaned up. About 950 families were relocated from the area, and remedial activities were completed by 1989. The cleanup took twenty-one years and cost $400 million. The Love Canal story contributed to the fervor of environmentalism in the 1970s.[2]

What Are Worldviews?

George Lakoff, a retired professor of cognitive science and linguistics at the University of California, Berkeley, faced a paradox. How could people who were pro-life also be in favor of capital punishment? How could life be viewed as sacred before birth and dispensable later in life? It did not make sense to him. Similarly, if single-payer health care saves money while providing health care to more people, why would cost-conscious conservatives oppose it?

Lakoff was determined to find some internal logic behind these apparent inconsistencies. We grow up in families, he reasoned, so our family experience gives us our first metaphors and forms the basis for how we perceive the world. His research revealed that Americans see government and public policy through a family metaphor, where the government is a parent and we the people are family members. And family experiences, as Lakoff discovered, can be very different.

Lakoff's research is based on the way the brain works. We continuously take unconscious shortcuts in our brains. Thinking becomes a habit, following pathways of thought created early in life that we are no longer aware of. Neuroscientists currently believe we are unaware of as much as 95% of our brain activity. This is why it's possible to go through a morning routine or commute to work without recalling the details. What is called "common sense" is an example of habitual shortcuts in our thinking based on past experience and accumulated knowledge.

When learning something new, we think in terms of metaphors and thought patterns based on things we already know. When motor cars were first introduced, they were called "horseless carriages." People knew what carriages were, so logically a car would be a horseless carriage and later an "auto-mobile." Similarly, we first called the internet the World Wide Web because we understood human networks as a web of connections, and the internet was a virtual human network. Artificial intelligence technology is based on a logical sequencing of if-then statements, similar to human reasoning, or intelligence; hence the term "artificial intelligence." You get the idea.

Through his research Lakoff discovered two distinct family metaphors that are dominant in the United States: the "strict father" and the "nurturing parent." These unconscious metaphors organize our thinking in ways that have profound political ramifications.

THE STRICT FATHER WORLDVIEW

The strict father worldview is based on an authoritarian parenting style wherein one parent—usually (but not always) the father—is at the top of a family hierarchy. Other family members are expected to respect and obey the father. This worldview is based on the assumption that children will behave badly if left to their own devices. Children need discipline from parents and other authority figures to become good. Child rearing under the strict father worldview is focused on enforcing rules through discipline. Success in life is presumed to be based on how well people conform to a set of rules governing such behaviors as working hard and respecting authority. This worldview assumes the world is a dangerous place, and people—especially women and children—need to be protected. It is the father's duty to protect the family.

The strict father worldview is focused on individual responsibility. What happens to you in life is your responsibility. This means that if you are poor or unsuccessful, it is your fault for not paying attention in school, not getting a good education, or not applying yourself in some way. People who don't follow the rules and commit crimes should be punished. It is for this reason that most conservatives support capital punishment.

Government, as understood within the strict father worldview, should focus on protecting the nation's people from foreign enemies and natural disasters—threats that are large or far away, that an individual cannot realistically take responsibility for. This explains the conservative support for a large military and offering aid when a major storm or pandemic hits.

When it comes to government's relationship with individuals and businesses, the notion of individual responsibility and discipline takes precedence. Successful individuals are those who are disciplined, work hard, and play by the rules. Therefore, individuals and business leaders should be left alone to live their lives and do their work without government rules or regulations, which are seen as interference. If individuals have done their duty to learn and obey the rules of hard work, perseverance, respect for authority, and so on, they should not need the government to tell them what to do. In the strict father worldview, it is not the place of government to provide opportunities, assist people who need help, or prohibit businesses from doing harmful things through laws, rules, and regulations.

Businesses, from the strict father worldview, are considered trusted enterprises run by model citizens. Those who succeed in business have played by the rules, worked hard, been responsible, and created value. Successful businesspeople are respected and sometimes revered. Business owners and shareholders deserve to be rewarded and even get rich in exchange for taking risks, working hard, and deploying their energy to run a business. Progress and profit take precedence over caring for the environment. Besides, the idea that a business might act irresponsibly by polluting the environment, harming people, or taking advantage of them is generally unthinkable in this worldview.

The concept of hierarchy, which is part of the strict father mindset, is extended to the rest of life. Those holding strict father worldviews tend to view men as superior to women, parents as superior to children, White people as superior to people of color, humans as superior to nature, and industrial progress as superior to the environment.

Some people with a strict father worldview believe individual desires take precedence over any social or collective good. Those who refused to wear face masks during the COVID-19 pandemic are in this category. Even though wearing a mask was proven to reduce the risk of sickness and death in the community, some put a higher priority on their own desire to not wear a mask than on the health of others. This thinking takes the old earth story of domination to an extreme, where the individual dominates all other forms of life.

The strict father worldview can also result in situations where people fear an authoritarian leader to the point of giving up their own sense of moral responsibility. We have seen this in families, companies, and governments where people go along to get along and do not challenge authority, even when that authority is demonstrably causing harm. This is where authoritarianism takes root.

THE NURTURING PARENT WORLDVIEW

The nurturing parent worldview is diametrically opposed to the strict father worldview. It is based on parents as nurturers, where the emphasis in the family is on fairness and equality, not hierarchy. Parents with this worldview often see themselves as teachers who want to bring out the inherent goodness in their children. The lessons they teach are not about obeying rules or functioning within a hierarchy; rather, they teach empathy and respect for others. An underlying belief is that the world is a good and abundant place (as opposed to a dangerous place) and that most people will do well, if given a fair opportunity to succeed.

The nurturing parent worldview is focused on community and social responsibility, not the individual. What happens to you in life is mostly a result of the opportunities you've had. If you attended poor schools and experienced violence in your neighborhood, you were disadvantaged by social and community problems. If you didn't do well, it was not entirely your individual responsibility, but at least partly a result of your social situation. Those with nurturing parent worldviews tend to believe it is up to the community to address social problems.

Humanity, in the nurturing parent worldview, is seen as organized in a set of concentric circles, from neighborhoods and communities, to towns and cities, to state and federal government. There is a sense that everyone is a part of the collective or the common good. The nurturing parent worldview sees government as the collective will of the people. Government should ensure everyone has a safe, healthy place to live, and equal and fair opportunities to contribute to society and improve their lives. Government regulations serve to protect people and the environment. Good-quality public education and social programs are needed to assure that everyone has a fair chance to succeed.

Businesses are viewed in the nurturing parent worldview as capable of doing good, but not entirely trustworthy. The motivation to increase profits has too often led to harmful pollution, dishonest dealings, and poor treatment of workers. Most people with nurturing parent worldviews would like to see businesses be responsible to a wider group of stakeholders than just owners and shareholders. Business decisions should take customers, employees, suppliers, communities, and the environment into account, not just the owners' agenda. In the nurturing parent worldview, maximizing profits as the sole purpose of business leads to harmful effects on individuals, communities, and the environment.

UNDERSTANDING PATRIARCHY

Patriarchy is aligned with the strict father worldview. It is based on a hierarchy that awards economic and governing power to men and supports them in roles of leadership and authority. The word "patriarchy" is derived from the Latin *pater*, meaning "father," and *-arch*, meaning "to rule." At its root, patriarchy means putting men in charge.

Patriarchy is typically described as an unjust, hierarchical social system that subordinates and discriminates against women. Because it is hierarchical, it also discriminates against races, genders, ethnic groups, and social classes. Patriarchy has been a tradition in many cultures, countries, and religions. Men have been in positions of power for generations, and sharing power doesn't come easily.

Riane Eisler, a social systems scientist and author, speaks of the shift we need to make as moving from a domination (patriarchal) economy to a partnership economy. She describes a domination system as "a system of top-down rankings ultimately backed up by fear or force—man over man, man over woman, race over race, religion over religion, and man over nature." Her alternative, which she calls "a partnership system," consists of:

> A more democratic and egalitarian structure in both the family and state or tribe, equal partnerships between women and men, and with this a high valuing (with)in women and men, as well as in social and economic policy, of traits and activities stereotypically considered feminine, such as care and caregiving; a low degree of abuse and violence, because they are not needed to maintain rigid rankings of domination. *A system of beliefs that presents relations of partnership and mutual respect as normal and desirable.*[3] (italics added for emphasis)

Women in Western cultures have fought patriarchy for two centuries. It was seventy-two years from the first gathering devoted to a woman's right to vote in the United States to the signing of the 19th Amendment, which established the right of Black and White women to vote in the United States.[4] It was an additional twenty-three years before Asian American immigrant women could vote.[5] Slowly women have made gains in various professional fields. Still today, women represent just 20% of corporate board members[6] and 7% of CEOs of Fortune 500 companies.[7]

Patriarchy plays out in many ways. When I was in ninth grade, I was an excellent squash player. I played the boys on my school's junior varsity team after school, and I often won. I asked if I could join the team. I was told I wouldn't be allowed to do that. When I asked why, the answer was: "If we allowed you on the team, it would take away a spot for a boy."

This revealed a spectrum of limited, sexist beliefs. As a girl, I had less or maybe no value to the team, despite the skills I had worked hard to develop. It also implied that boys would not want to play me and especially would not want to lose to a lesser kind of person—a girl! This would be a blow to the myth of male superiority. This kind of hierarchical thinking degrades everyone involved.

Patriarchal thinking and roles can sometimes be a matter of life and death. We have seen this from New Orleans to Kenya, where floods, storms, and droughts have killed more women than men. According to a report by the National Institutes of Health, in the wake of the 2004 Indian Ocean tsunami, surviving men outnumbered women by a 3:1 ratio in Sri Lanka, Indonesia, and India.[8] A 2011 study of natural disasters around the world found that women and children are fourteen times more likely to die or be injured during a disaster than men.[9] Causes include the fact that men are often away from home working, men are physically stronger and more likely to be able to swim, and women lose precious evacuation time searching for children and relatives.[10]

While the focus of this book is primarily on advocacy in the United States, it's important for environmental advocates to know that one of the most important ways to address global climate change is to *empower women through education and access to family planning services*. According to the

World Health Organization, *270 million women* would like to be able to choose the number of children they have, but they don't have access to reproductive health services.[11,12] Seventy-four million unwanted pregnancies a year are the result. Women everywhere want to have a choice about their family size. Access to family planning for women worldwide would reduce the long-term population growth rate. By reducing unwanted births, there would be an estimated 848 million fewer people on the planet by 2050.[13] This would save the resources needed to feed, house, and clothe more people, and it would reduce carbon emissions.

International governments have recognized gender equality as an important part of climate policy. In the seventeen sustainability goals of the United Nations, goal #5 reads: "Achieve gender equality and empower all women and girls."[14] Nine specific actions and fourteen indicators support this goal. Also, the 2019 UN Global Climate Conference unanimously adopted a five-year Gender Action Plan to promote gender equality and gender-responsive climate action in all UN member countries. This was applauded as a major achievement.

No conversation about world population and women's empowerment would be complete without mentioning the disparity in consumption of natural resources between industrialized and non-industrialized nations. Americans make up less than 5% of the world's population, but we consume 20% of the world's energy. A family in India would have to have 10 children or more to match the energy consumption of an American family with one child.[15] *Both* overconsumption and women's empowerment need to be addressed in order to sustain life on the planet.

Women's voices must be heard, and women need to be a part of public policy decisions in order to rebalance policies and address the one-dimensional perspective of patriarchy. Patriarchy represents an imbalance of power, and environmental advocates must challenge patriarchal thinking and policies in order for men, women, and the earth to become whole.

Every person must question assumptions about the status of men and women and a power structure that values one above the other. People of all ethnicities, genders, sexualities, and religions, and those with power and those without, need to come together in solidarity to share power and end patriarchy. Then we can have an honest conversation about how to create a more balanced future for ourselves and our children.

Communicating across Left and Right

When I'm teaching or speaking, one of the most frequent questions I hear is: "How do I talk with those who hold a different worldview from my own?" It's not always easy. But it can be done. Disagreement can have a positive outcome when people seek to understand each other.

One of the first things to do in a conversation with someone who holds an opposite worldview is to check in with yourself. Are you coming from a place of curiosity, or a place of fear? I know when my nephew told me that Americans would be safer if everyone carried a gun, I felt fear. For me, the idea of going to a shopping mall knowing everyone is armed is a terrifying thought. In my fear, I gave up my personal power, and I could not carry on the conversation with a sense of curiosity allowing me to listen and learn. It shut me down. The only thing I could do then was to say that I felt very uncomfortable with what he said, and I would not be able to continue the conversation. You, too, need to recognize when you have lost your emotional balance and can't have a constructive conversation. It happens to all of us.

Personal, heartfelt stories are a key to breaking through people's worldview biases. Imagine a farmer telling a story about converting his dairy herd from conventional to organic management. One requirement for organic certification is that cows must graze outdoors every day in spring, summer, and fall. This farmer might mention how his cows are much more cooperative after being outdoors, allowing milking machines to be hooked up without resistance. He might also say how occurrence of disease under the organic protocols is much less than under conventional farming protocols. This is a true story from a Maine farmer, and it illustrates the value of expanding his business's mission from maximizing profit alone to placing value on animal health too.

Another key to communicating with people who hold different world-views from you is to speak directly and supportively to *their personal experiences.* In Maine there is a great gulf between people with right and left worldviews. While some people are retrofitting their homes with heat pumps and solar power, others are denying that climate change exists. In light of this, the Maine Climate Table, an organization that seeks to engage people in addressing climate change, sponsored research on how to talk to Mainers about climate change. Focus groups and surveys were conducted statewide to better understand people's views.

A major finding was that recognizing local and personal experiences of climate change opens the door to good policy discussions. For instance, Maine lakes melt in the spring ten to fourteen days earlier than they used to. Maine has experienced Lyme disease brought by deer ticks not seen before. Maine's shrimp season has been canceled for four years running because the shrimp have moved north to colder waters. Mainers have personally observed and experienced these things.

Beginning conversations with lived experiences is a great way to introduce policies to address climate change. What climate changes have people personally experienced in your area? You might say things like, "Have you noticed that we are getting more [or less] rain than we used to?" Talking about local changes in the weather or other direct experiences of climate change is your opening to communicating across worldviews.

The flip side of speaking supportively to someone's values and personal experiences is to never, ever contradict them! If you contradict or threaten someone's experience or values, they are likely to shut down and not hear what you are saying. Many climate change deniers are afraid of environmentalists because they believe environmentalists want to take away things they hold dear. They may feel that certain aspects of their lifestyle, like driving a large pickup truck, are threatened. Your position as an environmental advocate may be threatening to some people without your saying anything. You can bridge this worldview divide by starting a conversation with curiosity about someone's experiences and staying away from challenging their values.

One thing I've observed over and over in policy work is that people want to be heard. Many *assume they will not be heard,* especially by government agencies. I spent many late nights responding personally to comments and inquiries sent by citizens to my government agency. I gave an honest and specific explanation in response to each question, regardless of whether I agreed or disagreed with their view. I did this to demonstrate that our agency was listening. It worked.

Advocacy groups should follow similar practices and respond personally to questions and criticisms they receive. Often people will go along with policies or decisions that they don't agree with, as long as they truly feel heard!

It works best to talk and listen with respect without trying to change someone's view. Listen to understand where an opposing person is coming from. Ask why their views are important to them or if they had an experience that led them to their view. Showing true interest goes a long way toward defusing what could become a misunderstanding or shouting match.

Going further, you should work to understand the worldviews of those opposed to you and then try to create a *bridge* from their worldview to the issue you want to discuss. The gun safety lobby has generally misunderstood how gun owners derive a sense of control and power through gun ownership. We live in turbulent times, and gun ownership provides a sense of safety to many. It's an effective strategy when gun safety advocates acknowledge this. A gun safety advocate might begin a conversation by saying, "I understand that gun ownership is important to you and your safety, and I would never want to take your guns away. But I'd be interested in your thoughts on how we can keep guns out of the hands of children." In this way, you have acknowledged their values and created a bridge to the issue you want to talk about.

Disagreement can be positive when we are open to learning from each other. True understanding has great benefits, including finding solutions that work, and fully understanding the consequences of a decision.

If a disagreement is going nowhere, you can agree to disagree and then change the subject. But if someone intentionally baits or mistreats you with no intention of listening, that's abuse. If this occurs, you might ask the person why they are being that way and listen to the answer. You might also say how the mistreatment affects you and derails the conversation.

Sometimes in these situations, it's best to end the conversation. A technique that works well is to quietly say, "I don't speak with people who are shouting [or trying to impose their view on me]. I'd be happy to speak with you at another time, if you're interested in a dialogue where we both can share and learn from each other."

Climate Change: Bringing People Together

The discussion in this chapter is based on broad generalizations about worldviews. But individuals cannot be generalized. Each of us is unique, with a unique experience, and based on that experience, a unique point of view. While people lean toward one of the two worldviews described above, most have a mix of worldviews within them. A person might discipline children according to authoritarian rules at home while belonging to a union that makes collective decisions at work. Or a person might be conservative in supporting an authoritarian style of policing but liberal in allowing women the right to choose an abortion. Lakoff calls this "biconceptualism" and says almost everyone is biconceptual to some degree. Models like Lakoff's can aid our understanding but should never be used to totally define a person.

As you probably have guessed, the two worldviews described in this chapter correlate with the underlying thinking of conservatives on the right (strict father worldview) and liberals or progressives on the left (nurturing parent worldview). I am hopeful that, as we did in the 1970s, humanity will again see the environment as a nonpartisan issue affecting everyone. We must make a shift in consciousness wherein everyone, regardless of worldview, realizes we must care for the earth and each other if we are to survive as a species. There is emerging evidence that this shift is happening.

Pope Francis' encyclical, which we mentioned earlier, introduced the idea that caring for the earth is the responsibility of Catholics everywhere. There are an estimated 1.2 billion Roman Catholics in the world.[16] Other religious denominations have also been active in addressing climate change and environmental issues, including the Episcopal Church, the United Church of Christ, Quakers, and Unitarian Universalists.

Evangelical Christians who are politically conservative have typically avoided or denied the issue of climate change. Recently, however, led by the younger generation of church members, evangelicals are starting climate groups. They are calling their movement "Creation Care," and their rationale is based on the Bible, where God calls upon humanity to care for His creation, the earth. There are approximately 100 million people who identify as evangelical Christians in the United States, and 619 million in the world. The Creation Care movement supports a carbon tax. Could they also support corporate responsibility for pollution? Protection of the earth from harmful practices? These are questions for both the right and the left to explore. Imagine how powerful it could be if this sector were to fully embrace a vision of a healthy planet. Environmental advocates should engage evangelicals as important participants and allies in solving climate change and toxic pollution.

Hunters, fishermen, and outdoor enthusiasts are beginning to speak up for the environment, too. People in this sector are passionate about their personal freedom, and most of them hold conservative political views. They are seeing the outdoors they love change around them. Some who previously held anti-climate-change views are starting to organize to protect their favorite hunting and fishing grounds. A group of forty-one hunting and fishing organizations and gear manufacturers came together recently to urge Democrats and Republicans in Congress to do more to combat climate change. They support measures to preserve and restore wildlife habitat, lock carbon out of the atmosphere, incentivize farmers to sequester carbon by planting grasses, and set aside space for birds, deer, and other game.[17]

The American Climate Contract is a conservative response to the progressive Green New Deal. Started and promoted by Benji Backer and a group of college Republicans, the contract relies heavily on market incentives, new technologies, and infrastructure upgrades to address climate change. It calls for passing fourteen climate-related bills that have been languishing in Congress in recent years. The Climate Contract is a positive development, but it is an incremental approach, not a visionary one. You won't find a carbon tax or environmental justice mentioned in it. If all of its platform is enacted, carbon emissions would decrease. But even if carbon emissions were reduced significantly, we would still suffer from toxic pollution, deforestation, soil depletion, and environmental racism and inequality. Still, the contract might capture the attention of Republican lawmakers who have resisted other efforts to address environmental issues. It could give them a path to consider climate policies that are supported by young Republicans.[18,19]

While conservative Republicans in Congress have largely rejected the economywide climate measures proposed by Democrats, many are beginning to support specific measures to tackle climate change. The Theodore Roosevelt Conservation Caucus was formed in 2019 by Republicans in the House and Senate to "promote constructive efforts to address environmental problems."[20] The Climate Solutions Caucus is a bipartisan Senate group formed to "explore bipartisan policy options that address the impacts, causes, and challenges of our changing climate."[21] The formation of these groups is a response to pressure from environmental advocates and the increase in climate-related events in recent years. As of this writing, there are numerous bipartisan climate and environmental bills in Congress. Here are a few examples:

- The **Kigali Amendment** supports an international agreement to phase out chemicals widely used in air conditioners and refrigeration that are potent drivers of climate change.[22]

- The **Growing Climate Solutions Act** is a bill to establish protocols and incentives for farmers, ranchers, and landowners to develop projects that can use carbon dioxide–absorbing practices to generate carbon offset credits. This initiative would provide the financial basis for investments in reforestation, regenerative agriculture, and carbon sequestration.[23]

- The **Trillion Trees Act** calls for planting 1 trillion trees globally by 2050.

- The **Recovering America's Wildlife Act** would provide $1.4 billion in dedicated annual funding to state and tribal fish and wildlife agencies.[24]

Will the emergence of conservative climate activists and innovative legislation lead to sweeping policy change? It hasn't happened yet. But my gut tells me that climate change could be the issue that brings people and politicians together in this decade. President Biden's climate policies and the increasing pressure on Congress from a broad spectrum of voters and citizen advocates are hopeful signs.

Going further, in order to heal damage done to the earth and sustain life for future generations, humanity *has no choice* but to come together and care for the planet. We must recognize too that climate change is only one of several critical environmental issues that must be addressed. We could eliminate carbon emissions completely and still perish from deforestation, toxic pollution, soil depletion, lack of clean water, or disease.

To restore the environment to health, we don't need 100% agreement, but we do need critical mass, like we had in the 1970s. Ten percent of the population showing up on Earth Day in 1970 was enough to move Congress to pass the Clean Air and Clean Water Acts and other major environmental legislation. In a Harvard University study of three hundred campaigns and revolutions around the world that sought to change regimes, every campaign that had active participation from at least 3.5% of the population succeeded, and some succeeded with less.[25]

Today, in our polarized bickering we are essentially asking, "Which worldview should predominate?" The right and the left have argued back and forth endlessly over this with little progress, as seen over the past few years in Congress.

It is now time to change the question. Instead we should ask, "How can we accommodate our differences and work together to heal the planet?" This question can lead to new, life-affirming policies about how we care for each other and the earth. Environmental advocates are perfectly positioned to initiate these conversations and take action.

5

Developing Environmental Policy

It's not enough to know. We have to act on what we know.

—ANGAANGAQ ANGAKKSUAQ,
Eskimo-Kalaallit elder and shaman

Worldviews and Environmental Policy

When President Trump appointed a coal industry lobbyist as secretary of the EPA, liberals were aghast. For people with a nurturing parent world-view, the EPA was created to protect citizens, communities, and the environment from the harmful effects of industry. The coal industry in particular has been notorious for removing mountaintops to extract coal, storing mining waste in toxic ponds, exposing workers to toxic coal dust, and producing acid rain and carbon emissions when coal is burned. To liberals, appointing a coal industry executive to head the EPA was allow-ing the fox to guard the henhouse. This appointment and the subsequent weakening of EPA laws, rules, and enforcement was outrageous and immoral, from their point of view.

But conservatives welcomed Trump's choice. People with a strict father worldview felt that having an industry executive appointed to head the EPA would ensure that the agency wouldn't constrain industry with too many regulations that punish good, successful people for doing what they are supposed to do. From this worldview, environmental regulations serve to prevent businesses and the people who run them from pursuing their interests. To restrict the freedom of good and enterprising people, including those providing coal—a valuable fuel—is immoral.

Here we have an example of deep polarization based on opposing moral values. Neither side can hear the other, because they are rooted in opposite views of right and wrong.

People with strict father worldviews tend to see the earth as a resource that should be exploited to support human life. Humans are at the top of life's hierarchy. Therefore, we should be cultivating, extracting, and harvesting without worrying too much about other species or effects on local communities. Yes, we should be good earth stewards, but we should not let that get in the way of human enterprise, which is valued above all else. This view fits squarely with the story of domination as described in chapter 3. And it's not all bad. This thinking has provided us with a growing economy that has provided food, fuel, transportation, medicine, and jobs for an extended period of time.

The problem is that this view is not sustainable and is causing great harm. Resources cannot be extracted forever. And industrial pollution from resource extraction and manufacturing has harmed communities who live nearby, causing sickness and death. Unfortunately, poor communities and people of color have been the most adversely affected.

It should not be a surprise that those holding nurturing parent worldviews tend to see the earth as our life-giving mother who should be protected from harmful human activity. This worldview correlates with the new earth story of interconnection described in chapter 3, in which humans are not at the top or center of life; rather, they are an integral part of life. The story of interconnection calls for humanity to work with nature and care for the earth while meeting human needs. It calls for human creativity and for rewarding those who make a positive contribution. But the rewards are not just for the owners and shareholders. The nurturing parent supports business and human activities that affirm life' and benefit all those who are affected, including the earth itself. Let's see how the two worldviews play out in an actual policy issue.

In my classes, I have students do an exercise where they develop policy solutions for an issue, first from a strict father worldview and then from a nurturing parent worldview. What they find is that both the causes of the issue and the policy solutions are seen completely differently, depending on the worldview one holds. This holds true for every issue, from dental decay in children to renewable energy. In general, those with strict father worldviews favor *individual causes and solutions,* and those with nurturing parent worldviews favor *social causes and community-based solutions.* Two examples of these contrasting interpretations are shown below.

Childhood Dental Decay on the Rise[1]

STRICT FATHER CAUSES	NURTURING PARENT CAUSES
Poor oral health is an individual problem.	Poor oral health is a community problem.
Parents and kids need to be more responsible for brushing and flossing.	Many kids don't have access to dental services.
Doctors and dentists are self-interested, just trying to build their practices.	Only dentists are allowed to administer dental sealants, which are effective in preventing tooth decay, limiting access to these services for many.
Poor kids have more important problems to deal with than their teeth.	Poor kids are at greater risk of dental disease, so they need more help.
Parents shouldn't give their children sugary foods and beverages.	Children are constantly exposed to sugary foods and beverages through advertising, vending machines, and school cafeterias.

(continued)

STRICT FATHER POLICY SOLUTIONS	NURTURING PARENT POLICY SOLUTIONS
Educate parents to teach their kids to brush and floss daily. Educate parents about healthy diets for children.	Allow dentists, dental assistants, and doctors to seal teeth. Make this service available in schools.
Mount an educational campaign with public service announcements and brochures about brushing, flossing, and healthy diets.	Remove sugary drinks and candy from schools.

Landfills Overwhelmed by Plastics

STRICT FATHER CAUSES	NURTURING PARENT CAUSES
Recycling and landfilling plastics costs too much. There are less costly solutions, like shipping plastic waste to other countries.	There is far too much plastic produced in packaging, toys, and household goods.
People do not recycle plastics because it's unsanitary and inconvenient.	Municipalities are swamped with plastic waste and don't have a good way to pay for facilities to handle it.
STRICT FATHER SOLUTIONS	**NURTURING PARENT SOLUTIONS**
Stick with less expensive ways to dispose of waste.	Regulate packaging to minimize unrecyclable content.
Make recycling clean and convenient with roadside pickup.	Make packagers take back plastics they produce and reuse the material. Assess a fee on manufacturers and packagers to pay for municipal recycling and disposal facilities.

As you can see, the strict father causes and solutions are *linear*, suggesting single causes with direct solutions, and address symptoms rather than root causes. The nurturing parent worldview tends to see issues more *systemically*, seeking causes that address the root of the problem and then suggesting system-level solutions to address those causes. As Lakoff found in his research, direct cause-and-effect thinking is typical of those with a strict father worldview, and systems thinking is typical of those with a nurturing parent worldview.

Advocates gain power when they understand how people with different worldviews interpret policy issues. They can use this understanding to comprehend the issues at a deep level and develop policy solutions that are likely to gain support from the broadest possible range of people.

How Did We Get So Polarized?

So how did we shift from bipartisan support of environmental regulation in the 1970s to the partisan divide of today? A number of factors are at play, including the history of European conquest and colonial settlement in this country—a topic deserving more discussion than can be given here. But primarily, the partisan divide comes down to people in industrialized nations narrowing their thinking and policies about business, money, and profits.

Milton Friedman, winner of the Nobel Prize in Economics, famously said, "There is one and only one social responsibility of business—to use its resources and engage in activities designed to increase its profits." The idea that a firm's sole responsibility is profit became known as the Friedman Doctrine.[2] It is also known as the shareholder theory, since the profits accrue to shareholders. Colleges and universities have taught this theory and businesses worldwide have followed it since it was introduced in the 1970s. Right-wing think tanks also contributed by promoting business deregulation in order to maximize profits.

Then the Reagan Administration introduced "trickle-down economics" in the 1980s. This policy cut taxes for the wealthy and corporations, with the reasoning that benefits would trickle down to labor and the working classes as the wealthy invested in businesses. At the same time, Congress curbed spending on social programs and borrowed to finance the budget. The stock market did rise as a result. But unfortunately the net effect of these policies was to increase the income gap, making the wealthy wealthier and the poor poorer.

In addition, between 1980 and 2000 many companies moved manufacturing to other countries where labor was cheaper and regulations lax or nonexistent. Many American cities and towns were sacrificed in the pursuit of profits. In Maine I saw shoe factories, textile mills, chicken processing plants, paper mills, and precision manufacturing shut down, leaving communities and individual lives in shambles. In other places, steel, automobile, and parts and equipment factories left town, leaving many unemployed and cities and towns derelict.

As a result of business consolidation, many corporate headquarters were moved to large cities. This, along with moving manufacturing to other countries, meant that corporate operations were no longer transparent to local communities. When the corporate headquarters of a grocery chain moved from Maine to the Netherlands, many senior executives were no longer a part of the local community. We lost their personal support of community organizations, and we lost direct access to company policies and decisions affecting local businesses, workers, and municipalities.

Local communities and local media play a role in keeping companies accountable. When headquarters and operations move elsewhere, this local accountability is lost. This scenario has played out in many communities across the United States.

In worldview terms, the strict father took over the economy. Ronald Reagan served as president from 1981 to 1989, covering much of this period. He had the personal characteristics of a model strict father, a father-knows-best style complete with a deep, authoritarian timbre in his voice. The strict father economy has persisted through all of the presidential administrations since then. The power of the wealthy grew during this time through more tax cuts, and more money was spent on political campaigns to elect politicians who support the strict father economy.

The allure of a wealthy lifestyle and the need of many to identify with the elite for safety and acceptance have caused people to look for ways to justify the dominator class and prove its superiority. This has caused many to support people in positions of power, even when the policies and actions of those in power are counter to their own well-being.[3]

The narrowed focus of businesses on profits and the increased power of wealthy elite have affected the lives of many. Opportunities to grow a career are scarcer, especially for those without a college education. Rural communities and inner cities across America have suffered greatly as schools did not prepare students for a service economy, and good-paying jobs left for cheaper pastures. People of color have been especially hard hit. The middle class shrank and the gap between the wealthy and working classes widened. The resulting inequality is fueling polarization of the left and right, and giving rise to campaigns and movements demanding justice and equality.

Capitalism Today

Today's capitalism exemplifies the story of domination, patriarchy, and the strict father worldview. The unlimited pursuit of profits by corporations, which have been empowered by elites and governments, has marginalized many communities and caused the massive problem of global warming, not to mention resource depletion and habitat destruction.

The markets of today can hardly be called "free," because they are characterized by businesses that oppose free-market policies and seek to destroy or absorb competitors, often by overpowering government decision making through donations and lobbying. Author John Perkins calls this "predatory capitalism" or the "death economy," and he says it is characterized by these traits:

- Maximizing short-term profits to reward the owners
- Seeking to control public policy and markets through fear, donations, threats, debt, and lobbying
- Opposing taxes, public investments, and businesses that enhance quality of life
- Placing high value on nonproductive jobs and businesses (financial deals such as leveraged buyouts, stock manipulation, and speculation)
- Placing low value on jobs that enrich and support life (e.g., teaching, the arts, repair services, alternative healing therapies, local food production)
- Failing to value nature and causing massive extinctions, toxic pollution, global warming, and other environmental problems[4]

The opposite, which Perkins calls the "life economy" and which Riane Eisler and others call the "caring economy,"[5] has the opposite characteristics:

- Maximizing long-term benefits for people and nature
- Supporting democracy and markets by maximizing democratic participation and sharing power
- Supporting taxes, policies, public investments, and businesses that enhance the quality of life
- Placing high value on jobs that enrich and support life
- Placing low value on jobs that are nonproductive and provide no public value
- Valuing and protecting the natural environment and the quality of life[6]

People sometimes get lost here, thinking that there are only two alternatives: capitalism and communism. But both of these in their current form concentrate power and wealth in the hands of a few.

In supporting a life/caring economy, environmental advocates are supporting a wholly different alternative: social or democratic capitalism and its political sister, social democracy. While these concepts deserve entire books of their own, the important point here is that the life/caring economies empower people to be in partnership with each other because *caring for people and the earth is the principle on which trade and exchange of goods and services is based.*

Creating a Caring Economy

Much work is being done to elevate capitalism toward a caring economy. Ethical businesses are not predatory. Instead, they are based on voluntary exchange and creating real value for people and communities. Many businesses are dedicated to serving customers, delivering great products, respecting the needs of employees, and caring for the environment.

"Conscious capitalism" is a phrase coined by John Mackey, CEO of Whole Foods, and Raj Sisodia, a professor of marketing. It refers to a philosophy and a movement based on businesses "serving, aligning, and integrating the interests of all their major stakeholders in order to make a positive impact on the world."[7] Building on the foundation of traditional capitalism, conscious capitalism focuses on purposes beyond pure profits, and fostering a spirit of trust and cooperation among all stakeholders.

L.L.Bean, a manufacturer and retailer of outdoor gear and clothing, provides a good example of a company seeking to balance their actions with the effects of those actions on the company's stakeholder communities. Instead of taking action based only on the bottom line, the company has pledged to consider the impacts on six stakeholder groups—customers, employees, vendors, community, shareholders, and the natural environment—in setting corporate priorities and making decisions. This philosophy was established by CEO Leon Gorman in the 1960s.[8]

In considering a decision about the time required to ship items to customers, L.L.Bean sought to balance the needs of all six stakeholder groups. Company dialogue revealed that retaining employees depended on offering reliable schedules, with two consecutive days off each week. Having two days off yields a happier, healthier, more productive workforce. In making their decision, the company found that employee needs outweighed both customer desires for short shipping times and the company's desire to match the short shipping times offered by competitors. L.L.Bean chose to guarantee two-day shipping, not overnight or one day, in order to support their employees and guarantee two consecutive days off.

L.L.Bean's shipping decision may be better for the environment and delivery workers, too. When shippers have ample time to plan their routes, they move goods efficiently. But when overnight delivery is guaranteed, shippers might end up sending a truck out multiple times a day on the same route, even if the truck is only 10% full. It may also result in truck drivers working overtime or driving during storms or other unsafe conditions.

L.L.Bean's approach to this decision is different from most businesses. Making profits, meeting short-term revenue goals, and paying shareholder dividends usually take precedence over all other considerations. The effects on soils, forests, air, water, workers, customers, residents, or communities are not given much—if any—weight in business decisions. It is easy to see how under the old earth story of domination, corporations have been able to extract, harvest, and pollute, without regard to our health or the earth.

There are many organizations working to help businesses adopt earth-friendly, sustainable operations. One of the largest is B Lab, a nonprofit organization offering benefit corporation ("B Corp") certification for companies that meet an extensive list of sustainability criteria. B Corp certification is a seal of approval for businesses that are trying to do well by doing good. It's also a way to measure and report on corporate achievements other than profit. The B Corp certification process is rigorous, requiring assessment surveys, extensive documentation, and recertification every three years. To date, the vast majority of certified B Corp companies have been small, with fewer than 250 employees.

But B Lab has recently certified several multinational and publicly traded companies. Realizing that they must work with large corporations to make major changes in the way the world economy operates, B Lab has developed B Movement Builders, a new program specifically designed to help large companies transition to operating practices that are more people- and earth-friendly. There are more than 3,500 B Corps in seventy-one countries now. B Lab states its vision for the future as follows: "One day, all companies will compete to be the best for the world."[9]

Similarly, there are laws in thirty-seven states that provide a legal definition of a "benefit corporation." These laws provide legal protection to businesses with expanded missions that include both financial and social goals. Benefit corporation laws protect these companies from investor lawsuits claiming they are not maximizing profits as they carry out their expanded missions. While benefit corporations are voluntary, the laws defining them are a step toward encouraging and implementing a caring economy.

Riane Eisler says one of her favorite quotes is "caring pays, in dollars and cents." What she means is that caring businesses actually do well financially, and in many cases they do better than predatory businesses. Investors are finding stability, good management, and steady positive returns from companies that meet environmental, social, and governance criteria that specify how companies must care for people and the earth. As caring businesses continue to gain a reputation for good financial performance, the world will shift toward a more caring economy.

A movement to divest fossil fuel stocks from investment portfolios is well under way. The New York State Pension fund is currently divesting from fossil fuel investments worth $12 billion and will sell its shares in other companies that contribute to global warming by 2040. According to Divest Invest, a group that monitors divestments, 1,246 institutions and nearly sixty thousand individual investors have committed to shedding their investments in fossil fuels. These actions are the result of an eight-year campaign by forty climate advocacy and retiree organizations. The UK, Ireland, and Sweden have adopted fossil fuel divestment plans, and the UN secretary-general has urged other governments, foundations, and universities to follow suit.[10]

There are many businesses, consultants, and nonprofit organizations working to bring us the caring economy we need. The question is whether these efforts will be enough, soon enough, and whether they will succeed in changing the practices of the worst polluters—oil, gas, chemical, and agribusiness companies, for example.

"The lure of higher profits time and again has proven irresistible to those at the top of the corporate pyramid," says economist Marianne Hill. She recommends a combination of encouraging socially responsible businesses, stopping subsidies and tax breaks when their costs outweigh their benefits, strengthening corporate charters to make more social demands of businesses, and shifting power away from the corporate elite and toward employees and communities, among other things.[11] Not a single bill to curb corporate excess made it to the Senate floor during the Trump administration. We are still at risk from a devastating oil spill, continuing toxic pollution from plastics and chemical plants, and increasing greenhouse gas emissions. We allow corporations the freedom to pollute as they do now at our own peril.

More grassroots organizing and advocacy efforts are needed to establish corporate responsibility for a clean and healthy environment. We need to challenge state and federal corporate charters that do not require social responsibility from corporations. We have leverage to do this because corporations must register with the state where they do business, and some are also registered at the federal level. We need to demand that corporations be responsible for damage they cause to the environment and human health. We have to rise and challenge what is considered the right of business owners to profit at any cost.

The Strict Father and Environmental Policy

The strict father economy has wreaked havoc with environmental policies and enforcement of them. According to the *New York Times*, over 100 environmental regulations were reversed during the Trump administration.[12] His administration weakened Obama-era limits on carbon dioxide emissions and repealed and replaced emissions rules for power plants and vehicles. Rules for clean air, clean water, and toxic chemicals were weakened or reversed. The Interior Department opened up more land for oil and gas leasing by cutting protected areas and limiting protections for wildlife.

Among the rollbacks was the weakening of the National Environmental Policy Act (NEPA), which calls for public review of large infrastructure projects. Environmentalists considered revising and weakening the fifty-year-old law to be "one of the biggest—and most audacious—deregulatory actions of the Trump administration."[13] Advocates have used NEPA to challenge coal terminals, oil and gas drilling, and pipelines. The new rules eliminated the need for federal agencies to analyze a project's indirect or cumulative effects on the environment. They also directed federal agencies to develop categories of projects that require no environmental assessment at all. These changes would have an outsized impact on low-income neighborhoods, which already suffer disproportionately from environmental hazards.

The Trump administration also rolled back rules that reduce auto and light truck emissions. A majority of auto manufacturers did not support this rollback, and thirteen states filed suit against the EPA to prevent the change. The state of California continued to enforce its own standards in opposition to new federal rules that revoked their authority to enact state standards stricter than federal standards.[14]

Another rule change with far-reaching effects was one that restricted the use of scientific studies that don't make the underlying raw data publicly available. Under this rule, studies that establish the role of air pollution in respiratory infections such as COVID-19, studies that link certain toxins to cancer, and studies of racial disparities in diseases would not be allowed in public policy decision making. Medical histories, hospital data, and even street addresses that are part of these studies should never be made public. The net effect of this rule is to greatly restrict the science on which public policy is based.[15] Fortunately for the environment, President Biden has pledged to reverse these policies.

The strict father economy plays out in local politics, too. In many places, local volunteers come together to create comprehensive plans for their communities. Participants are usually enthusiastic about crafting a narrative describing how they want their community to look and function. This is an example of creating a shared vision, an exercise that can be positive and energizing. Then the plan is codified in local zoning rules.

When a land owner or developer finds that their plans conflict with local zoning, they seek waivers or variances, or in some cases they try to overturn the rules. It has been very difficult for communities to sustain their vision and stick with their rules in the face of opposition from developers, who can afford good lawyers and are skilled at promoting the economic advantages of their projects. As a result, we've seen historic neighborhoods torn down and replaced with strip malls, and industrial plants built adjacent to schools and low-income neighborhoods.

These examples illustrate how the divergence of worldviews affects environmental policy. In a strict father worldview, US environmental rules have curbed growth and made businesses less competitive in a global economy, and therefore should be rolled back. In a nurturing parent worldview, environmental rules protect Americans from disease, protect the natural environment from destruction, and are essential to the future health of the planet.

Advocates Must Build Bridges

White supremacy, racism, patriarchy, and authoritarianism arise from an extreme form of the strict father worldview. The story of domination described in chapter 3 aligns with the strict father worldview. Because of the destruction that story has caused, many condemn the strict father worldview. And they are justified in doing so.

But the truth is, advocates must work with a variety of people, including those who hold different worldviews, in order to create policy change. The goal of environmental advocates and activists is not to condemn the views of others. It is to persuade a critical mass of people that *policies that affirm life on earth are essential to our current and future well-being and should be given top priority.*

Not all who hold a strict father worldview are extremists. Because American culture heavily emphasizes individualism and capitalism, most Americans (including liberals and progressives) hold at least some strict father views. What advocates must do is seek and define common ground, and from there persuade moderates to support life-affirming public policies.

The positive aspects of capitalism provide a starting place for finding common ground. Capitalism has stimulated innovation and led to advances in medicine, communications, energy, education, transportation, and technology. As a result, life expectancy has risen and poverty has decreased worldwide. So while the strict father economy is not sustainable in its current form, its successes can be recognized by advocates in creating common ground. From there, advocates can build support for new policies that will bring us a healthier future.

Crafting Bipartisan Policies

An obvious place to begin building common ground is in showing how clean energy and sustainable products support the economy. Job growth in clean energy, for example, is growing 70% faster than other sectors, and these jobs pay more than the national median wage.[16] Sustainable products and services, such as clean energy, electric cars, energy storage, electric ferry boats, and 5G broadband infrastructure provide new business opportunities and employment. Environmental advocates should use this information in crafting environmental policies.

Areas where the two worldviews might intersect—where common ground can be found—are fertile ground for developing policy solutions that will gain bipartisan support. Take corporate responsibility for environmental damage, for example. Conservatives on the right clearly understand the concept of responsibility. In their view, a child must pay if they break a window, and a person who commits a crime must accept punishment given by a judge. Corporations that poison or pollute might similarly be held responsible for cleaning up the damage their business operations cause. Currently, most environmental cleanup is the job of government, using taxpayer dollars.

Could the right be persuaded that cleaning up environmental damage is the responsibility of corporations? Could they be persuaded that a clean environment is needed to preserve future business opportunities? Could they see corporate responsibility for environmental impacts as a reasonable expectation that doesn't overly constrain businesses? Could they support uniform environmental policies around the world, in order to level the business playing field? With an understanding of worldviews as a backdrop, environmental advocates can frame environmental issues in terms of the need for a stronger sense of corporate responsibility for the earth, appealing to both the left and the right. Research by the FrameWorks Institute shows that the value of responsible management of the environment has broad support.

Worldviews may also intersect on the value of environmental protection. The conservative right values protection of the family and the country. They have traditionally supported the military and the police as a reflection of the value they place on protection. The question for the environmental advocate is: could conservatives support environmental protection too? What if protecting the environment also protected families from harm?

Clearly, work would need to be done to show why the value of protection should be extended to the environment. In doing this, advocates must acknowledge that conservatives prefer less regulation. Using personal stories and targeting specific environmental issues, an advocate might acknowledge the value of less complex regulation, while at the same time pointing out the benefits of carefully thought-out environmental regulations that *protect families and the places they love from harm.*

Conservation Hawks, a conservative outdoor sporting group, uses this technique in several award-winning films. Their message to viewers is this: by protecting the environment and addressing climate change, rivers and streams prized for fishing will be preserved and protected for your children and grandchildren to enjoy.

It is difficult to forge bipartisan policies. But it can be done. Research from the FrameWorks Institute shows that careful framing can go a long way to finding common ground on environmental policies. More on this is presented in chapter 11.

Solutions: Regulatory or Market-Based?

In general, the right favors market-based solutions, and the left favors regulation-based solutions. Both have been successful. Both are needed.

The Regional Greenhouse Gas Initiative (RGGI) is the first mandatory market-based program in the United States designed to reduce greenhouse gas emissions. RGGI is a cooperative effort among ten states: Connecticut, Delaware, Maine, Maryland, Massachusetts, New Hampshire, New Jersey, New York, Rhode Island, and Vermont. Its purpose is to reduce carbon dioxide emissions from the electric power sector. RGGI obligates large fossil-fueled power plants within the ten-state region to reduce their carbon emissions. They can do this in one of two ways: reducing their emissions outright, or buying "allowances" from other plants that have reduced their emissions below the required level.

The key to reducing emissions is that the total allowable emissions (the "cap") is reduced every three years. The cap ensures that polluters don't use allowances as a way to continue to pollute. This market-based plan is achieving its goals: in RGGI states, carbon emissions from power plants have declined by more than 40% since 2005, while these states' economies have grown by 8%. The RGGI states have recently set a goal to further reduce emissions to 30% below 2020 levels by 2030.[17]

Another market-based environmental policy proposal is a carbon fee and dividend program, initiated by the Citizens' Climate Lobby. It's based on a system adopted in Canada and Switzerland. The backers of this proposal to Congress have intentionally designed a market mechanism they hope will have bipartisan appeal (note they use the word "fee" instead of "tax"). The program would assess a fee on carbon at the point of origin, meaning the oil well, fracking site, or port of entry. The fee would rise over time to the point where burning fossil fuels becomes less competitive than other fuel options such as solar or wind, causing fossil fuel use to decline. Some or all of the monies collected would be distributed to citizens as a "dividend," therefore not increasing the size of government and offsetting any increase in fuel costs to consumers. This proposal and other ways to tax carbon are market-based solutions that hold promise.

But some issues do not lend themselves to market-based solutions. PFAS (per- and polyfluoroalkyl substances) are a group of persistent toxic chemicals, called "forever chemicals" because they do not break down in the environment. They can cause liver damage, thyroid disease, and cancer. It is not enough to reduce these chemicals through market mechanisms, even if it were possible to do so. The only safe thing to do is to ban their manufacture and distribution, and then initiate programs to clean them up.

In Maine, PFAS have been found in milk and traced back to municipal sludge used to fertilize farm fields where dairy cows graze. Multi-generational farms have been put out of business, and farmers have been poisoned. PFAS have been found in drinking water supplies, too. Even though these chemicals are now banned, funding to clean the land has been difficult to obtain.[18]

Regenerative agriculture and forestry practices that restore soils and waters are not easily initiated through either market-based solutions or regulatory mechanisms. This is because they require an up-front investment that most farmers and forestry companies cannot afford. They therefore need subsidy, which has to come from some other source, either government, philanthropists, or corporations.

Restoring our planet will take new market mechanisms, carefully thought-out regulations, and new investments. *All three approaches are essential.* There is no getting around it.

Environmental advocates need to embrace all solutions and find the optimal solution for the problem they are trying to solve. In developing environmental policies, advocates need to work with supporters, opponents, and decision makers on both the left and the right. By using their understanding of the two prevailing worldviews, environmental advocates can develop public policies that will gain broad support, and bring us a healthier, more equitable future.

6

Pulling Together Your Vision

A shared vision is not an idea. It is, rather, a force in people's hearts, a force of impressive power.

—PETER SENGE, *The Fifth Discipline*

Why Vision?

In the late 1930s a soda company in Maine was offered the rights to bottle Coca-Cola. The rights included the recipe and regional distribution, worth millions today. But soda was only consumed on hot summer days, which lasted about three weeks in Maine at the time. The bottler could not visualize the future popularity of soft drinks. He turned down the offer, saying, "You can't give away Coca-Cola in the winter." This is a perfect example of how a lack of vision results in missed opportunity.

As humanity faces a dangerously warming planet and a population approaching eight billion—that's *eight billion* people to feed, clothe, and house—a vision of how we will thrive in the future is not just helpful, it's required.

We are at a turning point. We either face the existential threat of climate change and address it, or we perish. Future generations will look back on this time as a pivot point in history: Are we going to go forward with a vision of the future that is positive and life affirming? Or are we going to decide that our problems are too big, people are too entrenched in the status quo, and give up our chance for a healthy future? We face this choice now.

Human experience is based, at least in part, on what we can imagine. For if we cannot imagine something, we won't recognize it. If we can't recognize it, then we can't take the steps needed to create it. It's imperative that we articulate a positive vision, if we want a healthy future.

The Source of Vision's Power

The power of vision comes from the tension between our present experience and our desired future. This tension pulls us toward the future we want. Peter Senge describes vision as being like a rubber band: as you stretch it, you create tension between the anchoring end and the fully stretched end.[1] The tension between police acts of violence against Black citizens, on the one hand, and a vision of a world where everyone is free from violence, on the other, is fueling the solutions being developed and implemented around the world.

Every media story we hear of cruelty to people or harm to the environment causes tension within us, whether we are conscious of it or not. The tension comes because these stories are not aligned with the loving, compassionate world that we know deep within is possible. The tension we feel based on the distance between compassionate and destructive behavior motivates us to take action. Taking even small actions aligned with our inner values can ease our tension. I encourage those of us who feel stressed to take small actions today that support the healthy and compassionate world of the future. Even the smallest actions will make a difference.

Connecting with others through a shared vision eases the tension in a larger, more lasting way. When people take action that is aligned with the needs and leadership of those directly impacted by environmental destruction, real progress is possible. A shared vision is powerful because it provides an umbrella under which many groups can be inspired to act. In this way a shared vision becomes a unifier.

An economy that invests in people and their well-being, instead of investing only for the highest return on the dollar, is a vision many share. This economic vision has been implemented in Scandinavian countries and is often referred to as the Nordic model. Within the Nordic model, Scandinavian countries have implemented a livable minimum wage, universal health care, and high-quality public education for all. Homelessness, chronic untreated diseases, and environmental degradation are almost unknown in these countries. They have created and carried out a vision of democracy that values people and the environment, while allowing businesses a reasonable but not unlimited profit. They've invested in people and have received a positive social and financial return on their investment.

Why *You* Need Vision

No matter the scope of your advocacy project, you need to have a vision or at least what you would call an overarching goal. Having a strong sense of where you want to go is what keeps you motivated. Life events, unexpected opposition, or other setbacks will occur, and when they do, your vision is what will keep you going.

A compelling vision of what you are working toward inspires hope. It helps you bear the inevitable frustrations and setbacks. It keeps you from the temptation to give up, compromise, or change direction. Like a child earning money to buy the bright shiny bicycle in the store window, it keeps you from forgetting why you're working so hard.

Positive versus Negative Vision

A true and positive vision is based on what we want to create. It is not a slogan or pronouncement by an authority figure. It's an exciting, long-term view of what our town, organization, state, or country could become. It comes from the heart and engages us. It is based on love, belonging, and a desire to work together to make positive change happen. Positive vision is a powerful force for change.

A negative vision is one that wants to stop or avoid something. The war on poverty, the "just say no to drugs" campaign in schools, and gun control are examples of negatively focused goals and campaigns. Environmentalists have a reputation for being against things—against coal, against local developments, against clearcutting, against toxics. I would argue that these are not true visions, because they are based on negativity.

Negative campaigns can accomplish short-term goals but are seldom successful in creating long-term social change. A stronger way to approach these issues is to frame them in positive, visionary language: "equal opportunity for all" instead of a "war on poverty," "drug-free America" instead of a "war on drugs," "responsible gun ownership" instead of "gun control," "clean energy" instead of "ban coal and oil." We need to focus on *what we want* in order to generate enough human energy, creativity, and power to create lasting change.

How to Think Differently

It's not easy to imagine a different future when you are anchored in the present. I've asked my college students to imagine themselves on a day twenty-five years from now, after a Green New Deal or some other far-reaching environmental legislation has passed and a fairer economy is in place. What is their experience on that day? I give them fifteen minutes to write a description of their day in the future.

The results are disappointing. Students say things like "we all drive electric cars." This is probably true, but hardly visionary. I was hoping to hear things like "every community generates their own fully sustainable energy" or "I take my kids to school where they get a wonderful education that stimulates their creativity and is tailored to meet their personal needs." Vision needs to include detail and depth, so you can feel it viscerally.

Imagining something completely new is hard. When America's rivers were polluted sewers, people couldn't imagine that these same rivers would one day become the site of high-priced waterfront real estate or picturesque walking trails. Not many of us today can imagine ubiquitous artificial intelligence that helps us think and, in many cases, replaces human reasoning. But getting your health diagnosis from a holographic doctor on a computer screen is only a few years away.

There are many ways to stimulate vision. These include joining online webinars and discussion groups, attending conferences, visiting cities or towns that have initiated new programs, and creating partnerships with groups you can learn from. One of the best ways to stimulate vision is to travel to a new place and experience something different.

Several years ago I organized a trip to take Maine leaders to Denmark to learn how the Danes have reduced their fossil fuel use by about 75% since the 1970s. I recruited fourteen state, local, and business decision makers to join me on a Denmark Climate Tour. We spent a week meeting with energy agencies, touring local energy co-ops, and visiting a state-of-the-art biogas plant, several wind farms, and an island where four villages had come together and reduced their carbon emissions to zero.

The group returned home with an understanding of what a small country focused on sustainability looks and feels like. The trip had a profound effect. Each participant has been guided by their Denmark experience to strive for sustainable initiatives in their jobs back home. *There's nothing more powerful than personal experience to change one's thinking.*

At another time, I organized a trip to Japan to introduce Maine fishermen to scallop aquaculture. Maine fishermen were opposed to aquaculture then, even as wild fish stocks were declining around them. They saw themselves as hunters of the ocean. The idea of farming was not only alien; it was threatening to consider.

Ten fishermen, a journalist, a university professor, and two organizers traveled to Aomori, Japan, to meet with fishermen who farm scallops on Mutsu Bay. This bay is about the same size and latitude as our home fishing grounds. It even looks very much like Maine, which helped us connect with what they were doing there.

We went out on a local fishing boat for a look at scallop aquaculture operations. Our group stood in a small circle as a net was pulled over the side of the boat and emptied on the deck. Out fell a pile of gigantic, fully mature scallops with shells nearly nine inches across. I looked around our circle and saw each person's eyes widen as they took this in. The scallops they saw were beautiful specimens that would sell for the highest price, twenty-five dollars per pound, in our home state.

In order to have a vision, you must be able to imagine something new. The fishermen came home from Japan and started working to establish scallop aquaculture in Maine—something they opposed prior to the trip. The vision of huge, twenty-five-dollar-a-pound scallops inspired them to spend thousands of volunteer hours working on their project. They've returned to Japan several times after that initial trip, and they continue to work toward this vision today.

Visions Are Needed in Every Sector

As you can see from the Denmark and Japan examples, various sectors need to develop their own visions. In fact, *every organization in every sector,* regardless of size, needs to create and implement a vision for a healthy future. Each organization that does this joins a worldwide vision of a more just, sustainable, and healthy planet. Below are examples of visions from a variety of sectors.

Many businesses, especially those that are legally registered as benefit corporations or are certified as B Corps, are driven by strong, proactive visions. (See chapter 5 for an explanation of these programs.) Here's the vision from Danone North America, a $6 billion food company: "We believe our world is ripe for a change in the way we eat, drink, connect, and do business. It's our job to find new, more sustainable ways of working to better serve this expectation and help reconnect people with the food they eat, nourish lives, and build a healthier world through food."[2]

Danone North America incorporated as a public benefit corporation and then declared their first priority was to become a certified B Corp as a way to use business as a force for good, balancing financial interest with the social and environmental benefits they want to create for people and the planet.

Oberlin, Ohio, is one of more than 100 US cities that has created and is implementing a climate vision and action plan. In 2010, the city and

Oberlin College signed a memorandum of understanding with the Clinton Foundation and the US Green Building Council to participate in the Clinton Climate Positive Development Program. This commitment elevated the city and the college to a "climate-positive community" that will not just neutralize its emissions; they will improve the environment with net emissions *below zero* by 2050. Their plan is comprehensive, covering energy generation, energy efficiency in buildings, waste management, water management, land-use planning, local food and agriculture, transportation, resilience to weather events, and education and outreach to schools and citizens. The program achieved its initial goal of reducing its greenhouse gas emissions by 50% by 2015, and it should meet its goal to reduce emissions to below zero by 2050.[3] Many cities and towns across the country have or are working on visionary climate action plans.

Congregations of all faiths are also stepping up and developing visions for reducing their carbon footprint while strengthening social equity. They are teaching their members how to do the same in their own lives and businesses. Communities of faith have been leaders of social justice in the past and are well positioned to lead on climate and environmental justice now.

The US Climate Alliance is a group of twenty-five states that have committed to implementing the policies that advance the goals of the Paris Agreement. They aim to reduce greenhouse gas emissions by at least 26%–28% below 2005 levels by 2025.[4] C40 Cities is a group of ninety-six cities (representing more than 700 million citizens and 25% of the global economy) committed to bold climate action. Their vision is to "lead the way toward a healthier and more sustainable future."[5]

The Green New Deal: A Vision for the Environment?

Green New Deal legislation is appearing at multiple levels of government, including in Congress, a number of states, and a handful of cities. Green New Deal initiatives link the well-being of people and the well-being of the planet. These initiatives recognize that poor communities suffer more from climate change and environmental degradation than wealthier people and places.

Green New Deal proposals aren't all the same, but they are all based on values of fairness, social and racial equality, climate justice, and a clean and healthy environment. These proposals give us practical programs to fight for, too—like free higher education, a federal jobs guarantee, a livable wage, universal health care, clean air and water, and justice for those most vulnerable to the effects of climate change.

Is the Green New Deal a vision? Absolutely! There is tension between the current reality in the United States and Green New Deal values and proposals. This tension has the potential to move us toward a different kind of economy—one that is more like the Nordic model and seeks a fairer balance between people, the environment, and profits. Seeing others, especially those who are different from us, as valued human beings is a step to realizing that all life on earth is worthy of respect and protection.

Awareness of climate change and climate justice has soared in the past several years, which is another good sign. The Maine Climate Table is a group that came together in 2013 with the question: "How do we talk to people about climate change?" At that time, the phrase "climate change" was scary to say, especially in rural parts of the country. It implied you were on the political fringe. You never knew how you might be received. Better not to bring it up.

Now, even in rural areas, Americans are not afraid to say those words. We've moved beyond introducing the topic. The Climate Table is now working to *address* climate change, not just talk about it. It's time to integrate care for the environment with care for diverse and vulnerable people, and to create a culture and economy that work for everyone.

The Sunrise Movement launched in 2017 with a vision of "decarbonization, jobs, and justice" and has "hubs" in forty-nine states and Puerto Rico. It has the support of millions of young adults and has organized climate strikes around the country and the world. Sunrise has a multiyear plan to achieve the Green New Deal. During the coronavirus pandemic, they launched an online initiative to train thousands of people of all ages in how to take action. Through Sunrise and thousands of other community organizations, awareness, understanding, and action on climate change and social equity are accelerating. This is good news for all of us.

How a Shared Story Can Lead to Vision

During our weeklong Denmark tour we visited many organizations and groups. There was one story we heard at almost every stop. After we heard the story at three, four, and then five different places, we realized this was a shared story that led to their national vision of energy independence. The story was called "No Drive Sundays." It goes like this:

In 1973, the Organization of Petroleum Exporting Countries restricted world oil supply. The result was gasoline shortages and skyrocketing fuel prices around the world. Economists call this a "price shock." In Denmark the government responded by prohibiting both the sale of gasoline and driving on Sundays. This action aroused public attention. As No Drive Sundays became the norm, people began to envision an energy-independent Denmark—a different future when the country would never have to rely on imported oil again. From this larger vision, smaller visions spawned across the country to implement energy conservation and renewable energy projects. In time, the No Drive Sundays policy was replaced with energy independence.

Now, fifty years later, Denmark is the largest wind energy producer in the world. On windy days they export wind energy (in the form of electricity) to neighboring Sweden and Germany, making them completely energy independent on those days. In developing wind energy, they've become the world leader in the manufacture and supply of wind energy equipment.

In developing wind power, Denmark has also become the world's top innovator in wind energy public policy. Every wind farm in Denmark must offer 20% of its ownership to local residents in the form of affordable shares. While we were in Denmark, one of our bus drivers proudly told us about his yearly dividend from his wind energy stock. Towns where wind farms are located receive an annual fee. Denmark also established a process for property owners to seek compensation if they can prove property values have decreased as a result of nearby wind turbines. None of these policy innovations would have been possible without the vision of Denmark as an energy-independent country.

Visioning Sessions

Taking a group to a foreign country may not always be practical. Or perhaps there is no place in the world that has yet achieved the vision that you need, and you must start from scratch. Visions and new initiatives to implement them often start with a small group of people who share a common idea.

The Sunrise Movement, which has turned out an estimated four million people for climate strikes around the world, started with just eight members. They were recent college graduates who worked remotely for no pay. Several lived with their parents. They trained youth organizers and mobilized protests and rallies, beginning with small local actions.

But the vision of the eight founders was much bigger. They wanted to overcome what they saw as the climate movement's shortcomings, particularly a tendency to think small and introduce incremental steps. Sunrise wanted to build a culture of inclusivity, wield political power, and take climate action from being a matter of changing your light bulbs to becoming an issue that candidates and politicians must have a position on, in order to hold office. In just six years they have changed the national and global conversation about climate change, and they are now working to implement the Green New Deal in Congress and create change around the world.

In the policy and nonprofit worlds, it's common for organizations or communities to get together for a "visioning session" to craft a vision for their organization. The rules of storytelling apply here. All visions have roots in personal stories. Varshini Prakash, executive director of Sunrise, saw CNN footage of the 2004 Indian Ocean tsunami that killed 230,000 people when she was 11. Her parents were from south India, one of the regions devastated by the tsunami. This event formed her views on climate change. Another Sunrise cofounder, Sara Blazevic, clicked on a YouTube video and saw people standing on rooftops trying to escape an enormous flood in her home country of Croatia. The flood didn't even make the news in New York, where she was a college student. This fact motivated her to dedicate herself to Sunrise.

Heartfelt stories with dialogue and visual imagery create pictures in people's minds of a problem and of a new or improved future. If you are organizing a visioning session, you must make room for and encourage the personal stories that will connect people with an improved vision of what could be.

The Importance of Specificity

Questions are a simple and powerful tool because they focus people's attention. A well-focused and specific question can open a space for people to entertain a new thought. When I asked my students to imagine a day in their life twenty-five years from now, it was a very broad question—probably too broad. What if I'd said: "Imagine a day twenty-five years from now when you have a family with two school-age children. What kind of learning activities are your kids doing that day?" If I'd narrowed the question like this, I probably would have seen more creative, visionary answers. A clear and *specific* question is important if you want to get a clear and specific answer.

In Vermont, a local group called Huddlebury formed after the Women's March on Washington in 2017. They were troubled by the election of Donald Trump and wanted to bridge the divisions that had come to the surface nationally and in Vermont. The group read Naomi Klein's book *No Is Not Enough* and George Lakey's *Viking Economics*. As a result of their book discussions, they decided to organize a vision summit to begin developing a Vision for Vermont. One hundred people attended. They have been working on a big-picture vision for their state in the years since. Their vision encompasses a broad range of topics, including health care, the economy, education, environment, social equity, and immigration—a truly remarkable effort. Here is the introduction to their vision statement: "As Vermont moves through a time of transformation, we envision a future where Vermonters care for each other, their communities, and the earth; where the issues that matter to all of us are resolved in a way that protects our environment and combats further climate change; and where access to health care and economic, racial, and gender equity are assured for everyone. We are committed to a future where everyone has access to the best that Vermont has to offer."[6]

But after creating and refining their vision statement, the group stalled. This can happen with big-picture visions; they are so big that people don't know where to go next. The key to moving forward is to ask the next level of questions that flow from the vision. *More specificity is needed in order to move forward.* The next level of questions the Vermont group needed to ask were like these: What kind of health care system do we want? What's the basis of our future economy? What do we want our education system to teach? How would we create a culture that is more racially and ethnically inclusive?

Eventually the Vermont group did seek answers to the last question— how to create a more racially and ethnically inclusive culture—and invited a diverse group of panelists to answer it. The panel included an Abenaki woman, a US Marine who was an Iraq war veteran, a Black community organizer, and an LGBTQ organizer—all Vermont citizens. A daylong event with panel and breakout discussions were rich in detail about how diverse views could be included in the Vision for Vermont and be more fully recognized as part of Vermont's culture.

In order to move from a vision to public policy or social change, the next level of questions must be asked, as the Vermont group did in creating their diversity and inclusion panel. Those who have passion for and personal experience with the questions must be on hand to answer them. If you are contemplating a visioning session, whether for your company, your community, or your organization, articulating clear, concise, and specific vision questions is a prerequisite for success.

Visioning Pitfalls

One common visioning pitfall is failure to seek outside input. It's easy to work with a community group you know, or with colleagues within your workplace, to come up with a vision statement. But without the input and perspectives of the larger community, especially those most affected by the issues being discussed, your vision is incomplete and may be inaccurate.

Is your vision going to meet the needs of those most affected? The only way to find out is to invite those people to participate, comment, and give input. Alternatively, your group may want to join campaigns or movements led by those who are most affected by an issue and who come from the frontline communities. This was the case when US military veterans joined the Standing Rock Sioux in opposing the Dakota Access Pipeline.

The Vermont group's diverse panel was a great way to broaden their vision for Vermont. A business that is crafting its vision should gather input from all of its stakeholders: customers, suppliers, workers, owners, and the community. Many organizations I've worked with have created ways to gather input, including surveys, large forums, focus groups, and interviews with selected individuals. There are many good ways to gather input for your vision. No matter what format you choose, you will gain new insights, ideas, and feedback that will strengthen and inform your vision.

Another pitfall of visioning sessions is that people can devolve to telling stories only about what is wrong. They name opponents, articulate problems, and delve into the causes of the problems. While these discussions have value, all are at the "reality end" of the rubber band. They anchor you in the past and get in the way of moving forward. If they go on too long, they can be a turnoff, and people will become discouraged and disengaged.

If you're in a discussion that has gotten stuck on what's wrong, you can change its direction by asking a question about the future. If the topic is elementary education, you might ask, "What would a successful twenty-first-century school be teaching?" Or if the discussion is among subject matter experts, you might say, "In your experience, what changes in education have been successful? How might they be replicated?" From there, a discussion of a positive future—a future everyone wants—can grow.

Another hidden pitfall is that sometimes people love the vision but don't believe they can make it happen. It just seems too big and scary. Or people might feel, for legitimate reasons, that they can't commit their time and energy to it.

In a case like this, it makes sense to choose a smaller activity that people perceive as doable. This can be a starting place that leads to larger actions later. An example of this in the Vision for Vermont group is a project they call Sewing for Change. A group of women collect fabric remnants and use them to sew cloth shopping bags that they give away at stores as a replacement for plastic bags. During the coronavirus pandemic they made face masks along with the shopping bags. Through their website they've spawned Sewing for Change groups in other states. Their work has created new friendships and has empowered group members.[7]

Listen, Listen, and Listen

A key component to successful visioning and advocacy is listening. As soon as a person or group declares they have the answers, ideas stop flowing. It's particularly deadly when a person with decision-making authority provides the answers—or worse, imposes their vision on a group.

A shared vision is a story people *choose* to engage with and truly want to achieve. This is different from a vision imposed on others by political or business leaders. Like the fishermen who began developing scallop aquaculture, people need to *opt in and commit their energy to a vision* in order to achieve it.

Visionary ideas can come from anyone and often come from unexpected places. In one visioning session I led, a group of workers described the lack of security they felt in a poorly lit stairway they used to enter and exit the building where they worked. It turned out security wasn't just an issue for the stairway; it was an organizationwide issue for this public agency. The workers had raised an important issue, and as a result, the statement "We have a safe and secure workplace" became part of their organization's vision. In the short term, they fitted out the stairway with new lighting and locks. In the long term they implemented overarching policies to increase building, employee, and public security.

One mistake I've seen too many times is the idea of having a keynote speaker in order to provide "inspiration" for a visioning session. I love a good keynote address, and they have an important place in communications.

However, the problem is that any kind of lecture comes from an old model that features an expert at the front of the room addressing the "nonexperts" seated in the audience. People sit down and receive information. It is a one-to-many form of communication.

To stimulate the ideas needed for visioning, you need a many-to-many form of communication. People should not be sitting in seats listening to experts. Instead, they should be active participants. There are many methods for engaging participants in visioning processes. Most of them involve people working in small groups, wrestling with one or more questions. Some methods require predetermined questions and appointed facilitators. Others allow participants to create their own questions and are self-facilitated. Both can work well, and each has its place.

What works best is to allow people the time and space to tell their own stories, ask their own questions, and hear the answers. Generally speaking, the more autonomy and time given for people to listen to each other, the more productive they will be.

Visioning Process Tools

There are many methods for leading groups in visioning processes. *The Change Handbook,* a seven-hundred-page guide on my bookshelf, describes sixty-five of them.[8] If you have a passion for group process, you should own this book. But a simpler way to understand group process, which suffices for most of us, is to know that all change processes fall into one of two categories: opening and closing.

In opening processes, new ideas, solutions, or visions are desired. These are also called divergent processes. They are particularly favored by people who like to make new connections between ideas, people, resources, and programs. Brainstorming, visioning, creating idea maps, and organizing affinity groups all are opening processes. Asking a question where the answer is not yet known, and allowing time and space for people to thoughtfully answer it, is a simple and effective way to create an opening process that results in a vision or a solution.

Closing processes, also called convergent processes, are used when choices, priorities, goals, or decisions are sought. These processes are aimed at narrowing down the possibilities and making choices about how to move forward. Closing processes often involve voting, which can be done with technology tools or manually, using sticky dots, markers, or ballots. More elaborate closing processes can involve weighing options against multiple criteria or calculating the impact of various choices on a number of variables.

When designing a planning process, it's helpful to have in mind where and when you might be engaged in opening or closing activities. In many planning processes I've led, I will start with opening process tools. I will usually reiterate opening processes several times with various groups and various questions. Once all the ideas and potential solutions are gathered, then I'll move to a closing, priority-setting activity.

A public engagement process that combines opening and closing activities satisfies everyone—those who prefer diverging and those who prefer converging. And it usually satisfies the goal of moving the group from planning to implementation, as well.

Implementation

The most compelling vision goes nowhere if there aren't people and resources dedicated to carry it out. President John F. Kennedy's vision to put a man on the moon motivated NASA and Congress to take action. It succeeded because all the pieces needed to carry out that vision were in place: public and media support, congressional and federal budget support, and an agency with the necessary skills and technology to carry out the vision.

Too many visions get stuck on a shelf, or they are framed and hung on a wall, but they don't hold any real influence or meaning beyond the day they were created. This is because implementing a vision takes resources, commitment, and courage. It takes courage because not everyone is going to be supportive, especially if the vision is broad and far reaching. The Green New Deal is likely to experience strong pushback. It will be opposed by those whose living or investments are based on the fossil fuel economy.

To move our nation and the world toward a new vision, it will take grass-roots action and well-organized campaigns. It will take multiple campaigns in many places, culminating in a mass movement. It will take well-run organizations, good strategies for working with stakeholders, strong relationships with decision makers, and effective communications. It will take persistence over a number of years. Specific strategies, methods, and techniques for implementing a vision of a new economy, a healthy environment, and a just society are the subject of part II of this book.

PART II

GATHER YOUR POWER AND
TAKE ACTION

7

Using Power for Good

Power is infinite.

　　　　　　　　—ERIC LIU, *You're More Powerful Than You Think*

When a culture of dominance is broken, it activates power in all of us.

　　　　　　　　—MELINDA GATES, *The Moment of Lift*

What Is Power?

In physics, power is the force that moves an object over time. In human culture, power is the ability to achieve what you want. In advocacy, power is successfully persuading decision makers to do what you want them to do.

Power itself is neither good nor evil. But as we will see in this chapter, there are many ways to have and use power. Some of these are expansive, giving people more choices in how they live their lives. Others are restrictive or even abusive, limiting people's choices.

Advocates need to focus on two kinds of power in order to bring about the changes they seek: *personal power* and *organizing/community power*. Personal power comes from aligning what you do and say with who you really are. That's why personal stories and personal connections with the earth are the foundation of environmental advocacy. We are each an individual manifestation of love, life, and spirit. If our words and actions come from that deeper place within, they express true power. This is why all the great religions say that love conquers all.

Part I of this book described some of the different ways people define "reality." Understanding how you define reality, and how that may be the same as or different from those you need to influence, increases your personal power. When you use your understanding of earth stories and worldviews to guide you in communicating with different kinds of people, you increase your personal power.

Organizing and community power comes from drawing attention to what needs to change and building or joining coalitions powerful enough to make change happen. Organizing creates power where none existed before. *When people collectively speak up and take action, the power to create change has been awakened.*

Understanding the Power Structure

As environmental advocates create power through organizing, they must be aware of and understand the existing power structure. Politicians hold power because we gave it to them collectively, through our money and votes. The influence of political donors has grown enormously, excluding the voices of the vast majority of people. The power of the wealthy and the politicians that support them has accumulated over time, resulting in laws and rules that favor the wealthy. Examples include tax cuts that benefit the wealthy more than others, investments that are taxed at a lower rate than wages and salaries, and some hedge funds and corporations that pay little or nothing in taxes. Increased inequality is the result of the accumulation of power by the wealthy.

Corporations have accumulated vast power partly because they've been able to successfully lobby governments to get what they want, and also because of the large assets they own. The oil and gas industry has been using their vast resources to fight climate policies in at least sixteen states.[1] Many large corporations have more money than governments do, making it hard for governments to regulate them. Because many corporations source materials and labor from overseas, it is hard for customers and shareholders to know what corporate practices are. The resulting lack of transparency gives companies more power to do what they want and has resulted in great harm to people and the environment.

ANOTHER WAY TO LOOK AT POWER

Below is another way to look at power, as described in the Sierra Club *Movement Organizing Manual:*

1. **Visible Power**

   This includes the visible and definable aspects of power, such as formal rules, structures, authorities, institutions, and decision-making procedures.

2. **Hidden Power**

   This is the power to set the political agenda, including controlling the rules, setting priorities, determining who is at the decision-making table, including or excluding certain groups or points of view, and granting special access or influence to certain groups, such as donors.

3. **Invisible Power**

   This is the power to shape meaning and define "reality," including reinforcing social norms and beliefs, making assumptions about superiority or inferiority, defining what is normal and acceptable, determining what is important or unimportant, and determining which issues reach the decision-making table.[2]

It's important to understand the different levels of power, too. The power a politician holds is not the same as the power a schoolteacher holds. The power an individual advocate holds is not the same as the power an organized group holds. Similarly, the power a well-funded group holds is not the same as the power of a nonfunded group. When researching an issue or taking action, environmental advocates need to look around them and see where the power lies and how they might leverage it to make a difference. Tools advocates can use for mapping people's power and influence over their issues are described in chapter 8.

Abuse of Power

Discussing power can be difficult because power is often abused, leading to great pain. It's hard to fathom or accept that some people would let others die rather than lose money or political status, both of which are forms of power. What stories do power abusers tell themselves to justify such actions? The tobacco companies denied the science proving the harmful health effects of cigarettes for years. Oil and gas companies continue to make profits for their shareholders, despite scientific evidence of the environmental destruction they are causing.

Just recently, the EPA decided not to regulate perchlorates in drinking water, defying a federal court order to establish a drinking water standard for this chemical. Perchlorate is a component of rocket fuel, ammunition, and explosives that is known to damage fetuses and reduce IQ in newborns, according to the American Academy of Pediatrics. The secretary of the EPA gave this justification for relaxing perchlorate regulations: "This fulfills the president's promise to pare back burdensome 'one size fits all' overregulation for the American people."[3] There was no thought for the *health* of the American people. Those who abuse power don't want to face or acknowledge the results of their actions. To do so would be too painful for them to bear.

By the time my students reach college, most of them have experienced abuse of power. When I introduce the topic of power, they shift in their seats. Some avert their eyes. When I ask why, they say that power usually means exploiting others. They've known people who walk on others to get ahead. Some have witnessed the exploitation of the earth for profit. They've seen how the power of the economic elite overrides the needs of those with less. To varying degrees, they recognize White privilege. Many students in my classes have felt personally disempowered by racism or classism when trying to get ahead. Some have been bullied by teachers, coaches, or bosses along the way. Perhaps you have been too. Abuses of power are all too common.

CANCER ALLEY

The Cancer Alley story is a dark example of power gone awry at every level—local, state, and federal. Cancer Alley is an eighty-five-mile-long stretch of oil refineries and petrochemical plants along the Mississippi River between Baton Rouge and New Orleans, Louisiana. More than 140 oil refineries, plastics manufacturers, and chemical factories are located there. The plants emit tons of airborne pollutants, many of which are known carcinogens. People living in the area are fifty times more likely to get cancer than the average American.[4] There is also a cluster of COVID-19 deaths in the same area, with a death rate five times higher than the US average. The people who live there are predominately Black and poor, with more than 20% lacking a high school diploma.[5]

In 2014, officials in St. James Parish, which lies within Cancer Alley, closed a high school and post office and rezoned the land from Residential to Residential/Future Industrial. This was done to make way for a $9.4 billion Taiwanese petrochemical plant. The proposed plant would consist of fourteen separate plastics plants on 1,600 acres, just one mile from an elementary school, several churches, and a residential area. According to Courthouse News Service, roughly $1.4 billion in local property tax exemptions are part of the deal to lure the company to the area, to build plants that would employ 1,200 workers.

Local residents were not engaged in or informed of the zoning change. According to Anne Rolfes, the organizer and founder of activist group the Louisiana Bucket Brigade, "What we were trying to understand through the public record is who made these changes and how did they happen?"[6] Districts 4 and 5, where the plants would be located, have a total population of 22,100, and the districts' residents are 90% and 65% Black, respectively. This is an explicit example of environmental racism and classism.

Subsequently, the Louisiana Department of Environmental Quality (LDEQ) approved permits for the Taiwanese plastics plants, despite data showing they could double toxic pollution in the area. Models from the company show the plant would emit more ethylene oxide than just about any other facility in the country, exceeding the EPA benchmark for cancer risk.[7]

Following the issuance of state permits, the EPA got involved. The EPA Office of the Inspector General published a report stating that both the EPA and the LDEQ "failed to provide critical information to nearby residents about the ethylene oxide emissions and the elevated cancer risk associated with the chemical."[8] In response to the inspector general's report, EPA Secretary Andrew Wheeler demanded that the report be withdrawn, thus clearing the way for the plants to be built. This sequence of events shows little concern for the mostly Black residents living in the area. Local, state, and federal decision makers sided with the business, even though the potential harm is to American residents, with profits flowing to Taiwan.

Using Power for Good

Understanding how power works and using it for good is at the heart of effective advocacy. It makes the difference between feeling helpless about environmental degradation and taking action based on a vision of a better future. I'm talking about using power to defend wildlife, preserve forests, clean the air and water, stand for a more equitable society, overturn power abuses, and heal the planet. I'm talking about using power as a tool to work for the common good. I'm talking about using power in ways that respect the worth and integrity of people and all other life on the planet.

When it comes to power, I'm a pacifist. Property damage, smear campaigns, and even negative ads attacking someone's character are forms of violence. If your goal is to bring about a more peaceful, compassionate, and healthy world, then it's counterproductive—even hypocritical—to use violent means. The kind of energy people put into the world matters. If you want a more peaceful world, you are not creating it when you use weapons, whether they are guns or words.

Nonviolent direct action is aligned with this view. When people choose to break the law or put themselves in harm's way without violence, there is power in that choice. By not using violence, protesters are taking the higher moral ground, which challenges the morals of opponents and has more power than devolving to violence.

Nonviolent direct action shows opponents that activists are fully committed to their cause. They are so committed they are willing to put themselves at risk. This, along with the unpredictability of nonviolent campaigns, scares the daylights out of opponents. A typical response is: "If there's a group protesting in my office today, what will they do tomorrow?" Nonviolent direct action gets attention and cracks open the door to new conversations.

At the same time, environmental advocates can understand why some protesters become violent. Many marginalized groups have used nonviolent direct action campaigns for decades and continue to be ignored and abused by those in power. Their frustration sometimes results in resorting to violence to bring attention to their issues. Advocates should never condone violence, but we can strive to understand the pain of being ignored and silenced.

Student and community advocates have great power. By their presence in the legislature, city council, or town committee, they are sending the message that this issue matters to them. Just by their presence, they're saying: "When I could be enjoying myself with family and friends, I choose to be here to speak on this issue." This is using power for good.

Advocates and activists start from a place of power just by showing up. But just showing up isn't enough to effect change. Advocates and activists need to use their power to organize, strategize, and work with decision makers to move their issues forward. Later chapters in this book explain how to build powerful campaigns that succeed in making change happen.

Your Personal Power

You may not feel powerful. In fact, the majority of people feel powerless when it comes to global problems—climate change, toxic pollution, poverty, war, inequality.

Everyone feels moments of doubt and vulnerability. But, as we discovered in part I, your personal story of connection with the earth, your life experience, your knowledge, and your values are the roots of your personal power. You can let these roots nourish you as you step forward and speak your truth.

Young leaders across the country are speaking with grace and authority on climate change. Anna Siegel is a fourteen-year-old climate leader in Maine whose conviction grew from her love of wild animals. Her speeches on climate change are powerful because they come directly from her heart.

Autumn Peltier grew up in Wiikwemkoong Unceded Territory in northern Canada. When she was eight and attended a water ceremony with her family on a First Nations reserve, she saw a sign warning that the drinking water was toxic and unsafe to drink. She decided then that she needed to speak out for the people and the water. "Water is sacred, water is life," she says. "Mother Earth doesn't need us; we need her." Now in her teens, she has presented hundreds of speeches nationally and internationally and has been appointed chief water commissioner of the Anishinabek Nation. She was inspired by her great-aunt Josephine Mandamin, an advocate for the planet's water. Peltier's power comes from a place of deep conviction.[9]

Your personal power comes from your faith and convictions. I don't necessarily mean religious faith; I mean the faith that comes from what you deeply believe. I believe that no matter how poorly people behave, they have a good heart underneath. Although I have discouraging days and fearful thoughts, I also believe when people clearly see the choices before them, they will choose life. This is my faith in people. I draw on my faith to get through the tough times. You can too.

Staying Grounded

With continuous media attention to violence, accusations, and emotional turmoil, it's hard to stay grounded, confident, and calm. In recent years, I've found I need to focus more deliberately on maintaining my sense of calm and clearheadedness than I used to. You may be finding this, too.

I once had an office three blocks from the State House. As a professional advocate and lobbyist, I walked to the Capitol almost daily when the legislature was in session. As I walked, I would set aside my insecurities, personal agendas, and worries. There was a row of sweet lilac bushes along the sidewalk on my route. I would let my worries go as I stopped to smell them. By the time I opened the heavy doors of the State House, my attention was fully focused on the subject of whatever meeting I was about to attend. I was fully present and mentally prepared.

At first I was unaware that I performed this ritual. Only upon reflection did I see how important it was. As I walked through the echoing State House hallways, people would stop and give me the information I needed without my having to ask. Or I might stop and ask someone a question, and they would give me a full explanation. My open and listening attitude allowed me to easily discover and take in the important information I needed to do my job.

You could also initiate a ritual that will help you be fully present in the meeting spaces where advocates do their work. You could try some deep breathing as you travel to your meeting. Breathe from deep in your belly, and feel your breath as it goes in and out. Focus on your breath for at least five minutes. You might park a little farther away or get off the bus or train at an earlier stop, and then notice everything around you as you walk to your meeting. Give yourself a moment to relax and focus your energy. Listen for the birds. Watch the people. Do some stretches to the sky before you enter the building. Do the same thing before and after (and sometimes during) virtual meetings: step outside for some fresh air, breathe deeply, touch your toes, and reach to the sky. It will help.

Some years ago, I was engaged in a contentious issue. The public meetings I attended were hostile. Citizens were angry at and distrustful of state staff, who were trying to gather information. The leader of my team meditated before each meeting to help stay calm as she led the group. I struggled with the hostility. After a two- or three-hour meeting, the tension felt like a toxic substance in my blood. I would go for a walk or run both before and after the meetings to shake off stress. I kept a pair of running shoes in the trunk of my car so I could get some fresh air and calm down before the two-hour drive home. This helped.

You, too, should monitor your body and do what you can to manage the stress that will come up in your advocacy work. Public meetings can be long and tiring. City councils, town select boards, and legislative committees want everyone to be heard. This leads to lengthy meetings, often held in stuffy, crowded rooms or in tedious virtual meetings—a recipe for stress. I highly recommend finding the combination of exercise, fresh air, meditation, stretching, or yoga that works for you.

At stressful meetings, it also helps to refocus and remember the reasons why you're there. This will connect you with your heart and why you took on this responsibility in the first place. Another helpful technique is to clarify your desired outcomes prior to every meeting. Here are some examples:

- Do you intend to connect with a particular decision maker?

- Are you representing a group or a certain point of view? Are your talking points clear?

- Are you showing up to support specific partners? Who?

- Do you hope to solidify a relationship with another advocate or advocacy group?

- Are you looking to find out what position another group is taking?

- Are you watching for threats to your cause?

- Are you sizing up decision makers' responses?

You should ask yourself these kinds of questions as you mentally prepare for a meeting. If possible, you should write down a list of your desired outcomes prior to every meeting. If you can stay clear about your specific purposes for that meeting or that day, you will remain in a position of power and do a better job of representing your issue and your people.

Cultivating Optimism

Optimism is a choice. You can choose to focus on the future you want. Or you can choose to focus on what's wrong in our world. Optimists don't diminish the magnitude of the problems humanity faces. But they know that in order to solve these problems, they need to believe that change is possible and that people will recognize what needs to be done. There is power in choosing to be optimistic.

Although some people are natural optimists, many of us need to practice optimism in order to make it a habit. Fortunately, our minds are malleable. We can be active participants in our own thinking by noticing, refuting, and reframing. Optimism practice means recognizing when we feel defeated or deflated by bad news, and finding something more positive to focus on. To practice optimism means to refocus our thoughts over and over, until optimism becomes a habit.

It's true that corporations have emitted toxic gases into the air, causing injury and death. It's also true that many communities, like those in Louisiana's Cancer Alley, have spoken out against this and effected change. Which side of this story would you focus on to move toward positive change? The optimist focuses not on the size and scope of the damage, but on supporting those who speak out and on developing and implementing solutions.

Author Parker Palmer calls the difference between hard realities and what is possible the "tragic gap."[10] An effective and optimistic advocate stands in the tragic gap and lets it inform their actions. This requires holding the grief of environmental destruction without becoming cynical or depressed about it. This also means holding a vision of a better future without becoming disconnected from the hard realities. Optimists can use the dangerously warming climate and polluted lands and waters as the impetus to cultivate new ways of stewarding the earth and new ways of doing business. *Using the negative to power positive action is standing in the gap, and from there, you can cultivate optimism.*

Optimism is more than just hoping things will get better or focusing on the positive. Reframing your thinking from a negative problem focus to a positive solution focus is an important first step—a very important one in our negative and fear-based culture. But once you have shifted your focus to solutions, you must take steps to make things better.

In 2019, a man in Maine was killed when road construction equipment pierced a gas line, filling a nearby basement with gas and causing an explosion. The daughter of the deceased stepped forward and told her father's story to a legislative committee. In short order, they passed a bill to include gas lines in the "Dig Safe" laws that require utilities to mark the ground before digging begins. If this law had been in place, her father's life would have been spared. She spoke up so others would not have the same experience. Describing her experience was an act of personal power and was motivated by the optimism that grew from her personal tragedy.

You may have knowledge, a personal experience, or original ideas to add to a political discussion. Your experience, knowledge, and ideas give you power and credibility. What specific experience or knowledge might you contribute? Your past work, school, or family experience may be important for decision makers to hear, so don't hold back.

The Power of Commitment

Optimism and personal power lead to a sense of agency, which is defined as knowing we have the power to act. Small actions lead to larger actions, which lead to even larger actions. Once we find our agency, it grows.

Taking an action, even a small one, alters how we perceive ourselves. If you make a commitment to start recycling plastics at home, you're likely to find yourself separating your trash, compost, and plastics at a school or public cafeteria. By starting to recycle at home, you've begun to see yourself as someone who recycles. You want to act consistently with that belief, so you start sorting your recyclables wherever you go. People who are consistent are perceived to be honest and trustworthy. Conversely, people who are inconsistent are perceived as unreliable and untrustworthy. The motivation to be consistent is very high! This is the power of commitment.

Making a public commitment is even more powerful than making a commitment to yourself. Among registered voters, those who were asked the day before a presidential election if they planned to vote were 41% more likely to follow through with it than registered voters who were not asked.[11] Fundraisers use the same technique. They will ask for a small donation "just to show your support." If you give, later they will follow that with a larger request.

As an environmental advocate, your power will grow as you take action. And you can build power by asking others to join you. Consider asking someone to sign a petition. The petition itself may have little effect, but there is an effect on the signer; by signing their name they make a small commitment to the cause. You can build on this small commitment by asking them later to call or email their legislators. After that you might ask them to tell their story to the city council or legislative committee. This is using the power of commitment to build support for your cause.

Organizing Power

Power is created through organizing and building community, which is good news! This is what Eric Liu means when he says power is infinite. Organizing creates power where none existed before by awakening the dormant power within people and communities. This is a positive-sum process in that organizing creates new power, usually without taking it from others. Legalizing same-sex marriage created a new category of marriage and did not take away from other marriages (despite what some people argued). A clean river with a walking trail beside it doesn't take power from anyone.

Organizing amplifies the power of individuals. Strong, well-organized groups have successfully taken on large corporations, highly paid lobbyists, government agencies, city councils, state governments, and even Congress. To create major social change, well-organized and persistent campaigns are needed. As mentioned previously, twenty million people celebrated the first Earth Day in 1970. This massive participation combined with good organizing generated enough power to pass major legislation like the Clean Air and Clean Water Acts.

Solving the climate crisis today need not be a zero-sum game in which some people must lose in order for the environment to gain. However, the concept of scarcity and competition for limited resources is baked into our culture.[12] Scarcity thinking causes the people responsible for harm to dig in their heels and defend the status quo, even when environmental harm is well documented.

In Cancer Alley, people have been long aware of what is happening in their district. Citizens in Convent, a town in St. Joseph's Parish, successfully stopped a polyvinyl chloride plant from locating there in the late 1990s.[13] For the last several years new citizen groups have been organizing to stop development of more chemical plants, and reduce harmful pollution from existing plants. The Louisiana Bucket Brigade, the Gulf Restoration Network, the Center for Biological Diversity, RISE St. James, and 350 New Orleans have all stepped up to demand records and information related to the land-use change that would allow fourteen new plastics plants. They see the local problem, and they see the bigger picture of taking back their community and speaking out for environmental justice everywhere. "It's a battle in a small town. But this battle has ramifications for the whole world, and that sounds like an exaggeration, but it isn't," says Sharon Lavigne, president and founder of RISE St. James, one of the major organizers in St. James Parish.[14] Organizers in Cancer Alley continue to reclaim the power of their community.

You, too, can use the power of organizing, no matter the size or scope of your issue. If you can get others on your street to show up at town council meetings to support recycling or trash pickup or to oppose a harmful development, your power is much greater than if you showed up alone. If you engage in a larger campaign or movement, the power of an organized group can bring you through the inevitable struggles on the way to success. As Frederick Douglass once said, "Power concedes nothing without a demand."[19] Your demands need to be backed up with a well-organized coalition and campaign that create power where little or none existed before.

FARMWORKERS ORGANIZE TO CHALLENGE CAMPBELL'S SOUP[15]

Farmworkers picking vegetables for Campbell's Soup were abused, underpaid, and exposed to dangerous pesticides in the fields. Most of their incomes were below the national poverty level, and they lived in substandard housing. They were not provided with health care or medical insurance. They decided to organize to fight for their rights. They formed the Farm Labor Organizing Committee (FLOC), which at first was a small, informal group. They made an effort to speak with Campbell's about their working conditions. Their initial efforts were ignored. As a next step, 2,300 farmworkers walked off the fields and demanded a guaranteed minimum wage, an end to pesticide spraying while workers were in the fields, plumbing in the shacks they lived in, and worksite toilets.

Campbell's fought back. They said the growers were responsible for working conditions, not them. Behind the scenes, Campbell's helped growers bring in strike breakers and instructed them to use mechanical harvesters. The farmworkers responded with a call for a boycott of Campbell's soup products—an effective way to challenge the company's economic and political power. They mobilized churches, labor groups, and other organizations to support their campaign. They also organized a 550-mile march from Toledo, Ohio, to Campbell's headquarters in Camden, New Jersey. Communities along the way provided food, shelter, and shoes. Along the way they held a large public rally in Philadelphia and a Catholic mass in New Jersey, where fifteen priests washed the feet of the marchers in a gesture of support. Upon arriving at Campbell's headquarters they held another rally where they chanted slogans and sang songs calling for a national boycott of Campbell's products.

Following this, a group called Corporate Campaign joined the FLOC to devise a corporate campaign strategy, produce literature and mailings, and provide training and support to the farmworker organizers. After two years of negotiation, a historic three-way contract between Campbell's and the tomato and cucumber growers in the Midwest was signed. The contract recognized the workers' union and gave workers an equal voice in negotiating wages and working conditions. Workers were now guaranteed minimum earnings, a system of incentive payments, workers' compensation, unemployment compensation, and Social Security benefits.

Lengthy campaigns like this one have their struggles. At one point the AFL-CIO, one of the largest unions in the country, said, "The AFL-CIO has not approved a boycott of Campbell and does not support this corporate campaign."[16] Although this was a setback, FLOC organizers did not back down. And because of their persistence in using their power to organize, the balance of power eventually shifted, and they won their campaign.

The once "powerless" workers had established a direct voice in their employment and living conditions. As FLOC President Baldemar Velasquez said when the contract was signed, "It gives farmworkers choice in their own affairs."[17] They created power where none existed before.[18]

Community and Collaborative Power

Research confirms that our perception of how much impact we can have depends on our sense of community. If we feel we can join others and make an impact, we are likely to act. But if we feel overwhelmed by an issue and have little sense of community, we are likely to feel there's nothing we can do to make a difference.[20]

Many young people and college students are anxious and fearful about the future of our planet. While some are doing their best to ignore the issue and get on with their lives, others are motivated by their fear and anxiety to act. I hear the word "resilience" often these days. For youth, I think resilience comes from joining a community of activists or advocates and having faith that as a group, they can and will make a difference.

Collaboration occurs when people come together and contribute their expertise for the benefit of the whole, which might be a shared objective, project, or mission. True collaboration means all parties are fully focused on the common good, such that working toward a solution takes priority over individual or organizational agendas. Collaboration means giving up the fear of losing something or defending one's position. It means *working with and sharing power with others.*

When natural disasters occur, communities usually rise to the occasion and help care for one another. Stories abound about people contributing the skills and resources they have during storms, floods, and wildfires. Doctors and nurses might set up free clinics, churches and gyms might set up temporary shelters in their buildings, and grocery stores and restaurants might contribute meals.

Communities of people with shared experience, vision, and goals have depth and power. We see this in the response to natural disasters and also when policies are established to create and protect the kinds of communities people want.

Communities form around geographies, meaning neighborhoods, towns, and cities, as the Cancer Alley organizations have. Communities also form around issues that cut across geographic boundaries. The fishing community in Maine is a strong advocacy community. They appear in large numbers whenever an issue that threatens their livelihoods comes up. They are well organized, and their side almost always prevails. Almost every active issue has an advocacy community working on it, from mental health to education to climate change. The more diverse and well organized these communities are, the more effective they tend to be.

During the COVID-19 crisis, executives at many publicly held companies reduced their own pay to prevent layoffs of employees at lower pay levels.[21] A prominent example is Comcast, where the five top executives donated their salaries to COVID-19 relief, and the company pledge $500 million to help its employees during the outbreak. Similarly, top executives at Marriott, General Electric, Texas Roadhouse, Disney, and Airbnb gave up their salaries for 2020. Most donated the funds to help their employees.[22] Many people sheltered at home for long periods of time during the pandemic to reduce the risk of overwhelming hospital facilities. These are all examples of collaboration and cooperation in support of the common good.

The power of collaboration can be seen in the emerging sharing economy. Not everyone needs to own a lawn tractor, a swimming pool, a twenty-foot ladder, a car, a cabin on a lake, or a boat. Subscription services, memberships, and rentals are replacing individual ownership. This allows conservation of resources and access to products and services for more people. I believe we will see more sharing of resources in the future.

When facing environmental problems such as sea level rise, collaborative efforts between city government, university researchers, private industry, and community groups are essential. No one agency or group can succeed in addressing problems of this size and complexity alone.

Issues that cross national borders, like toxic air emissions or ocean acidification, need the power of broad international and intercultural collaboration to be resolved. This is why the Paris Agreement and the work of the United Nations are so important for addressing climate change. Single countries can never be as effective in resolving global environmental issues as an international collaboration.

Environmental Justice

As we saw in the Cancer Alley case, climate change and environmental pollution have a well-documented and well-known disproportionate effect on people of color. Hurricane Katrina killed 1,800 people and wiped out multiple Black neighborhoods in New Orleans when dikes there failed. Hurricane Harvey flooded Houston neighborhoods located in the hundred-year flood plain, home to many low-income residents. There are many, many examples where people living on less desirable land suffer the most from climate change and pollution.

The disproportionately high number of deaths among Americans of color during the coronavirus pandemic showed us once again that people of color are exposed to dirtier air, have unhealthier living conditions, have less access to health care, and have worse health overall than White Americans. This is due to a history of public policies that allow construction of industrial plants near low-income neighborhoods, and disparities in access to and quality of health care. It's also due to lack of good education and job opportunities for low-income people and people of color, necessitating their living in larger groups and in low-income areas. The following data illustrates this:

US RATES OF DEATH FROM COVID-19, BY RACE, DECEMBER 2020 (AGGREGATED FROM ALL STATES AND THE DISTRICT OF COLUMBIA)

- **1 in 750 Indigenous Americans has died** (or 133.0 deaths per 100,000)
- **1 in 800 Black Americans has died** (or 123.7 deaths per 100,000)
- **1 in 1,100 Pacific Islander Americans has died** (or 90.4 deaths per 100,000)
- **1 in 1,150 Latino Americans has died** (or 86.7 deaths per 100,000)
- **1 in 1,325 White Americans has died** (or 75.7 deaths per 100,000)
- **1 in 1,925 Asian Americans has died** (or 51.6 deaths per 100,000)[23]

Environmental justice is a movement that calls us to understand that all forms of oppression are connected: classism, racism, sexism, ageism, the burden of industrial pollution and effects of climate change, and so on. In order to heal ourselves and the earth we need to recognize and change the system that favors those who are in power over those who are not. It should not be "the money over the many."

Traditional narratives of the conservation and environmental movement excluded women, low-income people, Native Americans, and people of color. Environmental racism has manifested through locating polluting industries in areas populated by communities of color, displacing Indigenous peoples from their lands (sometimes in order to "preserve the lands"), exposing workers to toxic chemicals and materials, and polluting drinking water supplies. Historically, the US environmental movement was led and supported by middle- and upper-class White people. It wasn't until the 1990s that a racial frame, a gender frame, and a class frame for environmentalism began to emerge.[24]

How did environmental and climate injustice come to be? In the era of development following the Second World War and continuing to today, corporate decision makers, planning and zoning boards, and state and federal regulatory agencies found it easier to site landfills, factories, and other polluting facilities in low-income communities than in White middle- and upper-income communities. Until recently, low-income communities rarely had the tools, information, or connections to fight back.

History of the Environmental Justice Movement

In 1982, six thousand truckloads of PCB-contaminated soils were scheduled to be dumped in Warren County, North Carolina. Black residents in the area protested by holding marches and lying in the road to block trucks, and they gained national attention. Civil rights and Black church leaders joined local protesters. Five hundred were arrested. Although the people of Warren County lost their battle, this was the first environmental protest by people of color to attract widespread attention. It energized a new focus within the civil rights movement, drawing Black civil rights and church leaders to the cause of environmental racism.

Immediately following the Warren County protests, several studies substantiated the fact that people of color live, work, and play in America's most polluted environments. Rev. Benjamin Chavis, who had participated in the Warren County protests, went on to publish *Toxic Wastes and Race in the United States,* a research study showing that race was the single most important factor in determining where toxic waste facilities were sited in the United States.[25] Similarly, Walter Fauntroy, District of Columbia delegate and chair of the Congressional Black Caucus, tasked the Government Accounting Office with determining whether communities of color suffered disproportionately from siting of hazardous waste sites. The study revealed that three-quarters of hazardous waste landfills in eight southeastern states were located in poor African American and Latino communities.[26]

In the 1990s, environmental justice leaders began to push their agenda with traditional, primarily White environmental organizations. These organizations had focused on land conservation, endangered species, and clean air and water with great success, but they had not engaged in the environmental struggles of people of color. Environmental justice leaders challenged them to address racial bias in hiring, board recruiting, policy development, and toxic exposure in poor communities.

In 1991, the first National People of Color Environmental Leadership Summit met for three days in Washington, DC. In attendance were Black and tribal environmental leaders, as well as the heads of the Natural Resources Defense Council and the Sierra Club. The summit produced two foundational documents of the environmental justice movement: the *Principles of Environmental Justice* and the *Call to Action.* As a result of the summit and the growing awareness of environmental racism, a number of mainstream environmental groups developed environmental justice initiatives, hired people of color, and resolved to include environmental justice in policy development.

In response to environmental justice leaders, the federal government recognized environmental justice for the first time under the Clinton administration in the 1990s. A groundbreaking executive order directed federal agencies to identify and address the adverse health effects that federal policies and programs had on low-income people and people of color.

While much was accomplished in the 1990s and afterward, a landmark 2014 report, *The State of Diversity in Environmental Organizations*, highlighted the racial, gender, class, and cultural disparities in environmental organizations across the country. This study of 293 environmental nonprofits, foundations, and government agencies showed that people of color were grossly underrepresented in leadership, staffing, and volunteers. It also showed that leadership of established US environmental groups was dominated by well-educated White people, who held 89% of the leadership positions. The study found significant progress in hiring and promoting women—mostly White women—in environmental organizations, but men were still more likely to occupy the most powerful positions. Racial diversity lagged behind gender diversity. Recruiting of new hires was limited to a closed circle of networks and organizations that excluded people of color. Few of the organizations surveyed collaborated or partnered with low-income or racial minority organizations.[27]

The report was a wake-up call. Clearly, more work needed to be done to make the workplaces of these organizations more inclusive and welcoming. Since then, the Sierra Club and other environmental groups have taken action to increase diversity within their organizations. Many added environmental justice to their organization's mission and have taken action to support environmental justice. The Sierra Club's governing board adopted environmental justice principles in 2002. In addition, the organization mobilized members and regional chapters to better integrate environmental justice into their work on issues including clean drinking water, clean air, and land-use planning and zoning. They know diversity is essential to winning major environmental change.

The environmental justice movement has broadened environmentalism. The leadership of frontline communities—those most affected by environmental racism—is widely recognized today. Not only do we need to protect critical habitats, wildlife, and endangered species; environmental justice seeking equal access to healthy land, air, and water is crucial, too. Environmental organizations now realize the environment is not just a single item on a issue to-do list, or a list of places that need to be cleaned up; it is part of a larger, interlocking group of issues.

As we saw in earlier chapters, these interlocking issues are the physical manifestation of deeply held and often unconscious worldviews, earth stories, and beliefs. Recognizing and addressing inequality and exclusiveness is fundamentally connected to addressing climate change and toxic pollution. Advocates for environmental justice seek to clean up the environment *and* change the balance of power.

Environmental advocates must change the mental models and social paradigms we operate from in order to change the world. There are two things we can do to achieve this: look within and question our own thinking and motivations, and begin to work closely with people who hold different views and life experiences from our own. *By bringing diverse communities together, environmental advocates multiply their organizing power.*

Political Power and Social Equity

Following the Second World War, there was a period when most people in this country could expect a better life for themselves and their children than past generations had. The economy grew steadily as a result of public investments. The GI Bill paid for college education for eight million veterans returning from the war. The highways and bridges we use today were constructed then. A vast amount of housing was built to house young families, and the home mortgage interest tax deduction made it possible for many to afford them. There was a collective sense that our economy was fair and that hard work and education would be rewarded with a comfortable life. Many Americans called this the "American Dream." These things were true for most White people. Native Americans, African Americans, and other ethnic groups had some expanded opportunities, but nowhere near what White people enjoyed.

Beginning with the election of Ronald Reagan as president in 1980, public policies began to favor corporations over communities and individual success over the common good. As increasing amounts of money flowed to political candidates and professional lobbyists, ordinary citizens lost power. This imbalance has grown over the years, to the point where economic elites—the top 5%—have most of the opportunities now. Large corporations and the owners who profit from them have changed the rules to favor their agenda, which includes polluting the air, water, and earth as an "externality" in the pursuit of profit. As we have seen, the earth and the people living near industrial polluters suffer the consequences. The taxpayers often fund the cleanup, if there is any cleanup at all.

This fits perfectly with what Eric Liu calls the "first law of power": power concentrates, meaning that it feeds on itself and compounds.[28] If you start out rich, you get richer. If you start out poor, you may live to the median age if you're lucky. As more money flows into politics, the rules continually shift to benefit large donors and the wealthy. The Supreme Court's *Citizens United* decision in 2010 allowed corporate dollars to flow into political campaigns almost without limit. The Tax Cuts and Jobs Act of 2017 primarily benefited corporations and the wealthy.[29] We are seeing multiple efforts to make voting more difficult, such as requiring a photo ID and moving polls to locations that are less convenient for voters. These, too, are attempts to reduce the power of ordinary people.

Environmental advocates want to change the balance of power. They want to support the health and well-being of the majority of people on the planet, not just the wealthy and not just oil and gas companies. They want to bring power back to local communities so ordinary people's voices are heard and policies change as a result. They want healthy food, water, soil, and air to be available to everyone. They want equal opportunity for all and an end to racial discrimination. They want a government that focuses on what ordinary people need and want. They want corporations to be accountable for their footprint on the earth.

The COVID-19 pandemic provided a stark illustration of inequality in the United States. People working paycheck to paycheck could not afford to be out of work, so many worked at the risk of their and their family's health. Some had access to health care; others did not. For those in households with many living under one roof, quarantining or social distancing was difficult if not impossible. Many got sick and died. People of color have had higher rates of illness and death than White Americans. Many small and medium-sized businesses did not have the funds to sustain a lengthy closure and were ruined financially.

A broad movement to transition to an equitable, clean economy is what's needed to turn these trends around. This is why I'm writing this book: to help ordinary citizens and students learn *how to change the power structure*. We need a government and an economy that are truly of, by, and for the people, and for the earth on which our life depends.

From Power to Action

Part II of this book lays out specific ways in which you can build power for your issue or cause. Successful campaigns start small, usually with small actions and conversations among a few people. They typically grow organically, as smaller actions lead to larger actions, and support grows from a few individuals to larger and more diverse coalitions. Whether you are initiating a new campaign or joining an existing one, each chapter in the second part of this book lays out ways to strengthen the power of your group and move toward success in making the changes you envision.

Chapter 8, "Creating a Winning Strategy," shows you how to craft a focused strategy that will stand firm in the face of opposition and win the changes you seek.

Chapter 9, "Building and Managing Your Campaign," provides specifics for organizing a group or team, managing a coalition, and staging a successful campaign.

Chapter 10, "Working with Decision Makers," focuses on building personal relationships with decision makers so they will support your cause and become champions for the changes you want to make.

Chapters 11, 12, and 13—"Framing Your Message," "Communicating with Impact," and "Working with the Media and the Public"—go into detail on communications. These chapters provide the tools to frame, craft, and deliver your message effectively. Compelling communications and organized outreach cut through ambivalence and replace ignorance of your issue with well-informed support.

Chapter 14, "Epilogue: Eight Reasons to Be Optimistic in Troubled Times," describes what a healthy, peaceful, and compassionate future might look like, and it shows why I believe humanity is on the path to achieve it.

Creating a Winning Strategy

The most successful social movements I know developed clarity in three areas: analysis of the problem (research), an envisioned big picture solution, and a strategy for getting from here to there.

—GEORGE LAKEY, *How We Win*

Why You Need a Strategy

A friend of mine recently said, "I was disappointed in the 2017 Women's March, because nothing ever came of it." I sympathized with my friend. I too loved the energy of that day, and I marched locally with many men and women. I too hoped it would result in meaningful policy change. Then I explained to my friend that although the Women's March rolled out an ambitious agenda, there wasn't a focused effort with specific goals and a plan for making policy change. Without these, big changes would never result. Marches, protests, and platforms, as energizing as they can be, are never enough to accomplish social change.

Strategy consists of a specific goal and an identified path to achieve it. The Women's March's platform included calls to pass the Equal Rights Amendment, implement Medicare for All, and end violence against women, among many other important issues.[1] They achieved great visibility for these issues—an important accomplishment. Some local Women's March groups did take specific action in their jurisdictions, but the larger shift from protests, marches, and platforms to a strong organization with a specific advocacy plan didn't occur.[2]

The bottom line is that you must have a strategy in order to create change. You have to be clear about what you want and who can decide that. You must research your issue fully, becoming an expert on the subject and on the people who care about it. You have to have a clear goal and at least a simple plan to achieve it. You have to build a team and perhaps a coalition to support your goals. You have to work honestly with supporters and opponents. And you have to keep moving despite the setbacks. It's hard work and can take a long time to pull off a win. The process begins with building a strategy. This chapter shows you where to start.

Degrees of Separation

When choosing your issue and strategy, something to take into account is the idea of "degrees of separation." This concept was first elucidated by Hungarian author Frigyes Karinthy in 1929. He said all people are six or fewer social connections apart from each other.[3] The concept's relevance here is that you will gain faster and more complete results from your advocacy work if you work in arenas where you have fewer degrees of separation.

You might choose to work with smaller governments or corporations, where there are only one or two degrees of separation between you and decision makers. If your best friend has a parent in Congress, that reduces the degrees of separation and gives you the power to create change in this larger arena. With fewer degrees of separation, it is easier to get a personal introduction and establish relationships with influential people.

In larger arenas, like Congress or federal agencies, it can take years to move to a decision. Several of my colleagues in the fishing industry spent their entire careers organizing and advocating for locally managed community fisheries. This was in opposition to the National Marine Fisheries Service, a federal agency that manages US coastal fisheries. These organizers worked for *thirty years*, writing numerous reports, public comments, and letters, and driving hundreds of thousands of miles to attend meetings and make their point. The final result? When a new quota system that allocated fishing rights was finally implemented, a portion of those rights were allocated to local Maine fishing communities. A wonderful reward for their many years of work!

But with fewer degrees of separation, you can move your issue forward in a much shorter time. Ideally, you want to work in settings where decision makers can get to know you or your group personally, and will have the capacity to respond to your group's emails and phone calls.

It takes less patience to work at a smaller scale, too. The average time to get state or city legislation passed is two to six years, not thirty. If you are working in the corporate arena, smaller, more accessible companies will be easier to approach than larger ones, and changes will take less time to implement. If you have passion and patience for a much longer process, like the community fisheries advocates did, or if you have personal connections that reduce the degrees of separation, I say go for the big arenas. But if you don't, I recommend picking an advocacy arena where you can see results sooner.

Who Should Lead?

Political actions are ideally led by the people who are directly affected by their issue. This brings strength, credibility, and authenticity to the change process, leveraging the power of people's lived experiences.

Under this umbrella, there are three ways student and community advocates can work for change. One is to stand up and organize on an issue where you and your community are directly affected. This was the case with the fisheries organizers mentioned above, the farmworkers who organized against Campbell's Soup, and the Cancer Alley residents fighting the siting of chemical plants in their communities. What issues are arising in your area? What are you concerned about? You might join a group or start one yourself to advocate for an issue of local or regional concern.

A second way is to work with professional organizers in nonprofit organizations. The organization Defend Our Health, for example, works with people who have been harmed by toxic chemicals. The organization does research on these issues and then lobbies for policy change, with the support of community and student advocates. If you've been affected by or are concerned about toxic chemicals, you might work with them as a volunteer.

A third way to work for change is to join a movement led by others who are advocating for a cause that does not directly affect you, but where you want to join them in support. This was the case when military veterans, White activists, and Indigenous people from other regions joined the Sioux leaders in resistance to the Dakota Access Pipeline. This is also the case when White people join or participate in the environmental justice or Black Lives Matter movements. The appropriate leaders of these movements are those who have been most deeply and directly affected by the issues, i.e., the frontline communities.

Mainstream environmental groups are recognizing that workable solutions with staying power must come from people directly affected by the issues. In the Pacific Northwest, the nonprofit Ecotrust has often been the public face of environmentalism. Now, however, they are stepping into a support role, with the leadership and voices of frontline communities being central. As they say on their website, "We honor other ways of being and thinking, we recognize that we are on land that is not our own, and we respect the fundamental sovereignty of American Indian Tribes, First Nations, and Alaskan Natives. We work to shift power, resources, and privilege to disenfranchised communities, which is fundamental to the change we seek."[4]

You as a student, community, or citizen advocate are making a positive contribution by leading or joining a community initiative, or by joining and supporting frontline leaders who are leading a campaign or movement.

Researching Your Issue

The first step in creating a strategy is to research your issue. You'll need to understand the answers to these questions:

- Who worked on your issue in the past?

- What happened in past attempts to solve it?

- What are the key constraints that stand in the way of solving it now?

- What have other jurisdictions, local or otherwise, done to solve it?

To reiterate the last question, it's a good idea to explore how this issue has been approached in other places. Any lessons you can learn from other jurisdictions can help you avoid pitfalls and find new approaches. A good place to start is the internet. There's a wealth of information out there, including research reports and news stories from around the country.

Researching other jurisdictions was particularly important in developing a proposal to convert an investor-owned electric utility to a consumer-owned electric utility. In introducing this new idea to Maine decision makers, it was important to show that consumer-owned utilities have been successfully operating in other jurisdictions for years. It was also important to learn from others about the pitfalls in transitioning to a consumer-owned utility, so we could develop a transition process that avoided them.

After getting some basic research under your belt, you should get to know more people who are directly affected by the issue. People like to tell their stories and be listened to. If you are a community or student advocate, it will not be hard to find and talk to people directly affected by the issue you are working on. Even if you or your community know your issue well, taking this step will deepen your understanding.

Issue research is often called a "situation analysis." I encourage advocates to dig deeply into their issue and create a bullet-point situation analysis that summarizes the important points. An example follows.

SITUATION ANALYSIS: MAINE'S STATE-WIDE BUILDING AND ENERGY CODE

- Issue stuck for twenty years; multiple failed task forces
- Patchwork of codes, with different codes in every town
- No energy conservation standards for new and existing buildings
- Fire safety and two different national building codes competing to become the state code
- Seventy of 495 towns have a building code; <10% have an energy code
- Towns with codes refuse to update them; why?
- Shoddy and unsafe buildings everywhere
- "Home rule" vs. "efficient government" = competing values
- Many building contractors were trained on the job and are unfamiliar with codes
- Many towns have no capacity to enforce a code
- The number one consumer complaint at attorney general's office is bad building contractors—shoddy construction, and dishonest business dealings; consumers have no recourse

In advocacy work, the situation analysis is the basis for your fact sheet and talking points. A fact sheet is a handout that summarizes your issue and is distributed in print and online to supporters and decision makers. These are usually one to two pages long, with bullet points, with each bullet point sometimes followed by a one- or two-sentence explanation. Fact sheets are succinct and are designed to grab the reader's attention quickly. In-person meetings, website links to other resources, and longer papers (sometimes called "white papers") can provide more in-depth information. For more information about creating these, see chapter 12.

Elements of Strategy

To introduce the elements of strategy to groups, I often use a simple exercise. I ask participants to form teams of four or five people and then pick a topic; any environmental topic will do. They must identify who the decision makers are and what specifically the group is asking them to do. Once this is clear, they are to list three ideas for moving their issue forward. This exercise illustrates the fundamental proposition of advocacy: you're asking decision makers to do what you want them to do.

It also gives an overview of the three elements of strategy: articulating the "ask" that states your goal, identifying the decision makers, and designating a path to achieve your goal. The following sidebar gives examples. Thanks to George Lakey for teaching me this exercise.

STRATEGY EXERCISE

1. Your Specific Demand or "Ask"

What are you asking for? Is this your end goal?

Is it winnable?

Is there a vision behind it?

2. Who Decides?

Who makes the decision?

Is it an individual—CEO, governor, committee chair?

Or is it a decision-making body—school board, city council, legislative committee?

3. Series of Actions/Your Campaign

What series of actions can build support for your issue?

Keep in mind that single actions rarely have impact, but a series of actions that build on each other (a campaign) can strengthen support and help you achieve your goal.

Strategy Example: Dark Skies

1. Your Specific Demand or "Ask"

To pass a bill requiring outdoor lighting to be shielded, directing the beam of light at the ground and not into the sky.

The goal is to reduce light pollution in the state by 80%.

The vision is that all children will know the constellations, because they can see and learn about them.

2. Who Decides?

Environment and Natural Resources Committee of the state legislature (if they pass the bill unanimously, then it automatically passes the House and Senate).

> Rationale: Other possible decision makers include municipalities and the electric power company. Since shielded lighting products are available and cost the same as unshielded ones, the issue seems winnable at the state policy level. If shielded lighting was unavailable or would result in a cost increase, then asking the power company to offer incentives for installing shielded lighting and working with towns to make the change would be a more attractive strategy.

3. Series of Actions/Your Campaign

Draft a bill to require shielded outdoor lighting, and support it with these tactics:

a. Hold a Night Sky festival in a dark, rural location and invite decision makers to attend.

b. Create a video showing light-polluted areas contrasted with star-filled dark skies, and show it to decision makers.

c. Hold a press conference with educators, parents, and owners of businesses that have switched to shielded lighting as speakers.

Your *strategy* is the pathway between where you are now and the achievement of your goal. For your strategy to be viable, each of the three components—the ask or goal, the decision maker(s), and the overarching plan to get there—must be clear and achievable. You can test the clarity of your strategy by asking yourself, "Would my mother understand this?" Or ask someone unconnected to your issue if your goal and plan are clear and understandable to them.

The basic elements of strategy are similar for advocacy and direct action. Both need clearly identified decision makers and goals. The difference is in the process steps and tactics. Advocates working inside the system need to work closely with the decision-making process prescribed by the town, city, county, or state where the decision will be made. The official steps in the decision process determine your campaign deadlines. You will be given a date to present your proposal to the city council, for example.

Direct action campaign strategies and tactics are based on finding the best opportunities to bring attention to an issue. Effective organizers identify opportunities where decision makers can be directly influenced or where media attention is likely. After several years of implementing direct action events, the Earth Quaker Action Team attended the corporate annual meeting of a regional bank and directly made their demands to the bank's board of directors, for example.

Here is the step-by-step strategy we used in the campaign for Maine's Uniform Building and Energy Code (MUBEC):

1. Get study order from legislative committee (an order requiring us to study the issue, write a report, and submit draft legislation)

2. Research the issue

3. Build a coalition of support

4. Return to next legislative session with a draft bill

5. Work with coalition members and decision makers to campaign, lobby, and win!

Who Decides?

Effective advocates make sure they correctly identify the decision maker or decision makers for their ask. This often involves a strategic decision or two. Some of my students wanted to see more sustainable forest practices deployed in Maine's commercial forest lands. They quickly discovered this was a complex undertaking. Much of Maine's forest is privately owned. The state Department of Agriculture, Conservation and Forestry has jurisdiction over Maine forests. The legislature has oversight of the department and how it spends its resources. Several private groups offer certification to forest owners who manage their forests according to sustainability criteria. At the time, the Maine Climate Council was updating the state Climate Action Plan, which would include a section on carbon sequestration in Maine forests. All of these players have decision-making authority at some level, and any of them could be an entry point for working on the issue. Where to begin? That was the question the students wrestled with.

This example illustrates the need for research as a necessary first step in any advocacy initiative. You must fully understand your issue and become somewhat of an expert on its history and the decision makers and stakeholders who care about it. To be effective, advocates must take the time to assess the situation before making an ask of decision makers. Research is time well spent.

For the students in the above example, they needed to decide on an approach they could accomplish in the short amount of time they had to complete their class project. Since the Maine Climate Council was then in session, they chose to make a recommendation to them on forest carbon sequestration. This was the shortest path to reaching decision makers. Similarly, your team needs to tease apart the different levels of decision making on your issue and select an approach that matches your capacity, your timeline, and your personal connections.

Defense or Offense?

I'd been lobbying for years before I realized most of my work has been on proactive campaigns where something new is proposed. Among other things,

I crafted legislation to establish a uniform building and energy code, which hadn't existed before. I worked on legislation to add new elements to the Growth Management Act, which governs town planning and zoning. I joined others in creating a property assessed clean energy program that allowed homeowners to attach renewable energy loans to their property tax bill.

Proactive campaigns like these need broad and diverse coalitions of support to succeed. Strong sponsors and allies are also essential. Positive messaging showing all the benefits of the new program is needed. These campaigns can be long, because you are introducing new ideas that will take time to be understood and accepted. Opponents will line up and tell stories of the disasters that might happen if your idea comes into being. Proactive campaigns are especially hard to plan for because of the unpredictable obstacles that may be thrown in your way. As a proactive campaign leader, sometimes the best you can do is to stay alert and address threats as they arise.

Defensive campaigns are trying to stop something bad from happening or to ban something harmful. In a defensive campaign, your goal is to get decision makers to say "no." What's needed here is negative messaging showing the harmful effects of toxic chemicals, carbon emissions, clearcutting, or building a dam or oil refinery, for example. Your group will need to be present at each step of the decision process. Your tactics should be focused on delaying or overturning a decision. There are many ways to do this, e.g., more studies, more public process, new amendments, constitutional questions, lawsuits, and so on. Environmentalists often insist on environmental impact studies, which are part of the permitting process for large projects under the National Environmental Policy Act. Impact studies are a way to slow projects down and fully highlight the environmental impacts.

If you can slow a process down enough, the project may die. This was the case with the Atlantic Coast Pipeline proposed to carry natural gas 600 miles through West Virginia, Virginia, and North Carolina. Legal challenges brought by environmental groups prompted the dismissal or suspension of numerous permits, leading to increased costs and a six-year delay in the project schedule. Despite a victory at the US Supreme Court regarding a critical permit, Dominion Energy and Duke Energy abandoned the project. By the time the permit was issued, the project's delays and costs were too high to continue. According to Michael Town, executive director of the Virginia League of Conservation Voters, the project's defeat was "a huge victory for Virginia's environment ... and a testament to the power of grassroots action and hundreds of frontline advocates who never stopped fighting."[5]

In other cases where you are fighting against something, litigation may be needed. A group opposed a Pennsylvania law that gave local communities no say in siting hydraulic fracking operations. Neither legislative nor anticorporate actions had worked, so litigation was needed. An antifracking group sued the state of Pennsylvania for not enforcing a constitutional right to clean air and water, and the group won. This provided the legal basis to repeal state laws that allowed fracking without community input. The full story of this Green Amendment is told in chapter 2.

What's Your End Goal? Is It Winnable?

How deep do you want to go? Do you want to initiate a recycling program in your town? Increase the statewide recycling rate? Ban plastic packaging across the country? Or join a larger group working on one of these issues? How you answer these kinds of questions determines your end goal. You can start your advocacy work at any level and be successful. The key is to select an end goal that is motivating for you and your group. If you choose a modest goal, you can always raise your game later. *The key is to have a clear end goal in mind.*

Is your goal winnable? Thinking through this question can show you where change is possible. It can also save you frustration down the road. Maine had an extreme right-wing governor for eight years. He vetoed legislation to promote solar energy almost every year he was in office. Advocates chose to keep introducing solar legislation during this challenging time. But they had to adjust their expectations, because they didn't have enough votes in the legislature to override the governor's vetoes. They decided it was worthwhile to continue pressing forward, because it kept the issue alive and allowed them to fine-tune their bill. Later, under a more moderate governor and legislature, they passed the bill quickly with bipartisan support. It helped that the policies in the bill were fine-tuned and well known due to the earlier attempts to pass it.

Another winning strategy is to start small and scale up. This was successful in Maine with a ban on single-use plastic shopping bags. For eight years we had a governor who would not support a statewide plastic bag ban. So instead advocates worked on a town-by-town basis. By the time this governor's final term ended, eighteen towns had adopted fees and bans on plastic shopping bags. Retail chains began complaining that they had too many different town policies to comply with. After a new, more moderate governor and legislature were elected, a statewide ban was proposed. With the support of environmental advocates, towns, and retail businesses, it passed easily.

Similarly, state-by-state strategies have been used as stepping stones to achieve policy changes at the national level. This is the current strategy for a campaign to eliminate the group of toxic chemicals called PFAS (per- and polyfluoroalkyls), referred to in chapter 5. As of this writing ten states have passed a ban, and many other groups are campaigning for their states to do the same. When enough states have banned the chemicals, the door will have cracked open for a national ban.[6]

Strategy vs. Tactics

It's useful here to understand the difference between strategy and tactics. Strategies are the big-picture process steps: build a coalition, sponsor a study, pass a bill or an ordinance. Tactics are the specific ways to achieve those steps. If the goal is to build a new school in your town, the strategy is to get the approval of the town council and then pass the proposal in a town referendum. Tactics would include holding a public information session, printing a fact sheet, writing an opinion piece, and creating a website. Tactics are the fun part of campaigns. This is where you can get creative, interact with people, and feel like you are making a difference.

During halftime of the Harvard-Yale football game, protesters wearing Harvard and Yale colors staged a sit-in at midfield. They held banners and chanted "Hey, hey! Ho, ho! Fossil fuels have got to go!" Hundreds of football fans streamed onto the field to join the protesters. Most walked off after about an hour with a police escort; about forty who remained were arrested.[7]

This is an example of an effective tactic. Harvard and Yale alumni are major contributors to their schools, and they regard the annual Harvard-Yale game as an almost sacred event. Typically, fifty to sixty thousand people attend the game, and many more watch it on national TV. The combined endowments of Harvard and Yale are worth more than $70 billion. The demonstration perfectly targeted the audience with a clear message. It was a huge gesture in support of the goal to divest the Harvard and Yale endowments of fossil fuel investments.

Let's take a look at an equally creative but less impactful tactic. A colleague of mine once planned a "going-away party" for Central Maine Power Company, complete with a cake, costumes, and party favors. The purpose was to build support for a goal to convert this foreign-owned, investor-owned utility to a locally owned, consumer-owned utility. The party took place outdoors near the entrance to one of the company offices, with several speakers and a videographer present. Unfortunately, no media or decision makers were present. The event was colorful and well planned, but the impact was limited mostly to the twenty people who attended.

One of the pitfalls of organizing is that people often want to jump into tactics without having a solid goal or strategy in place. It is more fun to plan a creative event than it is to wrestle with the bigger-picture questions, like "What is the decision-making process to get Harvard and Yale to divest their endowments of fossil fuels?" The Harvard-Yale demonstration was a terrific tactic for getting the attention of donors. But how would that attention be used?

In this case, Harvard students launched a website urging alumni to withhold donations. Then an alumni group called Harvard Forward started a petition to nominate five pro-environment alumni to run for the Board of Overseers, which is just one step removed from the Harvard Corporation that runs the endowment. Three alumni were elected to the board. At Yale, environmentalist Maggie Thomas collected signatures to qualify for the ballot for a seat on the Yale Corporation, which governs the Yale endowment.

The *goal* was to get the endowment boards to divest from fossil fuels.[8] The *strategy* was to place supportive people on the decision-making boards of the endowments who could then build support and ultimately call for a board vote on divestment. The *tactics* were the demonstration at the football game, the student website, and the campaigns for board seats.

Stakeholder Analysis

To be successful, you must understand who will support your cause, who will oppose it, to what degree, and why. Answering these questions is called "stakeholder analysis" or sometimes "power mapping." The simple grid below is a helpful way to map your stakeholders.

You want to identify your stakeholders by group. If you are opposing a proposed new highway through your town, you would identify every group that is affected and every group that might support or oppose the project. In this case residents and businesses, the chamber of commerce, the state highway department, the town council, church congregations, and other groups in your town would be included in your analysis. By filling out the stakeholder analysis grid, you can identify your potential allies and coalition members, as well as your opposition. You will also identify how important each group is to your campaign.

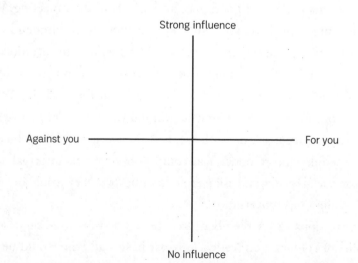

Another useful mapping tool is the fan-shaped model below. This model is helpful in identifying groups that are in the middle on your issue. Your middle people are the most persuadable, and they become the audience you are targeting in your effort to increase support.

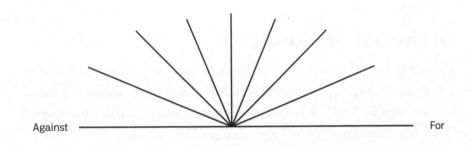

Against ———————————————————————————————— For

After identifying who the important stakeholders are, you will want to give some thought to *why* they support or oppose your issue. Rather than guessing, it is extremely helpful to talk to stakeholders and ask them how they feel about your issue. Informal conversations are best, and making yourself available to speak informally with stakeholders is an important part of advocacy work.

To reach stakeholders, you will need to use the personal networks of your team members. Even if your team has only a few connections, you can start with a handful of good ones and ask them for a meeting. When you're meeting with them, you can then ask them to recommend others you should talk to and whether they would be willing to introduce you. People are usually willing to help. This way you can expand your reach.

Social media tools are a handy way to reach out for feedback. You can use Facebook, an e-newsletter, or other digital vehicles to let people know you are seeking feedback on an issue, and then you can set up meetings with the people who respond. You could also create an informal survey, share it on social media, and ask people to indicate if they would be willing to have a follow-up conversation.

Organizations whose members are affected by your issue can also be a gold mine of contacts and feedback. Most have staff who would be more than willing to speak with you about your issue and help you identify important people to speak with.

When I worked on the Maine Uniform Building and Energy Code (MUBEC) issue, I met privately with eighteen different groups to talk about the proposal and answer questions. This kind of informal dialogue builds trust and support like nothing else. Once you have stakeholder groups on board, you will have a strong coalition that can help you win over decision makers. The key is to fully understand *why* people hold a certain position on your issue. In doing this work you will likely learn some surprising things. You can use these findings to refine your strategy.

As I got to know the stakeholders for the MUBEC, I discovered a fair amount of resistance from small homebuilders and contractors. Many of these tradespeople had learned their trade on the job and had never used codes. Codes are laid out in big, fat code books that go into great detail about building materials and construction specifications. They are quite technical. Some builders had no college education or hadn't finished high school, and they feared they didn't have the skills to use a code book. They were afraid of losing their livelihoods if a building code became mandatory; thus, they strongly opposed a statewide code. Our team had to accommodate this group. We did this by not requiring contractors to be licensed, and by offering free training courses in how to use the code after the law passed.

Another stakeholder group, the Maine Building Officers and Inspectors Association, saw the building codes as a way to professionalize their work. Most code officers were underpaid municipal employees with the difficult job of trying to enforce a set of rules. They saw a statewide building code as offering them an opportunity to move up in the world, with better recognition, perhaps better pay, and a clear set of rules to back up their enforcement decisions. It was no surprise that they strongly supported a statewide code. They sent representatives to all the public meetings, called their legislators asking for support, and had several volunteer lobbyists on hand in the State House. I would not have known that the code officers could be such a powerful ally if I hadn't gotten to know them personally.

Take Your Time with Strategy

Strategies, by their very nature, take time to develop. The best ideas come when you're in the shower, walking outdoors, or engaged in a routine task. Good ideas also come from listening to and reflecting on the experiences of a broad range of stakeholders. Planning meetings are good, but you want to give your strategies time to breathe and grow between meetings.

Sometimes you will know what the problem is but not how to solve it. This was the case for the Working Waterfront Coalition, a group consisting of industry, nonprofit organizations, and a state government agency. The group knew that development threatened water access for fishermen, aquaculturists, and boat builders. But how could they solve the problem?

As a coalition member, I worked with a partner for many months to develop solutions. We brought proposed policy solutions to coalition meetings where members asked questions, poked holes in our arguments, and sent us back to refine our ideas multiple times. This process went on for almost a year before we had a viable, well-thought-out set of solutions.

Sometimes you will need to present your strategy to others—a board of directors, organizational leaders, a committee, legislative staff, or donors. This is one more reason to spend extra time researching and working on your strategy: you want to make a credible and compelling presentation and then have it approved.

Do You Need a Written Plan?

Most campaign guidebooks say a written campaign plan is critical to success. I agree that a clear plan, with a goal, strategy, and tactics as described in this chapter, is essential to win. But whether a fully written campaign plan and timeline is practical or necessary needs more discussion.

If you are working in a complex coalition engaging many organizations and players, a written plan and timeline make sense. The written plan provides a reference that everyone working on the campaign can fall back on if there are questions or if things get confusing. If your campaign is grant funded, your funders are likely to require a written plan with clear benchmarks to measure progress along the way. If you are working as an advocate within the political system, you can determine when a bill may be introduced, heard, and voted on. You can plan ahead for these events, and a written outline of the steps and dates can be useful to coalition members.

But in many cases, particularly direct action and anticorporate campaigns, putting together a realistic plan or timeline is almost impossible. Yes, you may know you have to stop the pipeline before major permits are issued, which might be in two years. But with court appeals and countering actions by opponents and supporters, the timeline might be twice as long.

Anticorporate campaigns are hard to write a plan for because the inside power story within corporate leadership is so hard to determine. In an earlier example I cited Central Maine Power, which is owned by Avangrid, which is owned by Iberdrola, which is owned by shareholders around the world. In corporate structures like these, it is hard to determine where the decision points are and how long it will take to access them.

Your group should make a judgement on whether a written plan will serve you. If you decide to go forward with one, here's a list of typical plan components, in chronological order:

CAMPAIGN PLAN OUTLINE

1. Issue research/situation analysis
2. Goal or goals; the ask
3. Decision maker(s)
4. Strategies and tactics
5. Opponents and allies
6. Campaign assets and needs
7. Messages and messengers
8. Media and social media strategies

9. Budget and fundraising plan

10. Evaluation

11. Timeline

Strategy Summary

Campaigns can be won or lost based on strategy. It's important to remember that you are trying to get allies to step up and support you, to change neutrals into allies, and ultimately to persuade decision makers to do what you want them to do.

Too many campaigns get obsessed by every move their opponents make and become too problem focused to achieve their campaign goals. Others, like the Women's March, lack the organizational structure and strategy to move their issues forward. In order to succeed, organizers must keep campaigns focused on what they want to achieve.

In creating strategy and running your campaign, you'll want to work with a team of people you are comfortable with. Your group—even if you're only informally organized—needs people with the skills and desire to work together to run a compelling and well-organized effort. The next chapter will give you guidance on how to build and manage your campaign.

Building and Managing Your Campaign

As an activist you can echo the anger and hope of the disenfranchised. But to make institutional changes, you need an organization that can mobilize people to join together and support and work for an issue.

—NICK LICATA, *Becoming a Citizen Activist*

Getting Organized

Every campaign is in the business of creating power. By asserting a position and building the support of a diverse group of stakeholders, you are building community power and holding decision makers accountable. You are claiming and building power where little or none existed before.

To create and sustain enough power to evoke change, every campaign needs an organizational structure, with designated leaders and subgroups.

This is true whether members of your group are paid organizers, volunteers, or some combination thereof. Every effective campaign has a steering or executive committee or leadership team, usually three to six people who have made a commitment to be part of the team. This group works closely together and has the time and resources to commit to the work.

It also helps to have a sponsoring organization willing to provide amenities such as meeting space, online meeting software, a copy machine, and other support for the leadership team. Sponsors are usually organizations that are strong allies and supporters of your cause.

Establishing a leadership team is especially important in larger coalitions, where different people show up at each coalition meeting. It's nearly impossible to make decisions with fifteen to thirty people who may or may not have attended the prior meeting. But the leadership team can set the agenda and make decisions, with the input of coalition members. A skillfully led coalition with a strong leadership team has a great chance of success, even with a coalition membership that comes and goes.

What Coalition Leaders Do

One of the most important tasks of coalition leadership is to recruit, delegate to, and support other leaders. Appointing team leaders or committee chairs and delegating chunks of work to them is a way to share the creative challenges, which greatly increases the overall energy of your coalition. You should organize based on the skill sets of your people, and you should feel free to create teams or committees spontaneously, as needs arise. Here is the list of typical coalition committees or teams:

- Communications/media—responsible for letters to the editor, op-eds, media relations
- Social media—responsible for website, Facebook, Instagram, distribution lists, Zoom
- Fundraising—responsible for raising money
- Policy—responsible for specifics of policy development, campaign strategy, and drafting legislation

- Legal and technical—responsible for legal research if the issue is complex

- Events—you might have a team responsible for organizing specific events, such as press conferences

- Outreach—responsible for tabling at events, speaking engagements, presentations

Coalition leadership is also responsible for setting the tone in a campaign. This means leaders need to go out of their way to demonstrate the values they want to prevail. Coalition leaders can demonstrate inclusivity by seeking out different populations and stakeholder groups, to ensure broad perspectives are represented and heard. It helps if leaders are thoughtful and intentional about this.

Coalition leaders also demonstrate inclusivity by actively listening and responding to everyone, even if the comments being made are hostile or irrelevant to the topic at hand. An invitation to continue a conversation at a later time is appropriate when comments veer off the agenda.

Coalition leaders can demonstrate integrity by promptly following through on commitments and always doing what they say they are going to do. They can demonstrate humility if they can easily and publicly admit it when they are wrong. Leaders who admit they are wrong and who entertain the opinions and ideas of others create an atmosphere that encourages and deepens participation. Coalition leaders can demonstrate respectfulness by treating all stakeholders, including opponents, with respect.

In addition to recruiting, building, and supporting a leadership team, and establishing the tone and values of the campaign, effective coalition leaders do the following:

- Encourage teams or committees to generate and pursue their own ideas

- Problem-solve with team leaders or committee chairs

- Keep volunteers engaged on a regular basis through meetings and correspondence

- Close the communications loop by sharing results, new information, and interpretation of events with coalition members
- Translate complex messages and dynamics so all can understand them
- Bring in issue experts when needed
- Help recruit compelling messengers
- Manage the budget
- Manage the calendar
- Manage relationships with key partners and decision makers
- Craft agendas and schedule meetings

Why Diverse Coalitions Matter

The broader and more diverse your network of support is, the more power you will have. When US veterans joined the Standing Rock Sioux and their allies at Standing Rock in protest of the Dakota Access Pipeline, the protest rose to a new level of importance in the eyes of oil and gas interests who were behind the project, and the federal agencies who would authorize it.[1]

Building strong and diverse coalitions is critical to bringing about sweeping environmental and social change. As with the Dakota Access Pipeline, groups representing a variety of backgrounds and experiences can come together in support of an issue. When they do, they speak with a strong voice.

The Citizens' Climate Lobby is a national advocacy group committed to building the political will needed to address climate change. They have more than a hundred chapters, and they engage high school students, grandparents, and people from all classes, races, genders, and abilities in their efforts to lobby Congress. The organization knows they need a broad coalition to succeed, and they have reached out to communities of color and diverse organizations as partners. They offer numerous programs to recruit and train the broadest possible coalition, including diversity fellowships and scholarships, conservative outreach fellowships, college internships, and volunteer training. Their proposed congressional bill, the Energy Innovation and Carbon Dividend Act, is a market-based solution. They've succeeded in introducing the bill and enlisting members of both political parties to cosponsor it. Their large and diverse coalition keeps continuous pressure on Congress to pass the bill. You can learn more about this effort at the organization's website: https://citizensclimatelobby.org.

Finding Allies and Partners

Advocates often begin the process of coalition building by meeting and negotiating with other stakeholder groups. If the issue is to create incentives for solar energy, then you want environmental groups, the solar industry, electricity consumers, and the electric utility on board. You would want to reach out to all of them, meet with them, and find out who is willing to partner with you. Ideally, you would agree on which role each stakeholder group will play, and you would work together with your partners on strategy and tactics. It is helpful to agree on who will take the lead and how decisions will be made. If you are working to increase solar energy, you would need a strong coalition behind you in order to face the well-organized opposition of oil and gas companies.

Coalition building always begins with listening. You will want to approach potential partners privately in a safe setting—usually their premises—to discover their questions and concerns. All the stakeholders you identified as strong supporters in your stakeholder analysis should be contacted.

No matter how strong the support of your allies and partners, you should expect to make adjustments to your approach in order to accommodate them. Continuing with the statewide building codes as an example, we discovered that small, rural towns did not have the capacity to enforce a code. Some of these towns had just one or two part-time employees. To accommodate them, we made enforcement of the codes optional in towns with populations of less than two thousand. Even without enforcement, the statewide code would be in effect in these places. This meant that consumers there who experienced shoddy construction or dishonest contractors had an option to sue their contractor through the state attorney general's office. While this wasn't as ideal as local code enforcement, it was a step forward. We were happy to accommodate smaller towns in this way. This measure made smaller towns more likely to support us. It's a surprise to me that more laws don't allow varying standards for stakeholders with different capacities and needs.

Not all groups want to work together, but you must reach out and do the best you can to bring people on board. With groups that don't want to play, try to agree to disagree in a professional, nonpersonal way.

Many times stakeholder organizations are divided internally and can't support your cause. They may have to take a position that aligns with a majority of their members, even though some members do support you. In the case of the building codes, larger cities and towns were very supportive; but smaller towns, fearing that they could not meet the requirements in the proposed law, opposed it. The Maine Municipal Association (MMA) has a "one town, one vote" governance policy. There are many more small towns in Maine than larger ones, so the MMA had to honor the majority and oppose the statewide building code, even though larger cities and towns supported it. As an alternative, we worked with a coalition of mayors from the larger cities and towns to enlist those who did support us.

Working with Adversaries

Your relationships with adversaries are also a key to your success. All too often, advocates will vilify their opponents and fall into personal criticism of leaders on the other side. I've encountered plenty of cynical conversations about disliked opposition leaders. These conversations are detrimental to your cause and can be extremely unproductive, because they block the creative energy you need for your campaign to succeed. If you are drawn into these conversations, try to return to the cause you are working on and the positive reasons you are working on it.

Unsavory tactics, like personal attacks from your adversaries, can also up the ante and make it difficult to sustain a nonpersonal, professional relationship with them. One time a lobbyist personally attacked me. He sent an email to about thirty of my supporters and allied decision makers on a land-use issue. In the email, he called me unprofessional, unskilled, and untrustworthy, and he backed these accusations up with specifics. I was worried about what people would think. The following day, as I was walking the halls of the State House, several people congratulated me for being "flamed" by this person, as others apparently had been in the past. It turned out that being attacked by this person was a mark of distinction; it was evidence that you were making an impact!

You do want to prepare mentally for unexpected attacks. A famous example is Rachel Carson, an activist who opposed the chemical industry for the manufacture and distribution of toxic pesticides. The chemical industry and their lobbyists and supporters in Congress subjected her to vicious personal attacks. She was called disloyal, unscientific, unpatriotic, and hysterical. Even though Carson was a scientist, the media portrayed her as an amateur who was sentimental about nature. She knew her book *Silent Spring* would be controversial and she would be attacked, although she didn't know her book would become an influential best seller. She prepared for the attacks by getting fellow scientists and experts to review the book prior to publication. She also was prepared for attacks by her own certainty about what she had written, and her unwavering belief that harmful pesticides should be regulated.[2]

A good strategy is to try to head off attacks before they happen, as Carson did by having fellow scientists review her book. Another way to do this is to invite your adversaries to meet with you so you can hear their concerns and positions firsthand. Adversaries want to be heard, just like every other human. If you show that you care enough to listen to their point of view, you will at least have established a model of decorum for working on your issue. By engaging them directly, it's likely that you will discover new questions and concerns that you need to address.

I had a particularly cordial relationship with Rep. Henry Joy, a conservative from rural Maine. We disagreed on every policy issue, but we never made it personal. I went out of my way to greet him, and I understood his job was to represent his district, which consisted almost entirely of conservative Republicans. One day Joy introduced a bill titled "An Act for Aroostook County to Secede from the State." Aroostook is the northern-most county in Maine, with a population of sixty-seven thousand spread over a land area of 6,828 square miles—the size of Connecticut and Rhode Island combined. With so few people over such a large area, it could hardly survive as a separate state!

When the staff in my office saw this bill, they rolled their eyes. But I saw it as an opportunity. I picked up the phone, called Rep. Joy, and asked him about his intent behind the bill. Because of our good relationship, he calmly told me that he wanted to be sure the needs of his rural district would be recognized in all public policies. I let him know that I'd be testifying in opposition to the bill. From this short phone conversation, I quickly understood that he was using the bill to send a message—both to his constituents and to policy makers. Several years later, I recalled this experience and drew upon it to create the "no enforcement" standard, in which towns with less than two thousand people were not required to enforce the statewide building code. I had understood Joy's point and incorporated the intent behind it into the building code legislation.

I had an adversarial relationship with the MMA lobbyists, too. They had a firm position that no authority should be taken away from towns, while my job was to create more efficient government at all levels. The conflict was inherent. When it came to the building and energy codes, it made complete sense to me that the state could provide a building code that towns could use simply by downloading it. I calculated that this would save towns $5 million a year in legal and administrative costs, because they wouldn't have to go through a process of amending, updating, and adopt-ing local codes. This policy was a perfect fit with the idea of streamlining and simplifying government. In my view, it benefited towns.

But instead of seeing advantages, the MMA saw our proposal as a threat. They did not want the towns' authority to adopt codes to be taken away, even though adopting local codes was expensive and inconvenient. MMA was obligated to represent their members, the majority of whom are small towns who feared "unfunded mandates" from the state.

With this conflict at the heart of the issue, I made certain to reach out to the MMA lobbyists and include them on every meeting announcement. I actively managed the relationship with this adversary, answering all their questions and concerns—which were many—along the way. The result was more work for me and my team, but we also obtained a more robust policy in the end. Taking an adversary's concerns seriously can strengthen your campaign and the resulting policies.

Facing Organized Opposition

Sometimes groups that oppose you are sophisticated organizers who are familiar with the same strategies and tactics you might use. Sometimes they are better funded than your group will ever be, making it possible for opposition groups to drown out your messages with paid advertising and lobbying. Industry lobbying groups like the American Petroleum Institute (API) and the Partnership for Energy Progress are now fighting successfully in state and local political arenas. API has successfully fought laws and incentives to encourage electric cars in eleven states, slowing the growth of electric car sales. In Seattle, a proposal to ban gas hookups in new buildings met a wall of opposition, which turned out to be backed by Puget Sound Energy, Seattle's gas supplier.[3] In Colorado, the oil and gas industry spent $41 million to defeat a referendum question asking voters whether new oil and gas equipment including fracking wells should be set back two thousand five hundred feet from homes and other occupied buildings. The referendum lost. In the state of Washington, the Western States Petroleum Association spent $31 million to defeat a referendum to establish a carbon tax.[4]

Industry groups understand the principle of forming diverse coalitions with minority and citizen partners, too. In Pennsylvania, API has worked with AARP and the United Pastors Network to lobby for oil and gas infrastructure and against competitor opposition, including solar, hydroelectric, and nuclear power.[5]

Industry groups also use images and words that depict support for a clean environment, even though they oppose regulations on the oil and gas industry. The five largest publicly listed oil companies—ExxonMobil, Shell, Chevron, BP, and Total—spend about $195 million a year on branding campaigns suggesting they support action to address climate change. At the same time, they spend *$115 billion* on expanding oil and gas extraction.[6]

An example of marketing that brands the fossil fuel industry as climate friendly is API's "Energy Citizens" campaign. It features advertising showing American flags, happy workers and families, and beautiful scenery. Their Facebook page and websites encourage citizens to contact their representatives in support of gas and oil expansion and in opposition to renewable energy and regulation of oil and gas.

What can environmental advocates do about organized opposition? The first thing is to read the fine print. Postcard mailers, newspaper ads, and Facebook pages with beautiful wildlife images may not be from environmental groups. Stay alert, and be aware of whether any of your known opponents are privately partnering with larger allies to defeat you. And then be sure to make what you have learned public, using conventional and social media. When you communicate with decision makers, be sure to provide solid evidence of influence or funding from national and industry groups that support your opposition. Decision makers will appreciate this information and may use it in helping you build support.

The power of organized people telling the truth can beat well-funded foes. For example, New Jersey passed a $5,000 tax credit for electric cars, despite API opposition.

Stages of a Campaign

Campaigns grow and build over time. Although each campaign progresses differently, they generally follow three major stages, starting with building your team and securing allies and partners. Then campaigns build awareness and educate the public, supporters, neutrals, and decision makers. This second phase can take a few years to fully mature, as you educate and take actions to make your issue and your demands visible and understood. The final stage is to present your demands and negotiate with decision makers, getting them to agree to and codify the changes you want. The story of the Flint water crisis is a good example of how these stages build over time.

In 2014 Dr. Mona Hanna-Attisha, a pediatrician in Flint, Michigan, heard rumors about toxic levels of lead in Flint's public water supply. As a research and teaching physician, she began to collect data on blood lead levels in children. She was driven to do this by the fear of lead poisoning, which can affect children's growing brains and result in permanent disability.

For a full year she searched for a community of people who would support her in researching her suspicions. Local and county public health officials she contacted were indifferent. Requests for data from the state and county health departments went unanswered. At this stage, there was little awareness or sense of urgency about the issue. Motivated by fear for her patients and anger toward unresponsive government officials, she continued to work on gathering data at her pediatric clinic. But without a community of support, and without larger data sets from the state and county to prove her suspicions, she could not move the issue forward. The situation seemed hopeless.

Finally she met Dr. Marc Edwards, who had worked on a similar water crisis in Washington, DC. With his encouragement, she shared her preliminary research findings with a community group called the Children's Healthcare Access Program and at the annual meeting of the Michigan chapter of the American Association of Pediatricians. Members of both groups immediately understood the seriousness of the situation and offered to help. She now had a small community of support. But this small group was not strong enough to make an effective demand for change.

Her job and career were on the line. In order to be credible, her research needed to be bulletproof, and she needed a wider group of physicians and health care professionals to back her findings. Even though children's health and lives were affected daily, she still had to prove beyond any doubt that lead in the water was causing elevated lead levels in the blood of Flint's children. With Edwards's help, she was able to get the additional data she needed to complete her research. Through the media, speaking engagements, and personal outreach, she recruited more health care professionals and community leaders to support the cause. Once this added support was in place, she could go public with her findings, and she did so at a press conference.

Pushback from the city and state started immediately as they tried to discredit her and her work. This is where her community of support was crucial. They helped her fight back against lies and personal attacks. They joined her in recommitting to the original vision and purpose: to protect the health of Flint children. She created a list of demands—what Flint kids needed in order to thrive. She started a new study measuring lead levels in children more precisely by using GIS software to eliminate districts that didn't receive Flint water and could dilute her research results. She and her team gave dozens of interviews. Media allies did their own analysis and confirmed her findings. At this point, major public exposure and support were in place.[7]

One of the few bright spots of the Flint water crisis was the community response. Once the test results were made public, local residents, the Natural Resources Defense Council (NRDC), and other groups petitioned the EPA to launch an immediate emergency action in response to the crisis. When the EPA failed to act, the coalition expanded, with Concerned Pastors for Social Action and the American Civil Liberties Union joining Flint residents and the NRDC. This enlarged coalition sued city and state officials to secure safe drinking water. They took additional action to demand that all residents unable to reach clean water distribution centers have access to a bottled water delivery service or have a robust water filter installed in their homes.[8]

The growing community and coalition response finally generated enough pressure to force the city to declare an emergency. Ultimately they succeeded in persuading the city to change the water source and overhaul the public water system, replacing thousands of lead pipes. This was the result of a successful negotiation phase in which the parties agreed on measures the city had said were "impossible" months earlier.

By 2016, two years after Dr. Hanna-Attisha first heard the rumors about lead in Flint's water, the city's water system was declared safe, with lead levels testing below the federal action level. But questions remain today about replacing the remaining lead pipes and about bacteria found in household water tests.[9] As a result of the crisis, about nine thousand children suffered serious lead poisoning. Remedial programs have been implemented to support their cognitive development.

Each of the three phases of a campaign were important to this win. Without building an organized team of supporters, then building public awareness and putting pressure on decision makers, and then successfully negotiating with the city, the end result could have been much, much worse.[10]

HOW DID FLINT'S WATER SUPPLY BECOME TOXIC?

The story behind Flint's poisoned water ultimately came to light. Public officials had changed the water supply from Lake Huron to the Flint River to save money. The Flint River water was highly corrosive, and it leached lead from the old water pipes serving the city. Officials did not add antileaching chemicals required by federal law to prevent this lead corrosion. Omitting these chemicals saved approximately $80 a day. Officials had chosen a small cost savings over the lives and health of the community, even though it was illegal to do this. Many of these officials were fired. Eventually, the city's water source was changed back to Lake Huron, and most of Flint's lead water pipes were replaced.

Keeping Your Campaign on Track

Sometimes—especially when a deadline is approaching—the activity in your campaign can become frenetic. At these times you'll need to increase both in-person and online meetings to keep track of everyone's activity. You may also find it useful to keep a spreadsheet or use project management tools to track campaign activity.

At other times, momentum can slow down, and you will need to work to keep your issue alive. You'll want to generate stories in the media, keep your volunteers engaged, and continue to update and educate decision makers during slow periods.

To illustrate support for the Penobscot Nation's fishing rights on the Penobscot River, a Maine group organized and filmed a flotilla of canoes and kayaks on the river. Activists dropped colorful banners from a bridge over the river while Native and non-Native people canoed and kayaked below. This event took place during a period when Maine politics made it impossible to move forward on Native American rights, because neither the governor nor the legislature were interested in the issue. But the colorful flotilla and the resulting film showing a broad coalition of support for the tribes kept the issue alive during a down time. An unexpected benefit of this event was that the media used a photo of the banners hanging over the river for several years after the original event, whenever reporting on the river. You never know when you might be creating an icon!

There are also times when key decision makers simply will not move to support you. If this is the case, it's time to escalate your effort. The most common way to do this is to have constituents contact their representatives directly. In a small city or state, having ten people contact a decision maker about an issue is often enough to move a decision maker to your side. In larger jurisdictions, you'll need at least thirty or more. Having fifty people contact a decision maker is a landslide of support!

The key is to identify people who know decision makers personally, are campaign donors, or live in their district, and prepare them with fact sheets and talking points so their outreach will have maximum impact. Personal stories from people directly affected by the issue are particularly powerful. A private in-person meeting between constituents and their representative is often enough to work through the decision makers' questions and concerns and move them to your side.

If none of the above tactics work, it may be time for direct action—a protest or press conference in front of a decision maker's house, for example. In corporate campaigns, decision makers will often decline to meet with opponents. In this case, direct action is your best alternative. But publicly outing a decision maker should be a last resort. You will want to carefully think this through, because although you may succeed, you also risk stronger pushback from those whom you ultimately need to support you.

When You Need to Pivot

Inevitably, you will face unforeseen challenges as you move your issue forward. The bigger the change you are trying to make, the truer this is. Your sponsoring legislator may lose an election. The company you are trying to influence might be sold. A pandemic might close the city council or legislature unexpectedly. Or, more commonly, you just didn't have enough votes to win.

If your campaign is facing a significant change, you'll need to regroup, revamp your strategy, and make a new commitment. Sometimes giving up your campaign for now and postponing it until a more favorable time is the best strategy. Other times, adversity can re-energize your campaign and move it forward to success. The latter was true in the campaign to achieve ranked-choice voting (RCV) in Maine.

In RCV, people vote for multiple candidates in order of preference—first choice, second choice, third choice, etc. If a candidate wins a majority of votes, that candidate wins. But if no candidate wins a majority, then the candidate who did the worst is eliminated, and all the votes cast for that person are redistributed to each voter's second choice. This process is repeated until one candidate has a majority and becomes the winner. In this so-called "instant runoff" system, the end result is that elected candidates will always have a majority of the votes cast. In Maine, many elections have had multiple candidates (Republicans, Democrats, and Independents) where the winners were elected with less than 40% of the vote. RCV was designed to change that.

A successful signature-gathering campaign brought RCV to the state legislature. In response, the legislature passed a bill to delay RCV for four years. This lack of legislative support for a citizen initiative is rare. After that failure, organizers had three options: ditch the campaign, start over with a new petition, or exercise a "people's veto," a legal option that gives organizers ninety days to gather the required number of signatures to overturn a legislative decision. If a people's veto is successful, the initiative automatically becomes law without legislative support.

The organizers chose the people's veto. This was brave and risky, because the earlier campaign had gathered the same number of signatures in *twelve months*, not ninety days. It was also brave because the ninety-day period was from November 15 to February 15—the coldest time of year, and a time when people are busy with the Thanksgiving, Christmas, and New Year's holidays. The organizers hoped the steep challenge would energize the signature gatherers!

I was one of the signature gatherers for the people's veto effort. I stood in front of the flagship L.L.Bean retail store with a clipboard and a pen in ten-degree weather, asking Christmas shoppers to sign the petition. There was an army of volunteers all over the state doing the same thing. There are certain spots where I can't go now without recalling how cold my fingers and toes were as I explained RCV to passersby! It turned out that the organizers were right: the stiff challenge energized the team. We succeeded in gathering 82,609 signatures, far surpassing the required 57,277 signatures required to exercise a people's veto and make RCV into law.

Nuts and Bolts:
Running Productive Meetings

Coalition leaders usually develop agendas and schedule meetings. Teams or committees may also hold meetings, but one of the important functions of leadership is to keep everyone informed. Regular online or in-person meetings where teams or committees give updates and seek help are a good way to do this. Most coalitions I've been a part of have met monthly, and more frequently when an important decision or major event is imminent. Communication between meetings usually takes place via email, text, and phone.

Coalition leaders should always seek coalition member input on meeting agendas. They should ask in advance if anyone has anything to add or if there are any concerns. People need to feel included, and the best way to do this is to offer them not just a symbolic form of participation but a real chance to influence the agenda. Asking for input will also tip off coalition leadership if there are any missed items or serious concerns within their group. Leaders can then plan time into agendas to address these items, perhaps asking those who have raised the issues to lead these discussions.

Sticking to agendas and the allotted time for meetings is essential for keeping your group energized. This is especially true for online meetings, which can drain a group's energy if they go on too long. A particularly effective technique for creating meeting agendas is to start by asking yourself, "What are the desired outcomes for this meeting?" Write down the answers in bullet-point form. Once you have answered this question, specific agenda items should flow easily from there.

Someone should be appointed to run your group meetings. This can be a rotating role, or it can be done by someone who is respected and reliable as a meeting facilitator. If your group has paid staff, they might be designated to lead meetings.

Sometimes groups decide to bring in a facilitator from outside the group to run meetings. There are generally two reasons for doing this. One is when members of the leadership team wish to participate without the distraction of trying to run a meeting at the same time. If the purpose of the meeting is to plan, vision, or design a new initiative, having an outside facilitator to keep the meeting on track gives everyone a chance for input. This can be invaluable.

The other time to bring in an outside facilitator is when your group wants help in designing a process. Perhaps you want to gather input from several groups of stakeholders. Should you conduct focus groups? Hold a public forum? Meet with a homogenous group of stakeholders? Meet with a mixed group? What are the right steps for getting the results you want? A professional facilitator will be familiar with many process methods and tools and can help you design a process to meet your needs.

Clear agendas and agreed-upon ground rules will vastly increase the probability of having a productive meeting. Like playground rules, meeting ground rules establish expectations, include everyone, and make sure the activity is safe and enjoyable. Ground rules are agreed upon at the beginning of a meeting. As a meeting leader you can suggest ground rules, or a group can brainstorm ground rules on their own. The important thing is that everyone agrees to uphold them. Some common ground rules are:

- One speaker at a time
- No side conversations
- No need to repeat what someone else has said
- Keep remarks brief and to the point
- Respect the views of others, even if you disagree
- Everyone participates; no one dominates
- Listen to others; listen to learn
- Speak up if you disagree

Meeting agendas vary according to what needs to be discussed. It helps to try to estimate the time needed for each item. It also helps to put more important items earlier on the agenda to avoid losing people from important discussions who have either tuned out or need to leave the meeting early. Below is a very effective agenda template. It can be customized for just about any meeting.

SAMPLE TEAM MEETING AGENDA

1. **Introduce meeting leader(s) and participants.** This is especially important for online meetings, where some people may be on the phone and unable to see who is present.

2. **Establish the context for the meeting.** Discuss the lay of the land for your issue, and note any recent changes, updates, or developments. This brings everyone up to speed and lays the groundwork for topics to be discussed.

3. **Introduce the purpose of the meeting and the agenda.** Let people know which are the important agenda items and which ones need a decision or vote.

4. **Discussion topic A**

5. **Discussion topic B**

6. **Discussion topic C**

7. **Summary and next steps.** If possible, summarize the important points and any decisions made during the meeting. Then list the next steps specifically, including who will do them and when. Schedule the next meeting of the group.

Making Decisions with Your Group

Campaign teams have many decisions to make. Many groups use consensus decision making, meaning that everyone in the group is willing to go along with a decision, even if a few aren't 100% in agreement. But not every decision can be made this way, because it would take too much time and would get in the way of responding quickly to new developments.

It is helpful to get general agreement on strategy among coalition members so the leadership team and committees can then make routine decisions based on carrying out the strategy. The rule of thumb is to use consensus for decisions that are big picture, strategic, or longer term. Decisions that are shorter term or that carry out the agreed-upon strategy are usually made by the leadership team or committees. For example, the Our Power Coalition came to a consensus on how and when to present new legislation, but the details of the legislative language and a decision on which materials to hand out were worked out by the coalition's Policy Committee.

Even though your coalition members all support a common cause, disagreement can get in the way of progress. The strongest coalitions are unanimous in most decisions, with members willing to go along with the majority, even if a few disagree.

But if you have members who consistently disagree or block the group from moving forward, you need to pause and take some time to discern whether their concerns are relevant to your cause or outside its scope. If their concerns are relevant, they might be offered a chance to present them to the group. But if their concerns are not relevant, or if the problem is bad behavior and an unwillingness to abide by the ground rules, it is probably time for those members to move on.

You cannot afford to have your group held up by an individual or a small handful of members. Skilled leaders are usually able to spot trouble like this early and speak privately with disruptors. Members are usually offered a chance to change their behavior, but if they are unwilling to do this, they are asked to leave the group.

For Those Who Need to Act First and Think Later

Bill Moyer, a well-known activist and senior advisor to President Obama, once said, "Some people act their way into thinking, and others think their way into action." The Working Waterfront Coalition spent more than a year thinking before acting. This served them well, but this is not a path that suits everyone. It is highly likely you will have some action-oriented people in your group who are impatient with planning and strategizing. This is actually a good thing. Campaigns need both thinkers and actors.

The key is to provide opportunities for some people to act without compromising the cause—while planning, research, and strategy work is going on. Action-oriented people should be encouraged to take on a task. A very useful task would be to interview stakeholders and report the results to the rest of the group. There are always stakeholders whose perspectives need to be better understood. Other tasks might include building a website, setting up a social media presence, or drafting written materials for your group. It's important to recognize the different needs of people in your group and try to accommodate them.

Training

Training can play an important role in strengthening your coalition. Large coalitions and organizations like the Citizens' Climate Lobby, Sunrise, and the Sierra Club offer skills training to their members. Webinars and workshops on how to work with the media, lobby Congress, facilitate groups, and plan direct action events are offered and can be very worthwhile.

Smaller coalitions, campaigns, and nonprofits often use training and informational events as a way to build community and commitment among their supporters. A plethora of online events with panels, speakers, and documentaries are offered by nonprofits across the country. There are so many offered that it can be hard to choose which to attend. The quality of these presentations varies, but many are excellent.

In-person events where people can learn about an issue, see footage of outdoor adventures, ask questions, and network with others are a powerful way to build support for your cause or organization. These can be used to recruit volunteers and ask for donations. More information on public forums and conferences is provided in chapter 13.

What It Takes to Win

One of the most moving campaign stories I've ever heard comes from the disabled community. Back in the 1950s, most children with disabilities could not attend public school. Judy Heumann, who is today a disability rights activist, was told back then she couldn't attend public school in a wheelchair because she would be a "fire hazard." Later she was denied a teaching position for the same reason. Society treated people with disabilities as if their conditions were contagious. They were involuntarily sterilized, sent to live in state-run institutions, and denied the right to vote.

Starting in the 1960s, people with disabilities began to organize, and as the disability rights movement grew, Heumann became a lead organizer. This culminated in a twenty-eight-day sit-in at the San Francisco Office of the US Department of Health, Education, and Welfare. This is the longest sit-in at a federal building to date, and it was accomplished by 150 people in wheelchairs. The campaign was well organized, with a clear goal and well-planned actions. Campaign leaders gave direction and supported team leaders. Participants had clear roles, and the personal safety and health needs of disabled protesters were planned for and met. The result of their action was to establish meaningful enforcement of section 504 of the Rehabilitation Act, a section of law that had been ignored for years. The act was the first piece of legislation to use the word "discrimination," and it prohibited programs receiving federal funding from discriminating against people with disabilities.[11]

Although the same organizers spent years keeping up the pressure for enforcement of the law, discrimination persisted. The US Supreme Court ruled that a community college did not have to accept an applicant with serious hearing loss. Transit authorities interpreted the law inconsistently. During the Reagan administration, a task force on regulatory relief sought to roll back antidiscrimination laws, including section 504, because they were seen as a burden on businesses.[12]

In response, thousands of people in the disability rights movement attended protests, sent out alerts, spoke, lobbied, testified, filed lawsuits, protested, and got arrested, doing whatever they had to do for the cause. Businesses and churches opposed them, saying complying with the law would add cost and take away their freedom. After a remarkable show of support over a two-year period, the Reagan administration halted the proposed rollbacks.

But more work was needed. The disability community continued to be actively involved in Supreme Court cases and in proposing legislation to establish specific antidiscrimination policies. They were trying to win disability rights on a case-by-case basis.

By the mid-1980s, organizers concluded that sweeping civil rights legislation for people with disabilities was needed. They were able to build on their existing relationships with members of Congress and the administration. After two years of drafting and revising, they won civil rights for people with disabilities through the passage of the Americans with Disabilities Act (ADA). This landmark legislation was signed into law by President George H. W. Bush in 1990.[13]

As demonstrated by the twenty-year campaign led by disability rights activists, you must have a strategy, organization, persistence, and passion to win. You have to be clear about what you want and who the decision makers are. You have to work honestly with supporters and opponents, and you have to keep moving despite the setbacks. It's hard work and often takes a long time to pull off a win, as it did to establish the ADA. But the feeling of creating a positive change in the world is like none other—meaningful, empowering, and unforgettable.

10

Working with Decision Makers

In protest there must never be compromise. In politics, there is always compromise.

—BAYARD RUSTIN, civil rights activist

The Art of Lobbying

Advocacy, by definition, means working with decision makers. Notice that I said *working with,* not fighting against, and not trying to persuade in a one-sided way that leaves no room for questions or dialogue. This is critically important! Notice too that I avoid using the word "target." While it is common practice to talk about decision makers as "targets" in activist campaigns, using this word tends to dehumanize decision makers, who are, above all, human beings.

As an advocate working inside the system, you need to build a reputation with decision makers based on trust and respect. The advocate often has to present an opposing point of view, but they must do it in a way that engenders respect and provides a pathway for the decision makers to hear and support you. Decision makers need to be treated with care, as you would treat anyone you want to get to know. Whether you're advocating at city hall, the school board, a town council, the county commission, or the state legislature, it's important to establish a constructive personal relationship with the decision makers.

As an activist working outside the system, you have a very different role. The objective of an activist is to disrupt the status quo. You are, in essence, *rebelling* against authority. Many activist movements are *challenging* cultural beliefs and the system of laws and policies that support those beliefs. As an activist, your goal is to create an opening to present an opposing point of view. The story below illustrates how these two roles can work together in moving an issue forward.

Mark Harrington and Larry Kramer were activist leaders working on HIV/AIDS-related issues in the 1980s and 1990s. Millions were dying of this dreaded disease while the rigid and lengthy process of developing antiviral drugs cranked slowly through the system. As the death toll rose, activists escalated their protests. The AIDS Coalition to Unleash Power (ACT UP), formed in 1987, is regarded by many as one of the most successful grassroots organizations in history. ACT UP conducted numerous protests, including shutting down the operations of the US Food and Drug Administration for a day, storming the campus of the National Institutes of Health with one thousand ACT UP members, and demonstrating at the New York Stock Exchange to raise awareness of price gouging by Burroughs Wellcome, a maker of antiviral drugs.[1]

Because of their frustration over not being listened to, ACT UP protesters' language and actions became angry and confrontational. Their anger was needed to wake people up to the suffering of AIDS victims and their loved ones. Their argument ran as follows: If people were destined to die anyway, why not let them try experimental drugs? Why withhold treatments that might work?

At the time, medicine was paternalistic and conservative. Doctors believed they knew what was best for patients and did not seek patients' input on treatments. NIH and FDA doctors remained stuck in these attitudes and mired in their slow and rigid regimes for testing new treatments. Put off by the name-calling of angry protesters, they refused to hear their pleas for help.

Dr. Anthony Fauci (the same doctor who was a public voice during the COVID-19 pandemic), faced with mounting evidence that this cautious approach made no sense, reversed himself. He recalled telling himself, "Let me put aside the goth dress—the earrings and Mohawk haircuts and the black jackets—and just listen to what they have to say."[2] He invited protesters into his office and listened to them. From that point on, things began to change. He reached out and visited afflicted groups in New York and San Francisco to learn about their experiences. Over time, he gained their trust.

Fortunately, once they had an audience with Fauci, ACT UP leaders, including Harrington and Kramer, were able to tone down their language and shift from angry rhetoric to a softer tone more aligned with advocacy. They stopped calling Fauci "a murderer" and an "incompetent idiot" and began to urge him and the FDA to "move faster and with greater compassion for those who are suffering."[3] Harrington and Kramer eventually became trusted friends of Fauci's, and years later they expressed gratitude for his work.

As a result of the ongoing efforts of ACT UP and the negotiations with Fauci, AIDS patients were allowed to try experimental drugs, and the development process for new treatments was speeded up. Bringing about this change required a shift from anger and hatred to building constructive personal relationships between activists and decision makers. This example shows how direct action and advocacy can complement each other.

In a similar example, activist Greta Thunberg was visibly angry when she addressed the UN Climate Action Summit in New York in 2019. "The eyes of all future generations are upon you," she said, her voice quivering with rage. "If you choose to fail us, I say we will never forgive you." Her words were backed by millions of activists who participated in climate strikes around the world.

But it will take more than angry words to enact the changes climate activists demand. Specific policy proposals, a strong and persistent organization, and constructive relationship building between advocates and decision makers are needed. Most climate activists were disappointed with the results of the 2019 Climate Summit. While some progress was made, and activists drew attention to the climate crisis, more work is needed to fully address climate change.[4]

Many people are put off or intimidated by the idea of "lobbying." To some, lobbying suggests dishonesty and shady back-room wheeling and dealing. While this is sometimes true, most decision makers do adhere to their values and serve in public roles because they want to help people and make a positive difference.

If you put yourself in a decision maker's shoes for a moment, you'll see how difficult their job is and that you are actually in a position to help them. If you bring new information to a decision maker, you are helping them do their job. If you bring them an issue that appeals to important stakeholders or constituents in their district, even better. *Decision makers need you to inform them about issues that are affecting you and your community.*

This is the essence of politics: discerning how your issue fits with the decision maker's values, constraints, and goals. By practicing putting yourself in their shoes, you will see where your issue fits (or doesn't fit) for them, and that will make your job infinitely easier. With this knowledge, you will be able to frame and craft your message so it appeals to their interests. The pathway to educating and persuading decision makers will then be much less daunting.

Building Trust

Building trust with decision makers is critical to moving your issue forward. In order to do this, you must present your issue clearly and with a spirit of helpfulness. Even though you will have prepared talking points, your communications with decision makers should be a two-way dialogue. All too often, advocates read through their talking points without taking a breath, which doesn't allow the decision maker a chance to respond. You want to be a good listener, and you want to ask questions, so you can understand the decision makers' concerns.

A key part of building trust is honesty. You want to exemplify honesty, respect, and integrity. According to a saying attributed to Mahatma Gandhi, "Be the change you wish to see in the world."[5] There will surely be people you have to work with who are not honest and who are looking to find and exploit your weaknesses. But by focusing on and living from your values, you give others a chance to meet you on the same level.

It's always tempting to leave out information that is contrary to your cause or to gloss over questions you'd rather avoid. But if you're up front about *both* the pros and the cons of your proposal, decision makers will trust you more. The best approach is to anticipate objections and provide your best answers to them.

The proposal for a statewide Maine Uniform Building and Energy Code affected every town in Maine. Decision makers asked if towns in their district could amend the proposed state code. Since a primary goal of the proposal was to have a *uniform* statewide code, the answer was no. But in response to their concern, we added a process to our proposal where anyone could submit a code amendment to the state code board. We also required the state to review proposed code amendments in a transparent and timely way.

If you are asked questions you don't have an answer for, be sure to offer to track down the answers and get back to the decision maker quickly. Questions from decision makers are a gift to you, because the decision maker has just indicated what's important to them. You can and should develop additional talking points from your responses to their questions and concerns. You may even decide to amend your proposal based on feedback from decision makers, as in the building code example above. By listening, responding, and following through promptly on decision maker concerns, you will establish a reputation that you care and can be trusted.

Finding Allies and Sponsors

Snowmobiling is a very popular sport in northern Maine. In 2020, there were more than eighty-seven thousand snowmobile licenses issued, 280 snowmobile clubs, and $606 million in annual economic impact from recreational snowmobiling. The industry relies overwhelmingly on volunteers who donate the use of their land and maintain trails. I once met a man who groomed snowmobile trails for a small fee, and he was interested in raising snowmobile license fees in order to provide more money to maintain trails. He had done his research, and he knew Maine's snowmobile licenses were underpriced compared with neighboring states, the median income of the snowmobile crowd was high enough to absorb an increase, and if higher fees were used to improve trails, a majority of snowmobilers would support the increase.

So he went to his state representative and asked him to initiate a bill to increase the license fee. His representative agreed, and the man went to the state Capitol to testify in support of the bill. While he was testifying, legislators walked in and out of the room, worked on their laptops, and paid little attention to what he had to say. "A total waste of time," he called it. I agreed that this was rude and unfortunate, and I asked if he knew why his legislator hadn't built more support for the bill. He said he didn't know.

This example shows why it's important to find decision makers who will actively support your issue. This is true for every decision-making body, whether it's the local school board or Congress. In this case the legislator agreed to sponsor the bill but apparently had no interest in supporting it.

In selecting allies and sponsors, it's important to tell them what you need and then ask what level of support they can offer you.

This is where dialogue with decision makers is important. You want to know what questions and concerns may stand in the way of their support. In the best cases they will be enthusiastic partners who will help move your issue forward. In the worst, like the snowmobile example, they will put no energy into helping you.

Every legislative and congressional bill has a lead sponsor and a list of cosponsors. Local ordinances also need key allies on the committee or council that will decide on them. It is helpful to strategize in advance about who might serve as your key allies or sponsors. Do they have a passion for this issue or a track record of supporting similar issues? How much influence do they have with other decision makers? Are they a committee chair? A party leader? An informal influencer?

Your key ally or sponsor will be someone with the strongest connections to your issue and the greatest influence with other decision makers. That's why you'll see most major legislation being sponsored by party leaders. A major solar energy bill introduced in Maine in 2019 was sponsored by a prominent Republican senator and cosponsored by six other state senators and two representatives, including the speaker of the house, a Democrat. With such strong bipartisan sponsorship, it passed by a wide margin (32–2 in the Senate, 93–52 in the House).

Power-Map Your Decision Makers

It's also essential to understand the sources of influence on your decision maker. Where is the decision maker from? What is their background? Where did they go to school? What communities are they a part of? Who are their professional peers, campaign donors, and allies? What people or organizations do you know who might be able to influence them? Influencers can be used to persuade decision makers, so it is important to identify who they are.

A technique recommended by the Sierra Club is to "power-map" your individual decision makers. Using the same chart we used for stakeholder analysis in chapter 8, you can map the influencers on your decision maker:

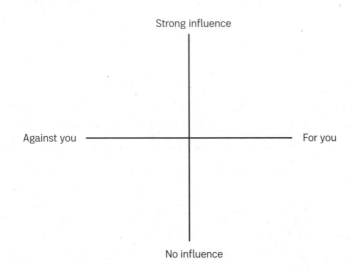

Strong influence

Against you — For you

No influence

You can then use this map throughout your campaign to strategize how to get influencers to persuade your decision makers.

Getting Started with Your Decision Maker

Communications with decision makers almost always begin one on one, either in person or online. As a first move, an advocate will typically try to make an appointment for a meeting with a decision maker. In Congress, you would call your congressional office and make an appointment. There it's likely you would be meeting with congressional staff, not the decision maker. Staff are typically skilled at listening and conveying your message to the decision maker, so in most cases you can rest assured that your message will get through.

In smaller governing bodies, you can request an online or in-person meeting with a decision maker and expect your request to be honored. You might call or send an email to get an appointment, or you might approach a decision maker in a public space—say at the end of a committee hearing or public forum—and introduce yourself. You can ask for their business card and follow up with a call or email to set up an appointment.

Whether in person or online, eye contact, body language, tone of voice, and physical presence are part of your communication with decision makers. This is especially important in your initial meeting. A neatly dressed person with a cheerful and helpful demeanor will begin a relationship on a positive note. An angry or hostile manner will create a hurdle to building trust that you will have to work to overcome.

On or Off the Record?

There's another reason why one-on-one communication with decision makers is important. Written conversations with decision makers, including emails and text messages, are part of the *public record*.

I am not talking here about hiding anything or being dishonest. I am simply talking about what is ready for public disclosure. As part of the public record, written communications with national and state decision makers are subject to freedom of information (FOI) laws. This means anyone can request and receive documentation of your written communications with decision makers. Journalists often request information under FOI laws and use it in published stories. The National Freedom of Information Coalition website lists the state FOI laws.

If you are having a preliminary conversation in which policy options are being discussed, you probably don't want a written record, and neither does the decision maker. It's too easy to take early comments and questions out of context. Imagine a legislator responding to your email by writing, "That's an interesting idea, but I have a few questions," and then having a journalist report that the legislator opposes your issue!

One technique that advocates use, particularly in writing emails, is to ask themselves if they'd want what they are writing to appear in a headline. If the answer is no, then don't write it! Most readers will remember what a big deal opponents made of Hillary Clinton's emails. You don't want to inadvertently cause a problem for yourself or your allies.

Decision makers may want to listen and comment privately at times. If you have any confusion or doubt about this, it is perfectly OK to ask, "Would you prefer to have this conversation off the record?" or to say the same thing more informally: "Shall we keep this conversation in the room?" If you are meeting online, you should avoid recording any conversation that is not ready for public disclosure.

What's Their Motivation?

Your issue research should include understanding the personal and political motivations of the decision maker(s). Is this someone who is new in their role and wants to make a name for themselves and take the lead? Is this someone who cares passionately about your issue or something closely related to it? Is this someone who needs to solve a problem for constituents at home? Does the decision maker need a win with their party? Or perhaps the decision maker is fed up with an issue, and your proposed solution offers a welcome way to move forward.

The latter was the case when I approached the cochairs of the Labor, Commerce, Research and Economic Development Committee of the state legislature about resolving the building and energy code problem. Both chairs were serving the last year of their terms in office. They had been hearing arguments about the codes for eight years without resolution. I recognized that the committee chairs were fed up with the complaints and would lobby in support of a solution—if they had one.

When I approached them and offered to craft a solution, they jumped at the chance. They asked me to write a "resolve," a bill calling for a study on how to develop and implement a statewide code. I wrote this up and gave it to them. The committee under their leadership passed the resolve immediately. I knew then that if I came up with a viable solution, these two committee chairs would work hard to pass it. This began a yearlong research and coalition building process that resulted in the passage of the Maine Uniform Building and Energy Code.

Politics

Sometimes a decision maker's priorities are counter to your issue. A decision maker may support your opposition, or they may stick with their party in opposition to your issue and thus be unwilling to consider your point of view. I had an experience like this with a particular conservative Republican in the Maine Legislature. She did not listen to advocates. She simply toed the line and voted according to her party caucus. She was not one to sponsor new legislation or even contemplate an issue not prescribed by party leaders. In a case like this, you should minimize your time with uninterested parties and work with decision makers who are more sympathetic to your cause.

As you look at the spectrum of decision makers, you'll see there's a continuum ranging from those who are solidly opposed at one end, to those who are more neutral in the middle, to those who are solidly in support of your issue at the other end. You will want to work with those who are persuadable—those in support and in the middle. It's no use to try to persuade people who will never share your view. For most decisions, a simple majority is what you need, not 100% consensus or even a two-thirds majority. So focus your effort on those who can be persuaded.

Sometimes factors that have nothing to do with your issue can prevent it from moving forward. This happened when I was lobbying on behalf of the governor for a bill called "Quality of Place." The bill required that natural resource assets be considered in state economic development plans. Under this proposal, an assessment of forests and water resources would have to be included in designating a development zone, for example. This was a difficult bill to lobby because it was conceptual, and most legislators are predisposed to concrete action. I knew it would be a challenge for it to pass.

After working on it for a while, I sensed the opposition stemmed from more than just the conceptual nature of the bill. Specifically, I was not able to get anywhere with Senate Republicans. I was representing a Democratic governor at the time, so it was not a surprise that Republicans would oppose it; but it appeared there was more going on. I had a good personal relationship with one of the Republican senators, so I took him aside and asked, "What's going on with 'Quality of Place'?"

He turned to me quietly and said, "We can't give one more thing to the governor right now." This was useful information. Seeing no chance of the bill passing, my team stopped lobbying and urged the committee to hold the bill over until the next session.

Factors unrelated to my bill had prevented it from moving forward. The following year, it passed. This example shows how a good relationship with a decision maker can yield critical information. You should do all you can to understand the contexts and motivations of your decision makers.

Preparing to Meet Your Decision Maker

Before you meet with a decision maker, you should meet with your team or group and thoroughly prepare for the meeting. As we saw in chapter 8, a first step in creating your strategy is to clarify your ask. You'd be surprised how many groups meet with decision makers without ever asking them to take action. Raising awareness is not enough to move your decision maker to act! You need to clearly articulate an action that the decision maker can take. This might be sponsoring a bill, voting a certain way, signing a letter or resolve, or writing a letter of support for a federal grant. You and your group need to agree on the ask and write it down.

You also want to make sure your ask is something the decision maker can act on. You'd be surprised how often a group asks for something the decision maker cannot make happen! Once there was a group of advocates who wanted to stop the importation of solid waste into Maine, and they wanted to submit state legislation to stop the practice. However, imports are governed by the federal Interstate Commerce Act, which state legislatures cannot change. A better strategy might be to prohibit facilities in Maine from accepting this waste.

Before your meeting, you should prepare a fact sheet—a one- or two-page handout describing the issue, your position, your main talking points, and answers to the most frequently asked questions about the issue. Short and simple is best. Talking points should cover the major advantages and positive outcomes from your proposed solution. Three to five talking points are ideal. A sample fact sheet can be found in appendix B.

SAMPLE AGENDA FOR MEETING WITH DECISION MAKERS

Here's a template for an agenda:

1. Thank your decision maker for the meeting and any support they have previously given your group or cause.

2. Introductions: a very brief "Who Are You and Why Are You Here?" story for each person in attendance.

3. Introduce the issue and the ask.

4. Review the talking points, with designated individuals on your team making each point.

5. Offer to take any questions.

6. Review any follow-up or next steps.

7. Thank the decision maker for the meeting.

It helps smooth the flow of your meeting if you determine who will address which points in advance. I also recommend rehearsing your agenda by doing a role-play ahead of time. This will help your meeting go smoothly and will be appreciated by a decision maker with a busy schedule.

Another important practice is to try to anticipate the questions a decision maker will ask. Advocates will often prepare a separate handout addressing frequently asked questions. If the decision maker requests more information, you should be ready to respond. If you don't have the requested information, you should agree to send it as soon as possible. A sample of a frequently asked questions handout can be found in appendix B.

Following Up

Once you've made your ask, you need to follow up with decision makers to see if they have followed through. It's best to do this in person or by calling or texting their cell phone. Emails often are missed in the avalanche of emails arriving daily. Phone calls and voicemails left at town, city, or legislative offices often don't get through, which is why a call or text to a cell phone or a message to a personal email is preferable. In my state home phone numbers and email addresses are available to the public. But if this is not the case in your area, you should reach out to your network or a local advocacy organization to get personal contact information for decision makers.

If the decision maker doesn't follow through or doesn't seem to support you, you'll need to nudge them. You can do this either directly or through an important constituent. If they used traditional funding for their campaign, having a donor call and speak about the importance of acting on your issue is likely to make a difference.

You may also want to nudge a decision maker through the media. Write a letter to the editor addressing the need for their support. You can also start a media campaign that demonstrates broad support that will influence the decision maker to act. You'll find more on media strategies in chapter 13.

Understand the Decision Process

Another key piece of an advocate's work is to fully understand the decision process for your issue. Those who know the rules are powerful. Those who make the rules are even more powerful! Rep. John Martin is someone who has made a successful career out of knowing every detail of the laws, procedures, and rules governing the Maine state legislature. He uses this information to swing decisions his way. He became so good at this that after he served thirty years (including fourteen years as speaker of the house), the legislature enacted term limits. Many say it was to term him out—which it did for five years before he decided to run again, and won.

Many congressional leaders have been able to control the agenda through knowing and using the rules. US Sen. Mitch McConnell is a recent example of someone who used the power of the majority party to set rules on which bills get a hearing. A famous case of this was when he delayed a hearing on Supreme Court nominee Merrick Garland, effectively disallowing President Obama from appointing a Supreme Court justice, and later allowed a hearing on Supreme Court nominee Amy Coney Barrett just prior to a presidential election, so that President Trump could add another conservative to the Supreme Court. These moves by McConnell will affect Supreme Court decisions for generations. These are extreme cases, of course, but the point is that effective advocates need a solid understanding of the rules of the decision process they are participating in. There is power in this knowledge.

What is the decision process for your issue? You will want to know who controls the agenda, what's on it, what's not on it, and what assumptions are behind it. Politicians usually set the agendas. The chairs of the school board, the town board of selectmen, the planning board, and legislative committee chairs set the agendas for their respective governing bodies. CEOs and board chairs set the agendas for corporate annual meetings.

Professional staff who serve these governing bodies can often provide guidance on the decision-making process. A town or city manager, a school superintendent, a city planner, or a legislative analyst are usually glad to help with this. You can ask them questions such as: How does the process work? What is the best way to approach the chair? How can I get my issue on the agenda? These staffers are usually glad to help.

Identify the Barriers

You also want to be aware of any barriers to your group's participation in the decision process. Are the agendas created in a private setting? In many states, legislative councils decide which bills will have a public hearing, without public input. In cases like this, you'll want to use your skills, creativity, and tactics to influence council members outside of the decision process.

Is the public comment period at midnight, following a three-hour meeting? Are meetings held at times and in places where those affected cannot attend? Where I live, daytime meetings are a problem for fishermen, farmers, and small-business owners who cannot take time during working hours to attend. Are there issues that will affect full participation of your group, such as inadequate seating, lack of wheelchair access, or lack of audiovisual capabilities in the public seating area?

There are many ways your group or issue can be marginalized in the decision process. You should stay alert to these possibilities and if your group or key stakeholders are marginalized, demand better treatment. You may not always succeed, but you gain nothing if you don't ask.

Know How the Decision Will Be Made

You will also want to know how decisions are made. In many cases, boards, councils, or committees meet privately to discuss the issue and may even decide it prior to or without holding a public meeting. In cases like this, it's especially important to work with individual decision makers outside of the decision process.

Conversely, the issue may be discussed and decided in a public meeting. In Maine legislative committees, this is mostly the case. Testimony is heard and questions are raised in a public hearing. Later a work session is held in which decision makers discuss the pros and cons, and then they hold a vote. Advocates may be called on to speak at work sessions, at the discretion of the committee. But since there is no guarantee you will be called on, it's important to give the committee in advance any information you want to be part of the public record. Fact sheets, reports, and testimonies are all welcomed and distributed to committee members.

Many decisions have formal criteria and processes. Effective advocates work within these formal frameworks. Aquaculture leases are a good example. Anyone wishing to set up an ocean aquaculture operation must obtain a lease from the governing body of the waters where the farm will be located. Like most places, Maine has a formal hearing process and decision criteria for obtaining a lease. The commissioner of the Department of Marine Resources, a state agency, is the final decision maker. There are aquaculture leases for salmon, mussels, and oysters. To obtain a lease, the proposed farm must meet these criteria:

- The lease must not interfere with navigation.
- The lease must not interfere with fishing.
- The lease must not interfere with significant wildlife and marine habitat.
- The lease must not interfere with ingress and egress of riparian (shoreline) owners.
- The lease must not interfere with public beaches, parks, docks, or conservation lands.[6]

There are no criteria for obstructing views from shorefront homes or businesses, but the majority of people testifying at aquaculture lease hearings focus on this aspect! These testifiers do have a stake in the issue, but the criteria do not include aesthetics, so their testimony has little or no bearing on the decision. A better strategy for these testifiers would be to learn who makes these rules and work with them to expand the criteria. I never knew whether the testifiers were simply unaware of the decision criteria, or if they hoped they could sway the decision makers with an emotional story. But I do know working to expand the criteria would have been a good strategy for their cause.

It's important to notice what's *not* on the agenda and what assumptions are being made. The fact that views from the land are not criteria for aquaculture leases is an example. The assumptions behind this are that the buoys, rafts, and underwater pens associated with aquaculture are not an eyesore, and that shorefront homeowners and businesses should not prevent aquaculturists from making a living.

A common assumption behind many policy decisions is that no budget increases will be considered. Knowing this, advocates should prepare by developing a funding mechanism to support their proposal, if needed.

In order to succeed, you need to do your homework and come to understand both the official decision-making process and the hidden ways an issue may or may not move forward. The better you understand the decision-making process, the decision makers, and the underlying assumptions, the more successful you will be.

Negotiations

After advocates have presented their case to decision makers publicly, a negotiation phase begins. At this point the lead decision makers negotiate with other decision makers in an effort to move toward a decision. Town select boards, school boards, county commissioners, and state legislatures all engage in this. Leaders of the school board may need to present to the city council and persuade them to accept their proposal. A legislative committee needs to come to a decision and perhaps work with party leadership to bring an issue to the full legislature.

There is no right or wrong way to negotiate at this stage. The process can be unpredictable and messy. Individuals will be working to persuade other individuals, and both advocates and decision makers will be trying to determine how many votes they have in favor or against. In political arenas, leaders will be working to move their council, committee, or party caucuses to a decision.

In campaigns that challenge corporations, the negotiation phase is less defined. There will be back-and-forth conversations between advocates and decision makers, with offers and counteroffers. The best approach is to select your best communicators to represent your group. Many groups hire a lawyer or advocacy group with negotiating experience at this stage, to guide negotiations.

The public policy advocates' role at this stage shifts. Behind the scenes, advocates will continue to lobby individual decision makers. Advocates will also be tracking votes in support or opposed, which is an important way to see where additional conversations with decision makers are needed. I recall many meetings where our team discussed how we thought individual legislators would vote and how we might move more of them to our side.

Then we would work individually with decision makers we thought we could persuade.

But at this stage in public policy arenas, decision makers are more in the driver's seat, with advocates taking a role in support of them. Advocates may be asked to track down information, attend meetings, make presentations, and answer concerns. Decision makers may also call upon advocates to write bill amendments and come up with ways to bring opposition groups on board.

The negotiation stage can be frenetic. Decision deadlines will be looming, while the opposition may present additional questions as roadblocks or stalling tactics. Good advocates stay in close touch with decision makers at this stage, answering questions and concerns and providing information. The most effective advocates try to use every opportunity—including questions from decision makers, requests for additional information, and moves by the opposition—as a way to build their case.

The Bottom Line

Politics is a human business. Decision makers are not weighing the facts on two sides of an issue and then making a judgement, as in a court of law. Instead, they are weighing how your issue might help them get re-elected, how your issue might bring them support from a group they haven't interacted with before, or how support for your issue positions them in their caucus or committee. They are also weighing your proposal against their own values.

You are offering them an opportunity to expand their knowledge and networks. You are offering them new information and a path to understanding an issue they may not have understood before. Your careful work to build trust-based relationships with decision makers will help you successfully navigate the complexities of public policy decision making.

Thank, speak, listen, respond, engage, ask questions, be flexible, thank, repeat. This is the basic recipe for lobbying and working with decision makers. If you are authentic, caring, and honest, most decision makers will listen and try to help. If you are offering solid, substantive information, you are moving an issue forward.

If decision makers ask you for more information, they are telling you what is important to them. If they ask you to reach out to another group or individual, they are telling you what other support they need in order to support you. If they ask questions, you will know what is important to them. In response, be sure to offer to follow up and then return with the information promptly. And then be sure to thank them for asking!

11

Framing Your Message

The dynamics of self-identity and tribalism play a major role in our ability to hear and believe information.

—MAINE CLIMATE TABLE TOOLKIT

Why Frames Matter

My college students get the basic idea that "frames are the mental structures that shape the way we see the world."[1] They also understand that we are *not* talking about framing as in "being framed," meaning someone has been wrongly blamed.

What the students may not realize is that framing is serious business that goes much deeper than words. *To frame an issue is to set the policy agenda.* By "setting the agenda" I mean establishing the words, images, and values that describe an issue. "Setting the agenda" means establishing public consensus for your version of reality, through repetition over time. As an environmental advocate, *you want to set the agenda.*

The conservative right has done a good job of setting their public agenda by framing policies in ways that align with their values. The phrases "tax relief" and "tax burden," for example, frame taxes as something painful from which people need relief. Scandinavians have a completely different frame for taxes, and they have some of the highest taxes in the world. They frame taxes not as burdensome expenses but as desirable investments in the future. In their view, taxes provide a stable, reliable economy where people have equal opportunity to succeed.

Conservatives have been effective in framing some environmental issues, too. They invented the phrase "clean coal." Yes, there are technologies to capture pollution from burning coal, like flue-gas desulfurization. But there is no such thing as "clean coal." In another example, conservatives frame hydraulic fracking for natural gas as a method for achieving America's "energy independence," which is partially true but completely neglects the fact that fracking produces hundreds of millions of gallons of polluted wastewater every year. Solar and wind offer energy independence too, but without the water pollution.

Environmentalists need to get to work framing environmental issues based on their values and scientific evidence. Then they need to communicate their frames firmly and repeatedly until the frames gain a foothold in the mind of the public. Repeating untruths or using words or frames in manipulative ways does not further a world based on compassion, respect, and equality. Repeating false or manipulative frames over and over will never make them true. But frames based on facts do need repeating so people will come to accept them and believe what is true.

To frame environmental issues with integrity takes in-depth research, reflection, and honesty. In this chapter, we will focus on what you can do to frame your issues and communicate about them truthfully and effectively.

Case Study: Maine's Working Waterfront Coalition

To help understand frames, we'll be looking at the example of Maine's Working Waterfront Coalition throughout this chapter. It took seven years for the Working Waterfront Coalition to preserve water access for Maine fishermen. While it's always important to have a clear message, in this case framing made the difference between success and failure.

The Working Waterfront Coalition began their work with research during the first year of the campaign. Here's what the research revealed:

- Just twenty-five miles of Maine's thirty-five-hundred-mile coastline remained available for fishing, aquaculture, and boat-related businesses.

- Maine's fishing industry is an important contributor to the economy, with more than $400 million in annual revenues, more than four thousand six hundred lobster licenses, and two to three million lobster traps deployed annually.

- Aquaculture of fish and shellfish is a growing industry, with revenues of about $30 million a year.

- Waterfront access is vanishing at an accelerating rate due to fishermen aging out of the industry, selling off their property to developers, and retiring.

- When fishermen sell their waterfront property for development, it's permanently removed from working waterfront status.

- Fishermen and aquaculturists can't afford to buy waterfront property due to high prices.

- Waterfront property was taxed at "highest and best use," meaning its tax value was its market value for development. Fishermen and aquaculturists can't afford the high real estate taxes on waterfront property.

- Marine businesses of all kinds are having a difficult time securing waterfront access due to low availability and high costs.

A group of five organizations formed the Working Waterfront Coalition to find solutions. The Department of Marine Resources, a state agency where I worked, was a founding member of the coalition. We knew what the problem was: fishermen and marine businesses were losing water access. But we didn't know how to solve it. We spent a year researching and developing policy solutions. Eventually we decided to change the tax status of waterfront properties, which would significantly reduce the property taxes fishermen were paying.

To do this, the state constitution would have to be amended. This called for a two-step process: passing a law in the state legislature allowing a public referendum, and then winning the referendum with a majority vote.

Our coalition organized successfully, pulling together a committed leadership team, attracting more than one hundred organization and individual members, and holding regular monthly meetings. We held press conferences and lobbied the legislature and the governor. We sailed to an easy victory in the first step of the process: passing a law to allow a statewide referendum.

The referendum proved to be more difficult. We did all the necessary things in our campaign—press conferences, tabling at events, speaking engagements, and so on. We were motivated and organized, and we built a strong coalition of support. With fishing, boat building, recreational marinas, and aquaculture businesses on our side, not to mention the support of the governor and the legislature, we should have won the referendum—but we didn't.

After our referendum loss, we regrouped and decided to try again. We worked with the legislature to pass a law allowing a second referendum. Then we launched a campaign to pass it. This is where we learned the importance of framing that spoke to our audience's values. We needed to revise our message so our audiences could vote for it. We got to work. The following fall the second public referendum was held.

The results were stunning: whereas our first referendum narrowly lost, the second won by a landslide. The only thing we did differently in the second campaign was to change the wording of the referendum question to appeal to the values of the voters. Here's how the two questions appeared on the ballot:

- Referendum question #1: "Do you favor amending the constitution of Maine to allow the legislature to provide for the assessment of land used for commercial fishing activities based on the current use of that property?" (lost 49%–51%)

- Referendum question #2: "Do you favor amending the constitution of Maine to permit the legislature to authorize waterfront land used for commercial fishing activities to be assessed based on the land's current use in a manner similar to treatment now available for farms, open space and forestland?" (won 73%–27%)

A closer look shows that the first question is narrow, referencing fishing only. Analysis showed that coastal voters supported it by a wide margin, but inland voters voted against it. To inland voters, the first question appeared to be a special interest group (fishermen) trying to get an exception to the tax laws.

The second question is broader, presenting the idea of "fairness" relative to farms, forests, and open space. Why shouldn't fishermen get the same tax benefits as other natural resource–based businesses? A vast majority of voters agreed, even if they didn't know any fishermen!

This is a crystal-clear example of why it is important to appeal to people's values in communicating your message. "Tax fairness among farming, forestry, and fishing industries" was a value voters could support. This is the essence of good framing and messaging: *understanding your audience and crafting a message that appeals to their values.*

Frames for the Ocean

Edge Research conducted a study to understand what millennials (people born between 1980 and 1996) think about the ocean. The purpose of the study was to help environmental groups learn how to recruit millennials to their organizations.[2]

They found that millennials interact with the ocean primarily by visiting beaches. "Beach visits" is their frame, and while at the beach they see cigarette butts and plastic debris, which are also parts of their frame. Environmental groups used this information to open their communications with millennials by talking about beach pollution. Once they had millennials' attention, the groups began to educate them about high-priority issues including ocean warming, acidification, loss of species, and coral bleaching.

Below are four different frames for the ocean, based on people and discussions I've engaged in. None are right or wrong; they simply illustrate the different ways people think about and relate to the ocean.

- **Spiritual/inspirational:** People holding this frame are filled with wonder about the ocean. Beautiful photos of sunsets, sunrises, storms, and marine life describe their frame.

- **Utilitarian:** People holding this frame view the ocean as a source of food. Almost all of northern Japan's and Iceland's coastlines are free from tourism development, because these societies have regarded the ocean solely as commercial fishing grounds for generations.

- **Recreational playground:** People holding this frame see the ocean as a vacation destination. Their frame includes beaches, trails, hotels, restaurants, marinas, boating, and cruise ships.

- **Living ecosystem:** People holding this frame view the ocean as an interconnected living system. Interactions among species, food chains, land, air, water, weather, and people define this frame.

The Power of Frames

Frames are powerful because they connect with unconscious structures of meaning in our brains. Author George Lakoff famously says to his audiences, "Don't think of an elephant!" Of course, we can't obey a command like that. In our brains, we have the idea of an elephant already formed. When the word is mentioned, our idea of an elephant automatically arises in our thoughts. This happens unconsciously, and we can't stop it.[3]

Frames are also powerful because they direct the policy positions we hold and the actions we take, even when we're not aware of the frames. A person who sees the ocean as a lucrative playground might support new tourism development, someone holding the utilitarian frame would want to preserve fishing access, and a person with a living ecosystem frame would want to protect important natural habitat from development. Framing affects every issue in a similar way: different frames describe issues differently, leading to different actions and policies.

As an environmental advocate, *you want to frame public opinion of what is right and good.* You want the thoughts and images you have created to come to mind when certain words are uttered. For example, if the subject of pollution comes up, you want people to think: "Good corporate citizens clean up after themselves." This is a reframe from: "Businesses provide jobs and are the engine of the economy. Waste cleanup is prohibitively costly, and we should support businesses and jobs by helping to clean up after them." Reframing changes public priorities and policies, and the institutions that carry them out. As Lakoff says, "Reframing is social change."[4]

One of the important things to know about framing is that negating a frame reinforces that frame. *If you use the language of the opposition, you are evoking a frame and worldview that may be the opposite of what you want.* Continuing with the tax example, you wouldn't want to frame a tax initiative as "fair taxes for all," because the right has already defined the word tax as a "burden." Instead, you would want to reframe the issue completely.

To create a new frame, you need to rethink your issue. On the tax issue, you might note that employment in renewable energy jobs is growing 70% faster than jobs in other sectors, which generates new income and corporate taxes. Taxes can support higher education, R & D funds to develop new technologies, and training programs for careers in energy efficiency and renewable energy. Taking these points into consideration, you might reframe your tax campaign by calling it "Investing in America."

The brain does not know the difference between negative and positive. It only knows that you've activated a thought, as in "Don't think of an elephant." This is why focusing on a problem tends to reinforce the problem in our minds. Focusing on solutions is the only true way to overcome a problem. When framing an issue or campaign, you'll have more success with positive, solution-focused frames. Likewise, as we saw in chapter 6, a positive vision is needed to generate enough energy to create change.

All too often, environmentalists focus on fighting against the frames developed by others. They find themselves responding or reacting to conservative frames, which only reinforces those frames. This is why you as an advocate want to think carefully about the words you use and what images in people's brains might be stimulated by those words.

Good Framing Reveals the Truth

We all have a tendency to focus on what we want to achieve. Nothing wrong with that. But to win on an issue, in addition to focusing on your goal, you need to understand and speak to your audience. You must understand what they believe, what they are afraid of, and what they want. As we've discussed, people hold conscious and unconscious beliefs. Winning campaigns do what they can to understand these, and then they meet people where they are. Knowing where your audience is mentally and speaking directly to their fears and values in your campaign messaging is a winning strategy.

The campaign for marriage equality is a great example of a reframing that reversed public opinion and policy. By 2010, thirty-one states had banned same-sex marriage through ballot initiatives or constitutional amendments. Clearly, the campaign for marriage equality was in trouble. Fact-based campaign themes of "antidiscrimination" and "equal rights" were not working. What could be done?

Goodwin Simon Strategic Research conducted in-depth interviews and focus groups to determine what underlying beliefs and concerns people had about same-sex marriage. Their research revealed that many people were conflicted about it. Many knew and loved gay, lesbian, and bisexual friends and family members. But this conflicted with their beliefs that same-sex relationships are promiscuous, exist only for sex, and are sinful or against their religion. Many perceived gay, lesbian, and bisexual people as deserting their families and engaging in antisocial behavior after they came out. Interviews also revealed that many could not understand why same-sex partners would want to get married.[5]

These findings led to reframing same-sex marriage away from a "social justice" frame and into a "love" frame. The social justice frame described same-sex marriage as an issue about equal rights and fairness under the law. The love-based frame described same-sex marriage as an issue about the committed, loving relationships of same-sex couples, and how they wanted to honor their commitment through marriage. This second frame effectively addressed the *misperceptions and fears* found in the research: that same-sex relationships were promiscuous and only existed for sex, and that gay, lesbian, and bisexual people were antifamily.

New messages were crafted based on the research and the new frame. Gone were ads about discrimination and equal rights. The new messaging focused on families, love, and commitment. In advertising, everyday people replaced politicians as messengers. A widely viewed advertisement featured Harlan and Dottie Gardner, a heterosexual couple who had been married for more than 50 years. The scene was a family dinner table where the Gardners spoke of their pride and support for their lesbian daughter and her fiancée, and their hope that someday the younger couple would be able to marry. The new messaging connected same-sex couples with the values of loving, committed families.

This reframing and revised messaging did the trick. Voters had a change of heart, and by 2012, four states had reversed themselves and voted affirmatively for marriage equality. This led to a landmark Supreme Court decision in 2015 to legalize same-sex marriage nationwide. The reframing and new messaging had turned public policy 180 degrees.

Tribalism

People constantly compare their thoughts, opinions, and beliefs with others within their social circles. This is one of the ways we inform and shape our identities. Our personal beliefs are strengthened or undermined by how others around us view the same issues. The internet has reinforced our tendency to align our beliefs with our social networks or tribes.

Because of our tendency to adopt the views of our social circle, we sometimes hold views that are in conflict with our personal experience. Some who cherish nature and have experienced the effects of climate change are climate change deniers because this is the prevailing view of their social circle. Similarly, some young evangelical Christians have joined with others of their generation in calling for solutions to climate change, even though many evangelical congregations continue to avoid or deny the climate change issue.

Messages that clash with a person's identity and social group often cannot be heard or accepted. Unfortunately for environmental advocates, tribalism has made climate change and other environmental issues so polarized that even straightforward information can be rejected.

People also have a tendency to find patterns and create meaning from them. The Greeks explained much of what they observed as a result of the actions of their gods. They created an entire system of mythology to explain the patterns they observed on earth. Today we still create explanations from patterns we see and experience. This can be a problem when people generate meaning that has no basis in reality. Most conspiracy theories fall into this category.

To counter tribalism and false explanations, it's helpful to return to people's lived experiences. Questions you might ask to explore someone's perspective are: Is the ice melting off local waters earlier than it used to? Are the summers hotter? Are we getting more rain? Have you seen changes in birds? Animals? What do you think might be causing these changes?

Advocates should work to understand views that are different from their own. Understanding the internal conflicts of others, the way the marriage equality campaign did, is a gateway to effective, heart-centered communication. You should dig deep to understand the emotions, values, and beliefs of your audiences, and then use this information as a tool to create impactful messaging.

How to Talk about Climate Change

Many myths persist about climate change and the environment. One of the most prevalent is that the warming climate is too big for us to really change. This belief, combined with the idea that we have to accept damage to the earth in order to have a robust economy, or that people will have to give up lifestyles they love in order to address climate change, keeps people stuck in the status quo.

The way to get through these barriers is to appeal to people's personal experiences and values. The Maine Climate Table, a group I'm a part of, commissioned a study to learn how we might talk to Mainers about climate change. A series of focus groups, surveys, and online feedback revealed how people viewed climate change. Three key themes emerged:

1. **Mainers take pride in their natural resources.** Natural resources are a core part of their identity and they want to be sure these resources are protected now and for future generations.

2. **Mainers are anxious about the economy.** Many Mainers would like to live a greener life, but they fear the costs are beyond their reach. Policies with significant costs are likely to generate pushback.

3. **The impacts of climate change are visible.** People are seeing impacts of climate change around them in unusual weather patterns, more extreme weather events, and changing wildlife.[6]

From this information, the consultants developed communication strategies. Below are highlights from their recommendations. Although developed for Maine, these can be applied in any region.

CLIMATE CHANGE COMMUNICATIONS STRATEGIES

- Keep it local and personal. Describe climate impacts that are readily apparent in people's lives, such as flooding, fires, increased or decreasing rainfall, etc.
- Establish local impacts before explaining climate change as the cause.
- Avoid speaking abstractly about climate change. If needed, acknowledge that climate change can be hard to understand.
- Emphasize the new opportunities and job creation that come with clean energy and green business.
- Build on past successes that people in your area are familiar with, such as eliminating DDT, reducing acid rain, and cleaning up the air and water under the Clean Air and Clean Water Acts.
- Emphasize proven local solutions and specific ways that individuals can take action.
- Use regular people as messengers, not celebrities or politicians.
- Say "climate change" instead of "global warming," because global warming has been shown to be more politically charged.
- Say "carbon pollution" instead of "greenhouse gases" or "carbon emissions," because people understand that pollution is caused by humans and is possible to clean up.
- Emphasize the importance of public health and the health and well-being of future generations as a reason to address climate change.

Climate Values You Can Use in Communications

Doubt about science has been growing in recent years. Many see financial or political objectives as motivating science and therefore don't trust the results. Others have difficulty understanding science because it is often presented in obscure ways. Most people with busy lives just don't have the time to study and understand science. The truth is, we can't be experts in everything in this complex world.

The FrameWorks Institute, a social science research organization, undertook several studies to understand and address the public doubt and lack of understanding about climate science. They began their work by interviewing climate scientists and citizens in four states. From this they determined that "the greatest communication challenge for climate scientists was a lack of consistent and complete storytelling."[7] They found that what was needed was a clearly articulated set of environmental values and understandable metaphors for explaining the phenomenon of climate change to the public.

FrameWorks then conducted a series of studies to test messages for communicating with the public about climate change and the ocean. They surveyed more than nine thousand Americans in their research. Below are the values and metaphors that tested best on measures of public attitude, prioritization, and support for policies that protect the marine environment.[8] They found these values to be universally appealing. You are encouraged to use them in communicating about your issues.

PROTECTION

The value of *protection* scored highest among all the values surveyed. It focuses on protecting the environment and people from harm, and the urgency of this protection. The specific message tested by FrameWorks was:

> It's important that we protect people and places from harm. We can do this by solving the issues facing our environment. This means stepping in to ensure people's safety and well-being to the best of our

ability and safeguarding the places we depend on. We also need to take measures to eliminate or reduce risks, making sure that people are able to go about their lives freely. Concern for the welfare of others and vigilance in preserving our habitats are the hallmarks of a protective approach. Simply put, we have a duty to protect our surroundings. Protection is the right thing for us to do.[9]

RESPONSIBLE MANAGEMENT

The value of *responsible management* and stewardship also scored high in the surveys. This value focuses on our duty to preserve and protect nature today and for the future. When combined with practical steps, like switching to cleaner fuels, "responsible management" frames a proactive, positive approach. It sidesteps climate denial, science skepticism, and feelings of helplessness by offering a positive and proactive framework. Further, this frame appeals to both liberal and conservative worldviews. Here's the specific message tested by FrameWorks:

> It's important we take responsible steps to manage the issues facing our environment. This means thinking carefully about problems and focusing on the best ways to deal with the problems we face. We also need to keep future generations in mind while we look at the best solutions. Open-mindedness and long-term planning are the hallmarks of responsible management. Simply put, we should take a practical, step-by-step approach that relies on common sense and uses all the evidence we have to take care of our surroundings. Managing challenges responsibly is the right thing for us to do.[10]

INTERCONNECTION

Interconnection as a value also tested well because people generally agree that all life is connected. But it's an abstract concept. In order to be effective in communications, it must be combined with concrete examples. People can grasp that the lobster fishery on the south coast of Massachusetts has ended because the ocean there is now too warm for this cold-water species.

Public health examples, such as the emergence of tick-borne diseases like Lyme, are also good examples that demonstrate the interconnection of climate, environmental changes, and people.

INNOVATION

The value of *innovation* also tested well because it speaks to human ingenuity and builds a sense of hope that we can solve environmental problems. It helps overcome fears that we must give up everything we love or choose between jobs and the environment. Like interconnection, this value must be combined with concrete examples to be effective in communications. Locally generated solar and wind energy are examples of innovations that support a clean environment.

One caution about using this frame is to avoid implying that science will save us and all we need to do is wait for science to solve our problems. Innovation must be combined with good environmental policies, regulations, and investment to reduce carbon emissions and address climate change.

Three Core Values You Need to Know

In addition to the values described above, there are three core values that advocates need to know and use in framing and communicating about environmental issues: equality, community, and investing in the future. Be sure to use these in framing and creating messaging for emerging environmental issues.

EQUALITY

Vice President Al Gore's documentary about climate change was titled *An Inconvenient Truth* based on the assumption that dealing with climate change would require unwelcome changes in our way of life. Subsequent research has shown that the opposite is true. Greater equality is a *prerequisite* for addressing climate change and is essential for improving the overall quality of life in whole populations.[11] The "new earth story" discussed in chapter 3 shows that we must enact policies based on caring for each other and the earth in order to sustain the health of the planet. If we do this, our lives will not be "inconvenienced"; they will be better.

The value of equality describes a culture of equal opportunity where all can succeed. Equality is reflected in a true democracy that would provide equal access to quality health care and education, fair treatment of workers, the ability to organize, fair trade policies, and protection from monopolies and harmful business practices. Equality also applies to businesses, allowing them to compete on a level playing field.

As an environmental advocate, you want to frame "equality" by defining specifically what it means with regard to your issue. If you are advocating for a public park, you might define equality as equal access to the park. If you are protesting a new chemical plant, you would define equality as the right of everyone to healthy, clean air to breathe.

COMMUNITY

Placing value on community recognizes our interconnectedness and the power of working together to solve problems. With strong community support, people can be cared for, and social and environmental problems can be solved. Even business ventures that have community support have a greater chance of achieving success.

Environmental problems are best solved by communities coming together with a shared goal for solving them. Environmental advocates need to continually emphasize the importance of communities coming together to do this. In communications, advocates should highlight the harm to communities caused by environmental damage, and *emphasize the community benefits* of pursuing and adopting specific solutions.

INVESTING IN THE FUTURE

This important value is critical as many countries rebuild their economies, regulatory structures, and cultures following the COVID-19 crisis. Young environmental activists are leading the way in demanding we clean up emissions and create a more equitable economy. We now have a chance to restructure our economy in ways that reduce the wealth gap, clean up the environment, and provide a healthier life for everyone on the planet. Robust policies on education, job training, health care, a clean environment, public infrastructure, and diplomatic relations with other countries can and should be framed as *investments in the future.* How might your environmental issue be framed as an investment in the future?

Some Useful Climate Metaphors

Metaphors link what we don't know to what we do know, helping us to understand something new. Whenever a new idea is introduced, it's described based on something familiar. The mathematicians who did the calculations for John Glenn's space flight in 1961 were called "computers." They didn't work *with* computers; they *were* the computers, making manual calculations. When the first automatic calculators were invented, they were called "computers" because they did what humans had done before.

Studies have shown that the public generally believes all environmental problems are caused by pollution from toxic and solid waste. Climate change is quite different and needs a new set of metaphors so the public can understand it.

As part of their groundbreaking research, the FrameWorks Institute tested metaphors and came up with several new ones to use in communicating about climate change, which are described below. Environmental advocates should use these metaphors in their communications about climate change.

HEAT-TRAPPING BLANKET

Since this metaphor was introduced in 2015, it has become widely used to describe the buildup of greenhouse gases in the atmosphere. Here's how FrameWorks describes it:

> When we burn fossil fuels for energy, such as coal, oil, or natural gas, we release carbon dioxide into the atmosphere. Carbon dioxide is a gas that traps heat. As CO_2 builds up, it acts like a blanket, trapping

in heat that would otherwise escape. This 'blanket effect' is warming the planet's atmosphere, disrupting the balance that keeps the climate stable.[12]

REGULAR VS. RAMPANT CARBON DIOXIDE

This metaphor helps people distinguish between naturally occurring carbon dioxide and harmful levels:

> Some carbon dioxide, or CO_2, is needed for life processes. We can call this regular CO_2. But CO_2 is not just something that we breathe out and plants take in. It's also something that can get put into the air when we use any kind of fossil fuel, when we burn coal to create electricity, or we use oil to fuel transportation or manufacturing. These things are putting a lot of CO_2 into the atmosphere and oceans. We can call this rampant CO_2 because there's too much of it and it's getting out of control. Rampant CO_2 accumulates in the wrong places, like the ocean, and causes a number of problems in the climate and ecosystems. We'll always need regular levels of carbon dioxide, but we need to start reducing rampant levels of carbon dioxide.[13]

CLIMATE'S HEART

This metaphor describes the role of the ocean in climate change, connecting it with weather, heat, and humidity:

> The oceans regulate the climate system the way your heart regulates the flow of blood throughout your body. The heart sustains the body by controlling the circulation of blood, making sure the right amount gets to all parts of the body—not too much and not too little. The oceans act as the climate's heart, sustaining the climate by controlling the circulation of things like heat and humidity.
>
> The ocean is at the heart of a circulatory system that moves heat and moisture through all parts of the climate system, including land, atmosphere, and bodies of water. As the heart of the circulatory system, the ocean regulates the climate by helping to control the earth's

temperature. By storing heat from the sun and emitting it back into the atmosphere, the ocean maintains a regular flow of heat and stabilizes the earth's temperature. Ocean currents and winds move heat and moisture to different parts of the world, which keeps the climate stable.

Burning fossil fuels damages the ocean's ability to maintain good circulation of heat and moisture. When we burn fossil fuels, we put a lot of stress on the ocean, which damages its ability to keep the climate stable—so sometimes the oceans pump too much heat and moisture through the system, sometimes too little. Burning fossil fuels weakens the ocean's ability to regulate the climate system.[14]

OSTEOPOROSIS OF THE SEA

This metaphor proved effective in explaining the effect of ocean acidification, by comparing it to the familiar condition of osteoporosis:

Ocean acidification is causing osteoporosis of the sea. Acidification is changing the chemistry of the ocean and, as a result, many types of shellfish have trouble building and maintaining their shells. This 'osteoporosis of the sea' causes the protective shells of these animals to become thinner and more brittle, which makes it hard for them to grow and survive.[15]

How to Frame Your Issue

Naming our coalition the "Working Waterfront Coalition" was deliberate. We didn't call it the "Commercial Waterfront Coalition" or "Fair Water Access for Fishermen" or some other name. We knew intuitively that the value of hard work would resonate with our audiences and would appeal to both liberal and conservative decision makers. We also knew that "Working Waterfront" is a frame that includes images of fishing piers, fishing boats, and fishermen unloading their catch—traditional activities that no one wants to lose. We had a winner with the "Working Waterfront Coalition" frame. The tag line "only twenty-five miles of working waterfront left" was strong, too, and helped propel us to victory.

You can frame your issue or campaign in a way that speaks to values held by your supporters and decision makers. Here's a simple four-step process for doing this:

1. Pick out the core values behind your issue or campaign, using the values described in this chapter or other values you feel are important.

2. Write down the public policy you are proposing based on these values.

3. Articulate the benefits and positive consequences of winning your issue (these will become some of your talking points).

4. Define who is "us" and who is "them" with respect to your issue and the values articulated above.

FRAMING SMART GROWTH

"Smart growth" refers to the concept of clustering human development in order to preserve wildlife habitat and open space, and foster stronger communities. Here's how the smart growth issue looks using the four-step framing process described above.

1. Core values

   • Build strong communities where people can interact easily.

   • Preserve open space, farmland, forests, and wildlife habitat.

   • Decrease traffic and carbon emissions.

2. Public policies

   • Offer incentives to towns that adopt plans and zoning ordinances that require developments to be clustered near existing centers of development.

3. Benefits and consequences

   - Safe, convenient, affordable neighborhoods
   - Decreased traffic and congestion, increased convenience, more walkability, more transportation options
   - Residents save time from driving less and can spend more time with families
   - Investment in existing centers strengthens sense of place
   - Protection of open space, farmland, forests, wildlife habitat
   - Less investment in roads and bridges, lower road maintenance costs, lower taxes

4. Who is "us" and who is "them"

   - "We" are the local smart growth organization made up of residents, businesses, and political officials who support these policies.
   - "They" are landowners and developers who want to build homes and businesses on undeveloped land outside of our existing town and city centers.

Framing beyond Words

Your actions are also part of how you frame your issue. Advocates working inside the system can frame their issue using values and metaphors. They can also frame their issue by bringing certain people to speak at a press conference. The Working Waterfront Coalition's press conferences featured fishermen who trucked lobster traps for many miles to get to the water. This provided concrete images that illustrated the difficulties fishermen had in finding water access.

Nonviolent direct action groups often frame their messages by acting them out. The Michiana Coalition Against Tar Sands anchored platforms to several pieces of construction equipment being used in constructing an oil pipeline. Moving the construction equipment would result in dropping a sitter on the platform fifty feet to the ground. *This action framed the pipeline issue as a life-and-death matter for the environment.* Enbridge, the company building the pipeline, is a known polluter, and the pipeline under construction had ruptured earlier, causing a large toxic oil spill.[16]

The Key to Good Framing

The key to good framing and effective messaging is *understanding your audience.* Your audience includes decision makers, supporters, and people who may be persuaded to support your cause. You need to know what they believe, what they fear, and what they value. Focus groups, surveys, and interviews are good tools to find these things out. But if you don't have the time or resources to do in-depth research, you can reach out to a dozen people who represent your audiences and question them directly about your issue: What would it take for them to support your campaign? What might prevent them from doing that? Why is this issue important to them? When they think about your issue, what fears come to mind? If you've developed a name for your campaign or messaging, you can get their feedback on that, too.

As this chapter shows, framing your words and actions so they speak directly to your audience's emotions, values, and beliefs is what makes communications effective. Good framing can define how your issue is perceived, discussed, and decided, making it a critical factor in your success.

12

Communicating with Impact

Ambitions become bold social change with good, effective communication.

—KRISTEN GRIMM, founder and president, Spitfire Strategies

Now that you understand how to frame your issue in the big picture, it's time to take a more granular look at communications—how to choose the right language to get your specific ideas across. We'll also discuss how to communicate through emails, calls, and fact sheets, something every advocate does sooner or later.

Your job as an advocate is to persuade. In the words of author Doug McKenzie-Mohr, "One of the most effective ways to ensure attention is to present information that is vivid, concrete, and personalized."[1] Vivid, concrete, and personalized communications are the starting place for persuasion.

Use Visual, Active Words

The first thing your communications need to do is capture attention. Long, boring, and impersonal documents don't do this. Seems obvious; but when I started work at the Maine State Planning Office, the agency was in the business of producing long, boring, impersonal policy papers. The agency director and I immediately got to work and directed staff to create colorful brochures with photos of real people and places as presentation pieces for our public policy research. The brochures succinctly summarized our findings and directed readers to where they could find more detailed information. We still did the research and had detailed information available for those that wanted it, but we led with visual images and key findings, not the details.

Similarly, you need to capture attention with active, visual words. Multisyllable words like "sustainability" and noun phrases like "ocean acidification" tend to alienate and confuse. Not everyone has a clear idea of what sustainability, ocean acidification, or even climate change mean. To some, using words like "sustainability" or "ocean acidification" immediately identify you as an elitist. In using these words you might inadvertently put off people you want to connect with.

Simple words that evoke visual images work best. "Plant more trees" or "keep forests healthy" works better than "forest habitat preservation" or "forest ecosystem management." Metaphors like "heat-trapping blanket" are a vivid and memorable way to describe the buildup of greenhouse gases in the atmosphere. You want people to easily *visualize* what you are talking about.

Visual metaphors are powerful, especially when they illustrate size. A few years ago, an environmental article I read described disposable single-serve coffee containers this way: "If you lined up all the used single-serve coffee containers side by side, they would encircle the globe at the equator." I don't recall where I saw this or when, but the image has stayed with me. Similarly, an energy auditor might say, "Heat is leaking from around your doors and windows, and you should consider weatherstripping to seal the cracks." But what if they said, "If you were to add up all the cracks around and under your doors and windows, you'd have a hole the size of a football in your living room. Think for a moment about the heat that would escape from a hole that large. That's why I recommend you install weatherstripping." The latter statement is exactly what home energy auditors were trained to say at Pacific Gas and Electric in California. Vivid information stands out against other information and is more memorable. When the two above messages from the energy auditors were tested, more people weatherstripped their homes after hearing the more vivid description.[2]

Action words are better than passive words. The homepage of the Sunrise Movement website uses action words well:

> The Sunrise Movement is a youth movement to stop climate change and create millions of good jobs in the process. We're building an army of young people to make climate change an urgent priority across America, end the corrupting influence of fossil fuel executives on our politics, and elect leaders who stand up for the health and well-being of all people.[3]

Using verbs in the present tense and active voice, as Sunrise did, adds impact to communications. In the active voice, the subject is taking the action. In the passive voice, the subject is the receiver of the action. These two sentences illustrate the difference:

> We're building power by voting for leaders who support the Green New Deal. (active voice)

> The Green New Deal is supported by the leaders who we are voting for. (passive voice)

Be Courageous, Bold, and Personal

Being courageous and bold means communicating that you firmly and proudly believe that your cause is right and good. You must state your demands urgently and unequivocally. Rachel Carson exemplified this when she called out chemical companies in *Silent Spring*. Climate activist Greta Thunberg exemplified this when she called out the United Nations for not taking stronger steps to stop global warming. You can do this for your issues by communicating your demands clearly and urgently. Here are some examples:

- We won't back down until we see new regulations on lawn chemicals.

- We won't stop calling and writing our representatives until we get a personal response to our demands.

- How many more lives have to be threatened by climate change, when the solutions are clear?

As we saw in the prior chapter, good communications begin with identifying your audiences and what they care about. A corollary is that you want to address your audience personally, meaning speaking to their fears, beliefs, and values, and offering actions they can take. Yet many climate change messages are impersonal and knowledge-based, like this one:

Climate change threatens life for people around the globe. Access to food, water, and healthy places to live are all at stake.

A more effective way to reach people is to present a personal, action-based message like this:

Climate change is a global threat, but you can take a step to address it by weatherizing your home. Weatherization is a good way to reduce your heating bill and shrink your carbon footprint.

The first message is true, but it presents an abstract concept with no way for the reader to connect with it or do anything about it. It's disempowering. The latter message connects awareness of climate change with something a person can do and is thus empowering.

Use Emotions to Your Advantage

Emotions such as hope, admiration, pride, and anger can inspire people to take action. Appealing to emotions in communications is a longstanding practice in marketing and advertising. You can use this technique to inspire people to do what you want them to do. Sharing stories of people who have created urban gardens from empty lots, after-school arts programs for kids, and support groups for parents can inspire others in your community to take action. Nonprofit organizations that give awards to the volunteer of the year are doing the same thing—communicating hope, inspiring people to take action for their cause, and describing what a valuable contribution means for that organization.

People are naturally inclined to want to belong. This, too, can be used to motivate people to join your campaign, make a donation, or take action to support your cause. Messages that are welcoming and inclusive and that invite people to join a group of like-minded people inspire people to take action.

Extinction Rebellion (XR) is building its movement based on anger, outrage, a shared sense of urgency, and welcoming participation from everyone. They are a decentralized, nonpartisan group that takes action to persuade governments worldwide to address "the climate and ecological emergency."[4] According to their website, any person or group can organize autonomously and take action in the name and spirit of XR. What binds the movement together is a set of shared principles and values, which are clearly and succinctly stated:

1. **We have a shared vision of change.**

   Creating a world that is fit for the next seven generations to live in.

2. **We set our mission on what is necessary.**

   Mobilizing 3.5% of the population to achieve system change, such as momentum-driven organizing.

3. **We need a regenerative culture.**

   Creating a culture that is healthy, resilient, and adaptable.

4. **We openly challenge ourselves and this toxic system.**

   Leaving our comfort zones to take action for change.

5. **We value reflecting and learning.**

   Following a cycle of action, reflection, learning, and planning for more action. Learning from other movements and contexts as well as our own experience.

6. **We welcome everyone and every part of everyone.**

Working actively to create safer and more accessible spaces.

7. **We actively mitigate for power.**

Breaking down hierarchies of power for more equitable participation.

8. **We avoid blaming and shaming.**

We live in a toxic system, but no one individual is to blame.

9. **We are a nonviolent network.**

Using nonviolent strategy and tactics as the most effective way to bring about change.

10. **We are based on autonomy and decentralization.**

We collectively create the structures we need to challenge power.[5]

Communications and particularly videos are sometimes used to wake people up to the gravity of a situation. While useful, these communications present a risk: they may cause your audience to be overwhelmed and avoid taking action. To prevent this, *you need to combine grave messages with a sense of common purpose and community.* You need to offer constructive ways people can address the threat and join like-minded people who are working for change.

Chasing Ice and *Chasing Coral* are two documentaries that use time-lapse photography to show the melting of polar ice and the death of coral reefs. These and other climate change documentaries are difficult to watch because of their emotional content. Seeing images of acres and acres of dead coral is traumatic. Audiences can be easily overwhelmed by these images.

To mitigate this, *Chasing Ice* and *Chasing Coral* show people taking action to address the threats in the films. The producers also provide materials for school and community groups to use at movie screenings. The materials include discussion questions and exercises designed to stimulate groups to come together and take action.

Open with a Question

Using a question to open a conversation is an effective technique for gaining attention. An opening line I used when approaching people on the street with a petition for ranked-choice voting was, "Did you know that in Maine you don't need a majority to win an election?" When I asked this, people's eyebrows rose and they were ready to hear more.

Asking a leading question is a great way to start a conversation with someone who may not have thought about your issue. But the question must be neutral and of general interest in order to open the door to a two-way conversation. If I had opened the conversation on the street with "Do you support ranked-choice voting?" or worse, "Our election system needs to be reformed," I would have put all my cards on the table and closed the door to dialogue with most people. The point of opening with a neutral general-interest question is to arouse curiosity and encourage thinking, not to force people to take a position by making a challenging statement.

I recommend opening with a neutral general-interest question in all your communications—printed handouts, posters, mailers, emails, websites, and blogs. It's a great way to capture attention and engage your audience.

Be Focused on Solutions

No matter what your audience or issue, your communications need to focus on solutions. Your tone can convey the seriousness of an issue, but there should always be hopeful, positive, and encouraging language to accompany it. To get people to rally behind your cause, *you need to believe a positive outcome is possible.* Your audience will then perceive your "can do" attitude in your communications, and they will rally in support. Here are two examples of solutions-focused language:

1. Carbon emissions haven't just caused changes in the weather; they threaten our health and the health of the planet we depend on for sustenance. But that's only because we haven't fully implemented

the solutions. We know that once we fully implement renewable energy, practice regenerative agriculture and forestry, and reduce carbon emissions, we can address this threat.

2. Lawn chemicals seep into our water supplies and threaten wildlife and drinking water. But that's only because we haven't spoken out about it and demanded restrictions on the use of these chemicals. Once we call out this problem and establish new standards, we will stop this threat once and for all.

Solutions-focused communications can be stated positively or negatively. For instance, composting is a solution for food waste. But which of these statements is better to make?

- You should compost because it's good for the environment and you'll save on garbage collection fees.

- If you don't compost, you'll lose money because you'll have to pay more to have your garbage collected.

Similarly, you could say, "Help clean up our lake by reducing your use of lawn fertilizer and do a good thing for the environment"; or you could say, "If you continue heavy use of lawn fertilizer, our lake will fill with algae, and you will lose the chance to go boating and swimming." *Research shows that language that presents the loss of something due to inaction is more persuasive than language that emphasizes the positive aspects of taking action.*[6] Showing people what is at stake and specifically what they will lose adds impact to your communications.

Include a Call to Action

Many make the mistake of believing that building awareness is enough to create change. Social scientists call this the "information deficit model," which can be stated like this: "If people only knew more or had more information, they will be moved to do the right thing and support my cause."

Since the term was introduced in the 1980s, numerous social science studies have shown that the information deficit model isn't true. Studies on this have been conducted at universities including Oxford University and the University of Colorado.

I've had a longstanding dialogue with a friend about two old dams on a river near my home. He insists that once people see the sacredness of the river and understand how the dams prevent fish passage, they will support removing the dams. I disagree. Awareness and education about the river are not enough to bring about change. In addition to providing good information about the river, his group needs to ask residents to contact their town councilors and *demand they vote to remove the dams.*

Presenting town councilors with a petition from residents demanding they remove the dams would also work well in this situation. The point here is that your communications need to clearly communicate your purpose. If your purpose is to remove the dams, you need to say this directly: "Our group needs your vote to remove the dams."

You need a clear call to action no matter the size or scale of your effort. Your call to action could be asking people to recycle plastics in their home, or it could be calling for a ban on burning oil and gas nationwide. If you want people to take a specific action, you have to ask them specifically to do it.

Years ago, I worked in communications for a supermarket chain. While there I learned that even if your message is totally clear, a certain percentage of people will misinterpret it. If the store's grand opening is at 8:00 a.m. on Sunday, a certain number of people will show up at 8:00 a.m. on Saturday. If you need an appointment at the pharmacy to get a vaccine, a certain number of people will expect to walk in and be served without an appointment. I call this the "10% rule." If your message is clear, you can expect 10% of the people to misinterpret it. If your message is not clear, you can expect 50% or more to misinterpret it. You want to tilt the odds in your favor by making your call to action clear and direct.

Use Visuals Effectively

Visuals are a powerful way to communicate. Physical, in-person experience is the most powerful form of communication, which is why I took people on a tour in Denmark to learn about renewable and locally generated energy. But the next-most-powerful form of communication, falling just below personal experience and personal stories related in person, is visual communication. More than 350 million pictures a day are uploaded to Facebook, and more than 1.4 trillion photos were taken in 2020.[7] These days, photos and videos are a critical part of communications, especially if you want to reach younger audiences.

Two communications organizations, Climate Visuals and Resource Media, combined their research on climate images and videos. They used surveys and focus groups to test dozens of environmental photographs and videos with various audiences. Their research affirms many traditional communications principles. Here are ten core principles they recommend for using visual imagery, based on their research:

TEN TIPS FOR EFFECTIVE VISUAL COMMUNICATIONS

1. **Hook people at the beginning.**

   You must engage viewers right off the bat if you want them to continue watching a video or dig deeper into your report or website.

2. **Choose a credible character to whom the audience can relate.**

   Just as in selecting messengers for your campaign, characters in visual communications should be authentic, credible voices on the topic. People who are directly impacted by climate change or are personally reducing their carbon footprint make good characters. Whom does your audience trust? Whose fate do they care about?

3. Show real people.

In the research, audiences preferred authentic images over staged photo ops, which they saw as gimmicky or manipulative. Photos of politicians scored low on authenticity, although respected local leaders might score better. Showing real people doing real things works best and avoids stereotypes and generalizations.

4. Identify what emotions you are trying to evoke.

What emotions will get the viewer off the couch and inspired to take action? Anger about injustice? Fear that something precious will be lost? Inspiration to help restore or save something? There's nothing to be gained by downplaying the risks of climate change or toxic pollution. But, as mentioned earlier, potentially overwhelming images need to be coupled with images evoking hope through taking action. Solution-oriented images usually do the trick.

5. Tell new stories.

People tune out overtold or clichéd stories. Less familiar and more thought-provoking images can deliver a fresh message to the public. Go beyond polar bears and show people doing new things to address climate change.

6. Surprise, humor, and authenticity are the secrets to going viral.

Show your audiences something unique, unexpected, or delightful. Low production value doesn't matter if these qualities are present. Think of what you share online with friends and how that might be used in campaign communications.

7. Show climate causes at scale.

As we found in the chapter on framing, people often don't grasp the links between the causes and effects of climate change. Visual images can be used to make these connections. But to do that effectively, it's best to show these causes at scale.

Showing a congested highway conveys carbon emissions better than a single car on the highway. Showing a holding pen containing thousands of cattle conveys the scale of agricultural production more effectively than a single cow grazing or a plate of meat.

8. **Tap into your audience's values.**

   Determine your audience's values, and use those to drive your visuals. What are their worldviews, aspirations, and life-guiding principles? Do they value family health? Safety and prosperity? Food security? The outdoors? How might you convey these values in visual images?

9. **Include a healthy amount of tension.**

   Think about your favorite stories for books, films, or TV. Drama, conflict, and suspense are what keep you watching or reading until the end. Audiences want to know what will happen to the main character and will stay glued to their seats to find out. Use the same strategy in visual communications.

10. **Be clear about your call to action.**

    As we've said earlier, a specific ask is needed to motivate people to act. Your call to action should be repeated across all your platforms, from the caption of your photo to your website landing page to your fact sheets.[8]

Create a Core Message

If you are launching a campaign, you'll need a succinct core message that communicates who you are, what you are doing, and why it matters. This can be a sentence or several short paragraphs that answer these questions:

- What is the problem, and who is affected?
- What is the solution, and what should be done?
- Who are we, and what actions are we taking to solve the problem?

Here's an example:

SECURE AND SAFE FOOD AND DRINKING WATER

Many rural American families are denied a basic human right–affordable access to clean, safe drinking water. About 43% of all Americans draw their drinking water from the ground, and the vast majority of rural households rely exclusively on wells.

In some regions of the country, including Maine, one in five homes with wells have dangerously high levels of arsenic, uranium, manganese, and radon, which have been linked to lower IQ in children, and skin, lung, and bladder cancer over a lifetime. Yet fewer than half of well owners have tested their water for these toxic contaminants.

Defend Our Health supports model legislation to improve testing rates for wells, provides educational outreach, and secures funding to help low-income families afford water treatment systems. Public health scientists agree: we must give all children a healthy start by ensuring safe drinking water at home.[9]

Stay on Message No Matter What

Once you have crafted and tested your messages, you must stick with them throughout your campaign. This means educating your coalition members on your messaging, and reinforcing the messaging repeatedly. It means using your message consistently on every social media app, every printed piece, and in every presentation.

One of the challenges of staying on message comes when you face opposition. Research on your issue and meetings with adversaries should reveal the common objections to your issue. You should use this information to prepare for attacks.

Campaign leaders and advocates can get bored with their messaging and tired of answering the same objections over and over. Responding to the same questions and presenting the same information for months and years is an inevitable part of advocacy work. It helps to remember that your audience may have only heard the message once or twice.

Pause, Reflect, and Measure

It's pretty easy to fall in love with your clever taglines. Most people do. But are they working? It's important to pause and measure the feedback from those you are trying to connect with. Are people taking the actions you want? Donating to your cause? Showing up for events? Contacting decision makers?

One way to improve the success of your messages is to test them with a few members of your audience ahead of time. Remember that your planning team is not necessarily the audience. A good practice is to circulate messages you are considering to people who represent your audience, and ask them for feedback.

Many organizations and campaigns have a step-by-step communications pathway for engaging people. It might start with a website visit and then progress to attendance at an event, then a small donation, followed by attendance at a second event, then contacting decision makers, and then recruiting others to attend events and take action in support. You should consider how your supporters and decision makers receive your communications, and build in ways to measure their responses at each stage. Ways to do this include keeping attendance records at events, and using social media analytics to measure responses to online petitions, web visits, and surveys.

The key is to be honest with yourself about the effectiveness of your communications. If they are not resulting in people taking the actions you want, you'll need to review and revise them.

Select and Work with Credible Messengers

The messengers can be as important as the message. If you are running a campaign, you will need to select messengers who will speak in public, in front of a camera, or directly to decision makers. People who are part of your community, directly affected by your issue, and credible with the audiences you are trying to reach are best. This can be as simple as having a well-known decision maker speak in support of your proposal, which provides credibility and helps persuade other decision makers. Or you might ask people to publicly tell their personal story of how your issue has affected them.

Storytelling creates a platform for discussion and debate. A story's authentic messenger can convince people of the need for change and compel decision makers to act. The key is selecting messengers whom your audience can identify with and find believable. Your message has to be repeated as many as ten times before people will believe it, so you may want to engage multiple messengers to get your message across.

There's no best-practice model for engaging messengers and storytellers in your advocacy work, but a thoughtful and respectful approach will yield the best results. In community advocacy, people generally own their own stories, as opposed to having others tell their stories for them in case studies or testimony.

Nevertheless, advocates must be sure that consent for the use of a personal story is fully informed and freely given. Storytellers may have unrealistic expectations, e.g., if they tell their story they will get a visa, payment for injury, or ongoing personal support. If you will be using someone's personal story as part of your communications strategy, it is helpful to clarify the messenger's expectations ahead of time. In some cases you may want to create a written record of these expectations to refer to later.[10]

Inviting credible messengers to tell their story as part of your campaign empowers them. The very act of telling a personal story and being heard can be a powerful experience. A message delivered personally in a meeting, at a public event, or online is powerful and will have greater impact than written testimonies or case studies.

Talking Points, FAQs, and Handouts

Talking points are a succinct summary of the important points that describe your issue. They include your core message, a bit of background on the issue, and the benefits of supporting your cause. Talking points are used verbally in presentations, press conferences, and videos, and they are usually made available in written form on the web and as a handout. Their purpose is to give an overview to supporters and decision makers so they can grasp your issue quickly. They should be arranged with the most general or important points first, and more specific or supporting points following later. If possible, they should be limited to one page, and they should provide contact information for a designated person who can be reached for further information.

Advocates create talking points from their issue research (see chapter 8). As you learn more about your issue and address people's questions and concerns, you will probably revise and update your talking points. Anyone whom you've invited to speak or testify should be given your talking points as an outline for their personal remarks. Your talking points should include a clear call to action. Here's an example of talking points from a toxics campaign:

DESIGNATE PFAS AS A HAZARDOUS SUBSTANCE

LD 1923 will protect our public health and environment by providing access to federal funding to clean up toxic chemicals. Toxic PFAS are contaminating our lands and waters.

- So-called "forever chemicals," PFAS (per- and polyfluoroalkyl substances) pose significant health risks, particularly for pregnant women and children.
- Because PFAS do not break down, these chemicals remain in any environment they contaminate unless cleaned up.
- PFAS-contaminated sludge was spread on fields across Maine as fertilizer. Only a handful of the approximately five hundred farms that received sludge have been tested to date.

- PFAS have also been released into the environment through discharge of aqueous film-forming foam used by firefighters, contaminating both soil and water.

- The Maine Department of Environmental Protection needs funding to help clean up PFAS and other emerging contaminants. The hazardous substances bill (LD 1923) will allow the DEP to access federal funds for cleanup.

- Classifying PFAS as a hazardous substance would make contaminated sites—including fields, farms, and water—eligible to be targeted for cleanup using federal funds.

SUPPORT CLASSIFYING PFAS AS A HAZARDOUS SUBSTANCE. SUPPORT LD 1923. For more information, please contact XXXX.[11]

If your issue is complex, you should consider compiling a frequently asked questions (FAQ) list to post on your website and hand out at events. You'll need to provide answers to the questions, of course! An example of an FAQ handout is provided in appendix B.

Write a White Paper

If your issue is complex, you may also want to consider writing a "white paper," an article that gives in-depth background about your issue. The proposal to create a statewide consumer-owned electric utility is a good example. Talking points and shorter written pieces were not enough for decision makers to fully understand the nuances of this issue, so the coalition working on it wrote a twenty-five-page white paper to fully inform supporters and legislators. Different people wrote different sections of the white paper, with one person appointed as overall editor. This way, the workload was shared, and the resulting piece was consistent in format and writing style. The paper was circulated to legislators and made available on the web.

Send an Email

Writing clear, vivid, attention-getting emails is an important advocacy skill, especially when reaching out to decision makers. Here are some tips for creating effective emails.

The subject line or headline of your email—especially in emails to decision makers—is critically important. It can determine whether your email gets opened. A crisp subject line will make your email stand out in the deluge of emails flooding inboxes.

Your email subject line should be concise and active. Subject lines that work best are personal and suggest an action from the reader. There are many possible variations, such as:

Need Your Help

Reaching Out about X

Would Like Your Input

Quick Question

Two I use regularly are "Question for You" and "Connect with You." These signal that I need the receiver's personal help. People usually open these emails.

The body of your emails should be short and concise. You can always provide more information over the phone or through links. Bullet points convey a lot and are easy to skim through, so use them. The body of your email should include the subject or central question, a few relevant supporting points, and next steps. That's all. No one can spend a lot of time reading a single email. Yours need to be razor sharp.

If you're like me, you get invitations to join mass emails on issues every day. Here are several I received this week: "Let your representative know you care about the Arctic!" "Save the bees!" "Sign now and tell Congress: prioritize recovery efforts that protect communities." These emails are easy to do, and I encourage you to send them, if you are moved by the issue.

But be aware that a *personal email* always has more power than a mass email. It takes a bit more effort, but a personal message with a couple of lines about why you care about the issue and how it affects you and your community will make more of a difference.

Make a Call

Personal phone calls have a number of advantages over texts or emails. Emails can get lost in a thread or may be missed entirely among the overwhelming number of emails received in a day. Even more important, a phone call allows for two-way dialogue that can answer questions, generate new ideas, and establish camaraderie in a way that digital communications cannot. Phone calls should be used strategically, for example when you need to have a sensitive conversation or when you don't yet have the clarity to put your thoughts into writing.

Good phone communications are similar to email: leave a quick, to-the-point voicemail that begins with a strong opening line: "This is so and so calling, asking you to support the solar farm for the city." Then let the listener know when they can call you back with questions. It helps to write out your message before calling, so you are sure to get your key points across without stumbling or meandering.

One day I phoned my state representative to urge him to support solar legislation. When I first got him on the phone, he was extremely defensive. When I mentioned that I was calling personally because I had a longstanding interest in solar energy, his tone relaxed. After I said that, he was ready for a person-to-person chat. It turned out there had been a mass directive to call legislators that week, and he thought I was part of it. But I wasn't, and that cleared the way for an in-depth conversation that lasted forty-five minutes.

Thank-you calls are rare, but they can help build your relationship with supporters, opponents, and decision makers. Leave a simple voicemail saying, "This is so and so, and I'm calling to thank you for your support at the hearing yesterday." It takes just a few minutes, but the value of a thank-you call in building relationships is worth its weight in gold.

A CHECKLIST FOR
EFFECTIVE COMMUNICATIONS

☐ Frame your message in a way that aligns with the values, emotions, and beliefs of your important audiences.

☐ Use visual, active words.

☐ Be bold, confident, and focused on solutions.

☐ Make your message personal, and speak to your audience's emotions.

☐ Have a clear call to action.

☐ Use credible messengers.

☐ Use visuals wherever possible.

☐ Create a succinct core message for your issue, and use it everywhere.

☐ Test and measure your messages for effectiveness.

☐ Stay on message no matter what.

Delivering Your Message

Your framing and communications could be the sharpest in the world, and your messages could check each of the boxes listed above—but none of that matters if your messages never reach your intended audience. The next chapter will explain how to get your message into the right hands: those you want to influence.

13

Working with the Media and the Public

The media's the most powerful entity on earth. They have the power to make the innocent guilty and the guilty innocent, and that's power.

—MALCOLM X

Delivering Your Message

One winter afternoon while I was working on a petition drive for ranked-choice voting, I was driving down the highway with a stack of petitions in the back seat. I had the sudden insight that island commuters would be gathering at the ferry terminal right then, awaiting their boat home. Perhaps these commuters had already signed the petition; but perhaps no one had yet approached them. Making a snap decision, I turned off the highway and headed for the terminal.

When I opened the door to the lobby, I felt a blast of warm air on this chilly afternoon. The generous lobby was filled with commuters sitting on rows of benches. They were quietly chatting, knitting, reading, or staring off into space. It was about 30 minutes before their boat would board.

I got to work. Walking up and down the rows with my clipboard, I introduced myself, asked for signatures, and answered questions about the petition. I collected about forty signatures in thirty minutes—more than double the usual gathering rate, a veritable gold mine.

As this story illustrates, the key to effective communications is to capture people's attention *when and where* they can best receive your message. Going in person to the ferry terminal where people were waiting was the perfect way to deliver my message. If I'd advertised on the radio or TV during rush hour, or stood outside an office building at quitting time, it wouldn't have worked.

To deliver your message effectively, you need to think through the specifics of your audience: who they are, what their daily routine is, and how they get information. A helpful exercise is to walk through a typical day in the life of those you want to reach. Going further, you might ask people you want to reach for feedback on how and when they get information and how best to reach them.

Everyone is deluged with information these days. This makes it doubly hard to reach decision makers, supporters, and opponents—your audiences. This also makes it imperative to be strategic about how you spend your time. You could spend an entire day responding to emails, writing a blog post, writing an op-ed, sending an e-newsletter, or planning a public forum. But you can't do all of them in a day, so the question is: which investment of time will give you the best return? The answer lies in *who you are trying to reach and how they receive information.* You need to know these things.

This chapter addresses the when and where of communications. *You must deliver your message so your intended audience will receive it.* This is a complex subject with numerous strategies and tools. In order to use them well you need to have empathy: empathy for your audience as illustrated by the story above, and empathy for journalists by learning what they need and how they work.

Know Your Journalists

The days of print newspapers with rooms full of journalists checking facts and writing stories are largely gone. Many newspapers have gone under, merged, or migrated online. But real journalists still exist, and in our current world where anyone can publish anything, the value of true, researched journalism has never been higher.

I grew up in an era when journalism was called the "fourth branch of government." Journalism was the force that kept politicians, corporations, and anyone in power accountable to the people. Journalism still plays this role, but unfiltered, unresearched, and emotionally biased stories have grown up around true journalism, like weeds in a field of grain. Facts and opinions are mixed together in many written pieces, and it's sometimes difficult to tell the difference. Many people accept opinion as fact without realizing it, resulting in distorted views on the issues.

Even today, most true news stories begin with a newspaper. Radio, local TV stations, and community websites get some or all of their news from the paper. Many radio news broadcasts are nothing more than announcers reading the newspaper on the air.

In most places there are two kinds of papers: dailies and weeklies. These are quite different. City and regional dailies (which are rapidly replacing print with online versions) employ journalists who specialize in topics. These journalists know the issues and players in the topics they write about. Environmental advocates should seek out journalists who specialize in environmental issues, as well as those who cover city, county, or state governments.

The best strategy to get to know journalists is to ask for a personal meeting, either face to face or online. You can meet with an individual journalist or the editorial board, or both. You want editorial boards to know you and your issue so they will select your op-eds or letters for publication. You want individual journalists to know you and your group so they'll call you when they need information for a story. When I worked in a state fisheries agency, I got to know several fisheries writers. They would call me when they needed facts or data related to commercial fishing, and I was happy to provide it.

The purpose of meeting with journalists and editors is for them to get to know and trust you. A secondary purpose is for them to understand your issue. You want to get to know their backgrounds, too: where they live, where they went to school, what their areas of interest are. Even more important, you want to know their values, their frames of reference, the topics they focus on, and how they get information. According to a recent survey, 83% of journalists view Twitter as a valuable tool for engagement.[1] It's important to find out which communications channels they prefer so you can communicate with them effectively. You also want to be clear on who is a columnist writing opinion pieces, and who are reporters writing news stories.

Several years ago I joined a group that traveled to Texas to volunteer with immigrants coming into the United States from Mexico. When we returned, I contacted a writer at a local weekly, sending her photos and a press release summarizing our trip. The writer responded, and a descriptive story and several photos were published in the next edition of the paper.

At the same time, I emailed a well-known opinion columnist in our region and asked if he'd be interested in learning about our trip. He responded by asking if he could interview two of us, and we met him several days later at a coffee shop. We talked for an hour as he asked questions, took notes, and recorded the conversation. The result: a prominent opinion piece in the statewide Sunday paper. His column included where we went and what we did, but as an opinion piece, it also commented on US immigration policy and the difficulties it poses to immigrants fleeing to the United States.

Ideally, you begin building a relationship with journalists before you come out with a major initiative. If you do, they will be more likely to respond affirmatively and run your press release, opinion piece, or letter to the editor. If they know your group, they might send someone to cover your event. By proactively meeting with the newspaper and presenting your framing of an issue, you are setting the agenda. You hope to persuade the media to frame and cover your issue from your point of view.

But, like decision makers, journalists are independent, so you cannot control how they will cover your issue. They might write stories counter to your position; or, very commonly, they may have written a story and are looking to you to help fill in the details. But proactive work to build a relationship based on trust can help. Ideally, you want your group to be the go-to source for the media on your issue.

Many journalists seek to provide balanced and unbiased coverage, but all journalists have biases, whether acknowledged or not. All media outlets do, too, although some biases are more pronounced than others. Sinclair Broadcast Group is a large media conglomerate that owns 193 television stations, including affiliates of FOX, ABC, the CW Network, and others. They have chosen to run coverage of Republican events and campaigns leading up to elections, but they have not done the same for Democratic events.[2] Local TV and newspapers have more independence than national outlets, but corporate owners like Sinclair sometimes require them to run certain stories. As you build relationships with the media, you need to be aware of where they are coming from and what biases they may have.

According to a colleague who spent his career managing newspapers, many journalists enter the field idealistically, wanting to "comfort the afflicted and afflict the comfortable," as the saying goes. This is laudable. Unfortunately, news sources often manipulate cub reporters, and when their editors see this they may criticize the reporter's work, leading young reporters to feel manipulated and unappreciated. This, combined with continuous time pressure and short deadlines, tends to turn idealistic young journalists into disappointed, cautious, and sometimes cynical reporters.

Your honesty and your provision of good, in-depth information can help you surmount these obstacles. Still, you need to be aware of the constraints journalists are often under, and if they react to you negatively, don't take it personally.

On all the issues and campaigns I've worked on, media relations were handled by staff or volunteers of allied organizations. This is optimal, because your message is delivered to the press directly and unfiltered. Larger movements or organizations sometimes hire public relations professionals to help with media relations. PR people usually know a lot about specific media outlets and have longstanding relationships with journalists, and they can expand your coverage considerably. If you can afford a PR firm, I'd say go for it. But it's not necessary in order to get good press.

Local Weeklies

Local weekly papers can become your allies. There are four types of weeklies: free, paid, geographically focused (e.g., town or neighborhood), and issue focused. If you were to plot the four types, a chart would look like this:

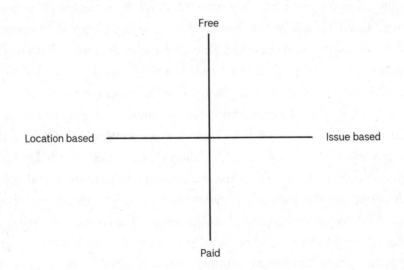

Environmental advocates should focus on geographically focused weeklies that cover towns or city neighborhoods. Weeklies or monthlies that focus on environmental issues are also worthwhile outlets for news and opinion about your issue. Free weeklies tend to be dominated by ads, with only a sprinkling of text. These are not worth your time. Issue-based weeklies and monthlies that don't address your issue, such as those with a health care theme, are not worth your time either.

All weeklies are strapped for cash. Writers are expected to turn around stories at lightning speed and don't have time for multiple interviews or detailed research. What they report is usually accurate, but they are relying on you for information. Writers who work for weeklies are looking for story ideas, so if you call them with a fresh story that has a clear connection to the communities they serve, you are bringing them a gift. This is easy to do. You can look in your local weekly to see who is writing stories you like, and then email or call them directly. If your story is interesting and relevant, they should respond right away.

Several years ago I was leading a project to install 128 solar panels on the roof of the large church where I'm a member. I picked a writer from the local weekly and emailed her about my solar panel story. I had a nice photo taken by the solar installer and offered that (with permission of course) to the paper, too. The result was a front-page story with a color photo.

Campus papers are a training ground for journalists. They are particularly useful if you want to reach students in support of your cause. But they tend to be infrequent, sometimes publishing only monthly and not during school breaks. Therefore, it's a good idea to use them to place features or opinion pieces, but not to organize events that are time sensitive. Contact information can be found in a campus paper available either on the newsstand or online, so you can reach out directly to the writers there.

Broadcast Media

Television is more powerful than print or radio because it delivers visual images. The key to getting the attention of TV news reporters is to build good visual images into your story. Early in my career, I used to be contacted by a TV station every year as winter approached, because I ran a store at the Maine Audubon Society. They would interview me outdoors next to a busy bird feeder on the topic of how to feed birds. Great visuals!

When you contact a TV news room, their first thought will be: how can we make a visual story out of this? The key to getting TV coverage is to offer a chance for local footage, featuring real people doing real things like picking up trash in a community cleanup or protesting on campus. If you contact a local TV station ahead of time, sometimes they will send a camera person to your event and follow up with a phone interview.

Don't expect in-depth analysis or coverage from local TV news. Time is of the essence on these programs. The average length of a local television news story is forty-one seconds. Prepare your communications for local TV as if it were a poster with a headline, a couple of points, and a photo. In contrast, national evening news stories average two minutes and twenty-three seconds long, and the most popular YouTube videos are four minutes and one second long.[3]

While public hearings and meetings sometimes get coverage, these are a lot less interesting visually than citizens engaging in activities. A colorful protest is more likely to get TV coverage than talking heads inside city council chambers.

If there's a public radio or TV station in your area, you will want to get to know them, too. Like weekly papers, public radio and TV stations are strapped for cash and need good stories. Public radio stations often have journalists who cover city, county, and state governments. Much of their work is done via telephone or taped interviews. It's a good idea to get to know them.

Reaching Out with Social Media

Social media is a powerful organizing tool. It gives you total control of your message and the ability to reach any group you want. Even authoritarian governments who want to discourage citizen action have difficulty controlling people who use social media to organize. Crowds can be organized in just hours to show up and make their voices heard.

Published and broadcast media are a one-to-many form of communication, where the broadcaster or publisher has full control of what you see and how it's presented. Even public responses (letters to the editor, guest columns, etc.) are controlled by the media outlet. The advantage to using published and broadcast media is the credibility you gain by having a third party determine that your issue is newsworthy.

In contrast, social media is a many-to-many form of communication in which participants select, present, and respond to each other. The concept is that people are free to post whatever they want, and anyone can opine on any topic. Examples of many-to-many communication include Facebook dialogues, blogs that allow for interactive discussion, and customer reviews of products and services. Most interactive forums are now limited to friends, followers, and subscribers in order to avoid hate speech or off-topic contributions. But many-to-many communication is why social media has become so powerful—and so dangerous in terms of accuracy.

The downside of social media is that your opponents can use it too. Most social media stories are unfiltered and unresearched, unless provided by a credible news outlet or a research organization. The true story about your issue can be distorted beyond recognition on social media. As a colleague asked me the other day, how do you respond when you say something is blue and your opponents say, "No, it's green"? When others are living in a totally different world from yours, communication can be difficult. The trick is to keep the discussion focused on the facts of people's real experience, and to address their fears directly, as discussed earlier. This will help keep the discussion grounded in the present.

During the coronavirus pandemic, I heard a story about a woman who had social media connections who believed the disease was a hoax. The woman was engaged in social media discussions with her friends about this while her husband was in intensive care with COVID-19. After wrestling with what to say, she finally came out and told her social media friends the truth about her husband. This took courage. But she was able to bring the discussion from an imagined reality back to the present by telling her true story.

Everyone needs to be more discerning these days. We need to check facts and sources before forwarding articles to friends. We need to question stories that lack credibility or attack someone's reputation. And we need to tell our true personal stories, as the woman above did. If we do these things, we will be inviting others to do the same.

As an environmental advocate, you can and should use social media to share information, hold meetings, provide webinars and trainings, and solicit feedback. A key concept in social media is your "platform." Your platform is your interlocking social media websites and applications that connect with and feed each other. You can share multiple types of content—photos, videos, and text—across multiple platforms, significantly increasing your impact. A common example is to use Twitter and Facebook to connect users to a blog, website, or video that provides more in-depth coverage of your issue.

Your platform is also the total number of followers and audiences you have on your social media sites. New social media apps, platforms, tools, and features are introduced continually. The four types of social media that advocates generally use are given below. You will want to be strategic in how you use these.

1. **Social networks:** best for posting short pieces, but can also be used for video events. Examples: Facebook, LinkedIn, Twitter.

2. **Video sharing:** best for sharing videos. Examples: Vimeo, YouTube, Pinterest.

3. **Blogging/community/forums:** these can be effective if you know which sites your audiences use. Examples: Tumblr, Reddit, Medium,

as well as blogs attached to news outlets, including city newspapers and online publications.

4. **Sharing economy networks:** best for fundraising. Examples: GoFundMe, Kickstarter, Patreon.

One of the obvious changes brought about by the coronavirus was the increased use of social media to work remotely, convene events, educate, socialize, and organize. Interactive features and tools will continue to improve. There are many advantages to the increased use of social media that are here to stay. When my church posted its worship services on Facebook, YouTube, and its website, its audience increased by more than 300%. A coalition I belong to organized an online fundraiser with virtual drinks and hors d'oeuvres, featuring several guest speakers. The coalition raised $25,000 in just over an hour. The cost? Zero.

A side effect of the increasing use of social media is the need to keep your distribution lists and social media sites up to date. For each e-newsletter I send out to my list of three thousand five hundred email addresses, about 5% bounce back. Some of these have to be removed manually from the list, and there are always new names to add—a tedious and time-consuming task.

When I was canvassing door to door to get out the vote, 95% of the names on the list I was given didn't match the people who opened the door. The area I canvassed in was mostly low-income apartments that turn over frequently. I enjoyed talking with the people who were there, but I was unable to collect data for the names on the list, which was part of the purpose of the activity. It would have helped greatly if the list was up to date!

There are three important tasks in managing your group's social media sites and activities: managing lists and contacts, creating and updating content, and managing technical functionality. There's nothing worse than having outdated information on your website or lists, or having site functions not work. This reflects badly on your organization.

Different audiences prefer and use different social media platforms differently, too. These preferences are changing constantly. In addition to managing the three tasks above, it helps to have a social media manager who can keep up with the changing landscape and make sure your messages are reaching the intended people.

In considering your group's approach to social media, you need to ask yourself how much time and budget you have to devote to social platforms. What social media platforms do your audiences use? And what is your purpose in using social media? Once you have clear answers to these questions, your group needs to appoint volunteers or hire people to make sure all your social media management tasks are covered.

Send a Press Release

If you are planning a press conference or a direct action event, you want to let the media know ahead of time. This is usually done through a press release sent three to four business days in advance. Your press release should be a brief document describing the issue, giving details of the event, and naming a contact person. Send your press release directly to journalists you know and to other media outlets in your area. Follow up with a phone call, text message, or email to the most important journalists to make sure they received it. The follow-up call is important; journalists can be deluged with information, and it's easy for them to miss your release.

To make your press release stand out, it helps to have a strong headline. Including the names of important people who will be speaking or the number of people you expect to turn out for your event in a headline works well. Use active verbs and specific points of interest in the headline, too.

Early in my career, I had to write press releases for supermarket grand openings. This was challenging because there's nothing controversial or interesting about a supermarket opening. To spice up my press releases, I included community stories using local celebrities. "Professional Hockey Players to

Greet Shoppers at Store Opening, Mayor to Cut Ribbon" was a strong head-line. Local weeklies actually printed this story! Keep in mind that the word "news" includes the word "new." The media are seeking things that are new and different and therefore newsworthy. Here are a couple more sample headlines:

Hundreds Expected to Protest Tuesday on Mandatory Vaccine Bill

Governor Mills Ready to Sign Statewide Plastic Bag Ban

The location of a press conference can also help make it newsworthy. If you are having a press conference about removing a dam, you might want to hold it at the base of the dam where fish are struggling to find a way to swim upriver. If your group is opposing a development, hold your press conference at the development site.

The body of the press release should be arranged in an "inverted pyr-amid" format, with the most important information at the beginning and less important details below. This is crucial, because publications will often cut a press release to fit the space they have, and the bottom paragraphs may not make the cut. Here's a graphic illustrating this format:[4]

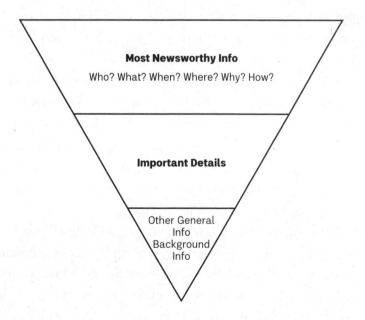

Your initial paragraph should cover the who, what, when, why, and where of your announcement and entice journalists to read further. This should be followed by several paragraphs providing more detail and offering one or two quotes from key spokespeople. You will want to say just enough to stimulate questions from journalists.

An advocacy secret is that you can write quotes yourself and then send them to the person they are attributed to for approval. They will either give their OK as is, or rewrite them in their own words. No interviews are necessary. In appendix B, you'll find a sample press release you can use as a template.

Hold a Press Conference

Press conferences are a great way to get the word out about your cause. With a press conference, you show decision makers there's strong support for your issue, which puts added pressure on them to come over to your side. A successful press conference will also build public support through media coverage. Press conferences can be standalone events, or they can be coupled with direct action. During the Global Climate Strikes in 2019, a press conference to call for action on climate change was held after a colorful march through the city to Portland's city hall.

In planning a press conference, you need to find credible speakers who can deliver your talking points. Typical speakers include supportive decision makers, key allies and partners, and citizens directly affected by the issue. Advocates usually prepare scripts or talking points in advance for the speakers. You hope to strike a balance between getting across key talking points and leaving room for speakers to share a related personal story or anecdote. Three or four speakers is usually plenty.

When selecting speakers, you want to identify people who are comfortable being interviewed on camera or on a microphone. Some groups offer media coaching to speakers prior to an event. Some people can tell their story credibly without coaching, while others may need some help. You should check in with each invited speaker to see what they need in order to become a star witness for your cause.

It's important that anyone speaking with the media have the framing and talking points of your group clearly in mind. Coaching should include reviewing and editing a script so the spokesperson is comfortable with it, and practicing reading the remarks aloud so the spokesperson can become comfortable delivering them.

To keep the audience's attention, you want speakers to be concise, limiting them to five minutes each. Your press conference is not a time for campaign speeches or discussion of unrelated issues. With some speakers you may have to be explicit about this.

One way you can reassure yourself and your speakers that all points will be covered is to plan multiple ways to provide information at your event. You can have plenty of handouts available, you can plan a Q&A session with the media, and you can provide online links to further information. The media will often interview individual speakers following a press conference. This is a time when speakers can elaborate in more detail, too.

In planning a press conference—or any event—it's important to appoint someone to be the media liaison. This person should reach out to journalists ahead of time to make sure they're aware of the event. At the event, this person should be 100% focused on greeting the media, providing information, and introducing them to people they may want to interview.

Write a Letter to the Editor

Letters to the editor (LTEs) are an easy and effective way to advocate. Instructions for where and how to send them and any requirements (such as maximum word counts) can be found on publication websites.

LTEs are very short pieces, usually limited by the publisher to 250 or 300 words. They are usually, but not always, in response to something published previously in that publication (which can be print or online). They contain just one or two supporting points. Here's a four-point template for writing an LTE:

1. **Grab the reader's attention.**

   Your opening line should summarize concisely what the letter is about and compel the reader to continue reading. Be sure to specifically reference the story or issue you are responding to.

2. **Make one, two, or three points that support your point of view.**

   This is the body of your letter. It should be concise and to the point. The focus should be on why you support or oppose the issue, or the positive or negative consequences of the issue or action.

3. **Summarize with a call to action.**

   What do you want people to do? What needs to happen? State this clearly.

4. **Sign your name.**

   Signing your name and town should be mandatory. Anonymous letters are weak and less likely to be published. If you have a title or position related to the focus of your letter, that should be included.

Here are two sample letters to the editor, with opposing views about the same article that appeared in the *Working Waterfront* newspaper.[5]

CRISIS CONFIRMED

To the editor:

Ideological media outlets have been pushing misinformation about science to unsuspecting people like the gentleman whose column "Media to blame for youth's eco anxiety" appeared in your December/January issue, and unfortunately he has been misled by their foolishness.

Contrary to what he wrote, there is indeed a consensus amongst the vast majority of climate scientists, and it is based on hard evidence. My wife, a marine biologist, and I lived on a marine research station on the shore of the Irish Sea during the 1970s, and we knew then that the evidence was overwhelming and conclusive.

All the science since then has deepened our understanding and confirmed the urgency of the crisis. Changes in the earth's climate caused by human activity are leading us toward environmental catastrophe, and society needs to take it seriously and act on it now. To do otherwise would be irresponsible.

David P. Lennox; Exeter, N.H.

RIGHT ON TARGET

To the editor:

Mark Preston's guest column, "Media to blame for youth's eco anxiety," which asserted "There is no scientific consensus on climate change," was right on target. The global-warming hysteria has gotten out of control. The "guesstimates" about this are absurd and are being promoted by people who know little about the climate and how it functions.

It is most unfortunate that Gov. Janet Mills is again wasting our tax money by having a thirty-nine-member climate change committee. Beware, climate change people will put whales before lobstermen and women. They will accomplish three things: increase our taxes, waste tax money, and give us dumb, unneeded regulations.

There always has been and will be climate change. Man can do nothing about it. God created climate and he is in charge of it.

The real problem is that in the past, and currently, development has been too close to the water. To help alleviate problems, garbage dumping in the oceans must cease, development in ecologically sensitive areas must stop completely, and wetlands must be preserved and enhanced.

Fred Hartman; Whiting

Letters versus Op-Eds: What's the Difference?

Op-eds are opinion pieces that usually range from five hundred to seven hundred words. They used to be published on the newspaper page opposite from the paper's in-house opinion pieces, and "op-ed" literally means "opposite the in-house editorial page." Many news outlets welcome guest editorials, opinion pieces, and guest blog posts.

The primary difference between LTEs and op-eds is that op-eds are longer and treat their topic in more depth. They are usually standalone pieces not written in response to previously published pieces, although occasionally there are exceptions. Op-eds often have three, four, or five supporting points instead of the one or two typical of an LTE. You can find sample op-eds by searching for "climate op-eds" or "environmental op-eds" online.

Participate in Hearings, Public Meetings, and Task Forces

Legislative committees hold hearings regularly. In most states, a legislative council decides which bills will get a hearing. In rural states like Maine, every bill gets a hearing, and bills on the same topic are heard at the same time. In cities, hearings on controversial issues are held, and committee chairs can be petitioned to hold a hearing if one hasn't been scheduled.

To influence a legislative council or city committee chair to hold a hearing, you'll want to contact campaign donors and people who have been affected by the issue and have them email, call, or write the committee chair requesting a hearing. An informal petition signed by supporters can also be helpful in moving a council or committee chair to call for a public hearing.

Many public meetings, including those held by town and city councils, county commissions, and legislative bodies, include a public comment period at the end. These are less formal than public hearings. If you attend in person, you might decide spontaneously to speak, or you might prepare comments in advance to present orally and submit in writing. Usually there's no required format for making public comments, although you should always identify yourself and any group or organization you represent. Both oral and written comments are usually accepted and do become part of the public record. Many groups will submit written comments in the form of a letter to the chair of the body hosting the comment session.

Asking that a task force be appointed is another way to raise your issue with decision makers. Task forces are an opportunity to thoroughly air an issue and consider multiple points of view. Task force members are usually appointed by the governing body, and you will want to be sure your view is represented. Directly contact the person or office making appointments and make the case that your organization should have a seat at the table.

In the best cases, a task force will be run fairly, with a chance for all to speak and deliberations made public both during and after meetings are held. In worst cases, task forces can be run by biased chairs who don't allow opposing views or have a predetermined outcome in mind. If this happens, you will need to make this known to the governing authority and perhaps the media. If you don't get results, you may want to activate your supporters to put pressure on those you need to influence, both directly with emails and calls, and on social media. The threat of public criticism is often enough to influence task force leaders and move deliberations and recommendations in your favor.

Task forces can be heavy on process, with numerous meetings, presentations, and interim reports. If you participate, you'll need to commit to the entire process. The end result of a task force is usually a set of recommendations on the topic discussed. A final report or presentation is usually given to the governing body that called for the task force. In some cases, a task force may be authorized to produce legislation that will then go through the legislative process.

If your group or point of view is not represented in a task force report, you may want to prepare a response. Many groups despair when recommendations don't include their views or go their way. But you always have the option of issuing your own report and using the media and social media to bring attention to it.

Give Testimony

Environmental leaders are often looking for people to testify in front of legislative committees or give formal comments in front of city or town councils. Or you may decide to testify yourself. Public hearings are formal opportunities to share your stories and heartfelt views on an issue. Both informal public comments and formal testimony need to follow the communications guidelines we've reviewed in this book:

- Articulate who you are and why you are here.
- Show persuasively why decision makers should support your position.
- Use clear, visual language.
- Include a call to action.

Formal testimony ranges from highly technical arguments presented by experts to personal stories related to the issue provided by citizen advocates. In hearings that are open to the public, anyone can testify. Remember that all testimony becomes part of the public record. This means your name, address, and written and oral remarks become available to anyone, including the press. These days, public testimony is usually available online following hearings. Examples of different kinds of testimony are provided in appendix A.

Oral testimony is often given a time limit, sometimes as short as three minutes. If this is the case, you'll want to give highlights of your testimony and focus on points that other testifiers haven't made.

Even if your oral testimony is abbreviated, your written testimony can and should provide a full explanation of your position. Formal written testimony follows an official format, which varies slightly by state, county, or city. All formal written testimony includes the following elements:

1. Address the committee chairman and committee members.

2. State your name, where you live, and the organization you are representing. This is your "Who Are You and Why Are You Here?" story.

3. Clearly state whether you support or oppose the resolution or bill, and be sure to identify the bill by its number and author.

4. Concisely summarize the reasons for your position. These are your talking points.

5. Share a personal story or anecdote that relates to the issue, if you have one.

6. Summarize your position clearly.

7. State your call to action, such as "I urge you to support XYZ bill."

8. Thank the committee for their time, and offer to answer their questions.

The following testimony illustrates these elements:

Required format {

IN SUPPORT OF LD 1923, "DESIGNATE PFAS AS A HAZARDOUS SUBSTANCE"

Before the Environment and Natural Resources Committee
January 24, 2020

On behalf of
Maine Council of Churches
Rev. Richard Killmer

Greeting the chairs and committee {

Senator Carson, Representative Tucker, and members of the Environment and Natural Resources Committee: I am Rev. Richard Killmer, a retired Presbyterian minister.

Who is he and why is he here {

The Maine Council of Churches supports LD 1923, "Designate PFAS as a Hazardous Substance." My denomination is a member of the council. The Maine Council of Churches has seven member-denominations that represent 437 congregations with fifty-five thousand members across the state.

State governments have a responsibility to protect the people of the state. We in the faith community affirm that task and view it as paralleling the work of God. Psalm 12:5 states, "Because the poor are plundered and the needy groan, I will arise, says the Lord, and I will protect them from those who hurt them."

Talking points {

I urge you to pass LD 1923 because toxic PFAS (per- and polyfluoroalkyl substances) is contaminating Maine's land and waters, and threatening the health of Maine children and families today and in future generations. This important legislation will allow the Department of Environmental Protection to finally prioritize and clean up contaminated sites, protecting Maine's most vulnerable populations from these dangerous chemicals.

Talking points (continued)

It is particularly urgent to address these so-called "forever chemicals" because they remain in any environment they contaminate unless cleaned up. We already know that PFAS-contaminated sludge was spread on fields across Maine as fertilizer, and only a few of the approximately five hundred farms that received sludge have even been tested to date.

Right now, there are farmers, families, and communities in Maine that have learned their land or water is contaminated with PFAS—yet the state is unable to even start the process of prioritizing sites for cleanup.

There is evidence that PFAS interferes with normal brain development in children. PFAS also increases the risk of some cancers, may lower a woman's chance of getting pregnant, and have been associated with liver problems and increased cholesterol levels. They are so ubiquitous that over 97% of Americans have these chemicals in their bloodstream—including newborn babies.

Summary statement

The council is especially concerned about the health impacts of toxic chemical exposure from PFAS on lower-income families as well as children and teens whose young bodies are developing and whose potential parenting years are well in front of them.

Maine needs LD 1923 to help protect our most vulnerable populations from harm to their health, and to preserve our farms and beautiful environment for future generations.

Call to action

Please support classifying PFAS as a hazardous substance, and vote to pass LD 1923. Thank you.

"Neither for nor against" Testimony

Why would someone testify "neither for nor against" (NFNA) an issue? This neutral position is a valuable tool. It is used when you have relevant information to add to the discussion but don't want or need to take a position. You would use it if your group is internally divided on an issue or if you wish to avoid impacting how decision makers might respond to another issue that's important to you. Or you might use it when the full implications of a proposal, bill, or resolution are not yet clear. When a proposal to transition the ownership of Maine's electric utilities from investor owned to consumer owned was introduced, many groups testified NFNA. A primary reason was that the specifics of this complex proposal were not yet clear.

I often testified NFNA when I was a lobbyist working in the administration for the governor. By taking an NFNA position, I could present pertinent information without directly involving the governor in the politics surrounding an issue.

Use Petitions to Let Governments Know What You Want

Citizen initiatives (also called ballot initiatives and public referendums) are powerful tools for voters to tell governments what they want. Not all petitions carry the same weight, though. Statewide citizen initiatives are formally defined and regulated by state law, and if they pass they result in policy change. Twenty-seven states and the District of Columbia have a citizen initiative process. There are no provisions for formal citizen initiatives at the federal level.

Many cities also allow formal citizen initiatives; 76% of the ten largest cities in each state allow them.[6] Citizen initiatives in these cities carry legal weight and result in policy change when successful. In Austin, Texas, four types of citizen-initiated petitions are allowed:

1. Citizen-initiated petitions that allow voters to propose a new ordinance

2. Referendum petitions that allow voters to propose repealing ordinances before they take effect

3. Recall petitions that allow voters to remove a mayor or a member of the city council

4. Charter-amendment petitions that allow voters to propose changing the city charter[7]

A citizen petition in Seattle stopped a development that would have turned 90% of the Pike Place Market into offices, hotels, and a parking garage. Volunteers gathered twenty-five thousand signatures in three weeks. Despite the developers' well-funded advertising campaign, the referendum against the development passed with 75% of the vote.[8]

Citizen initiatives were originally conceived as a way to allow voters to circumvent legislatures that were biased toward wealthy special interests. This is still true today. However, the cost of gathering signatures and mounting statewide referendum campaigns, particularly in large states like California, have made citizen initiatives too expensive for many grassroots groups.

Wealthy special-interest and corporate groups now use "citizen" initiatives as a tool to further their interests. In Washington state, agriculture interests including DuPont, Monsanto, PepsiCo, and Nestlé contributed $20 million to oppose labeling to identify genetically modified ingredients in food products. On the other side, in favor of the proposal, organic producer Dr. Bronner's Magic Soaps spent just $2.2 million. Voters rejected the proposal.[9]

Informal citizen petitions are not legally binding, but they are useful in influencing decision makers. These measures are especially effective at the city, county, and town level. If you want a community garden or a solar farm to be located on city property, writing up a petition and getting residents to sign it is a powerful move. It is not legally binding, of course, but what city or town councilor will ignore dozens of constituents asking for something like this?

Many environmental advocates have used informal petitions, often conducted online, to further their agenda. I am invited to sign petitions every week via email. Recent examples include "Help Protect the Right to Vote!" and "Climate Change: It's Time to Speak Up!"

How Formal Petitions Work

In cities and states that allow citizen initiatives, there are two ways to put a ballot question in front of voters. One is legislative, in which a state legislature or city council passes a bill to put a question in front of voters. This process is used in most states for funding large public projects, such as roads, bridges, airports, or stadiums. These ballot questions cite the cost and purpose of the project and how the project will be financed. In California and a number of other states, legislatures can refer three types of issues to voters as ballot questions: constitutional amendments, state statutes, and bond issues.

A question can also be put before voters as a result of a citizen initiative. In this case, a required number of signatures (usually a percentage of voters in the previous election) must be gathered and then certified by the city or state. If certified, the citizen initiative appears as a referendum question in the next election. Citizen initiatives are highly regulated, with slightly different rules in each jurisdiction that allows them. If a citizen-generated ballot question passes, then the city or state must hold a hearing on it and is likely to pass a law to implement it. Here are some of the reasons you might choose to gather signatures for a ballot initiative:

- It is required in order to amend a state constitution (eighteen states require this).

- Decision makers need to see citizen support before giving their support to an issue.

- A group is unhappy with a government decision and wants to overturn it.

- A group wants to raise the level of importance of their issue and build citizen support for it.

Regulations governing citizen initiatives vary by city and state, but the following eight-step process is typical:

1. File an application to conduct a citizen initiative with the city or state, along with draft petition language, which will become law if the petition and referendum vote are successful.

2. The state or city reviews the proposed language and amends or approves it.

3. The citizen group reviews amendments, makes changes, and gives final approval. (Steps 2 and 3 often take several iterations before language becomes final.)

4. The state or city prepares and prints petitions, with title, summary, and detailed language.

5. The citizen group gathers the required number of signatures. Campaigns usually gather more than the required number, to make up for any signatures that may not be certified. In California, campaigns must report to the state when 25% of the required signatures have been collected.

6. Submit petitions to the governing body for verification. Several levels of verification may be required.

7. Conduct a campaign to build voter support for the petition.

8. Referendum held on election day.

If you do decide to go forward with a citizen initiative, you will need a lot of people to organize the signature-gathering process, and many volunteers to gather signatures. It's important to know all the laws surrounding citizen initiatives. Failing to have petitions notarized, having inaccurate voter addresses, not following the prescribed process, or incorrectly filling out petition forms are just some of the ways signatures can be invalidated. You want to check the rules and make sure everyone working on your petition complies, so all signatures will count.

Sometimes groups hire contractors to gather signatures and pay them by the signature. While this might help you meet a deadline, paid signature gatherers are usually not well versed in your issue and may not represent your cause as well as you'd like.

Once I encountered a paid signature gatherer on the street who represented a petition falsely. His opening line was, "Do you want to sign a petition to increase education funding?" As I was about to sign, I glanced at the petition title at the top of the petition form. It read, "An Act to Permit a Casino in York County." I asked him what percentage of casino revenues would be used for education. He didn't know the answer nor where I could get more information, signaling that he was a paid gatherer. I'm not in favor of casinos, even if a small percentage of the earnings supports education, so I declined to sign. Volunteers who are passionate and knowledgeable about your issue are always your best signature gatherers.

Host a Public Forum

A great way to build support for your issue is to hold a public forum or a conference. Too often an issue only gets discussed when there is a decision on the table, awaiting action. This raises the stakes and adds tension to the discussion, as people take positions and defend their side. When there's pressure to make a decision, there's little room for a relaxed dialogue to discover the nuances and implications of an issue. In contrast, public forums and conferences provide an unpressured opportunity to explore an issue and all its ramifications. They are ideal for developing ideas and building consensus for public policy.

Public forums can range from informal, after-dinner neighborhood gatherings to full-day conferences with keynote speakers and breakout sessions. The reasons you might choose to host a public forum include:

- You need to educate your decision makers and show them the public supports your position.

- You want to raise public awareness, attract media attention, and build public support for your issue.

- You and your community of advocates want to learn from experts.

- You want to hear and share stories of people's experiences related to your issue.

- You want to lay the groundwork for developing public policy.

The simplest kind of forum is a neighborhood or community event to learn about and discuss a community issue. Events like this were common when I worked to improve internet access in rural communities. People would come together, often in the evening with several speakers, to talk about broadband options for their community.

Similar gatherings take place when communities want to take action on climate change. I've attended regular forums hosted in the home of a friend where there will be food, maybe a soup and salad, and an informal presentation and a question-and-answer session on a climate-related topic. These forums provide education and networking opportunities.

Small, focused community forums are easy to organize, cost little, and can be very productive. If you are trying to influence a decision maker, you can invite them to attend. If you are trying to learn from experts, you can invite them to speak. Most speakers will not charge for attending a two-hour community gathering, although you may want to compensate marginalized individuals. An offer of a free meal (if you are serving food) and compensation for mileage is the usual standard.

Larger conferences take a great deal of planning, usually beginning nine to twelve months in advance. While the details of conference planning are beyond the scope of this book, there are two important things to think about when contemplating a conference:

- Who is hosting it?

- Why would people attend?

I've attended numerous forums and conferences over the years. Those that are worthwhile always focus on a specific topic, include experts who can offer depth and perspective, and have ample time for participant networking and input.

Government agencies at the state and regional level will often host conferences. The people who attend these usually do so because they want their voice to be heard by the hosting agency. They want to be seen and have input. Attendees also want to know and respond to what other groups are saying on the issue. Many (but not all) government-hosted conferences can be informative and well worth your time.

Conferences hosted by community and nonprofit groups usually offer a chance to learn about and share ideas on a topic of interest. People attend usually because they want to learn from, share, meet, and network with others. Out-of-state expert speakers add stature to these events and will attract participants and media. Nonprofits and community groups will often partner as conference hosts, to increase and broaden participation.

Self-organizing forums can also be useful for gathering public input. In these forums, a general question or theme is announced, and then participants form their own breakout groups, based on their interests. Sometimes called "unconferences," "open space," or "open forums," these meetings intentionally avoid the hierarchical aspects of conventional conferences, including sponsored or expert presentations and prescribed breakout topics. Because self-organizing forums are focused on people's true interests and attendee participation, they tend to be highly creative and energized. They work best when a group is truly seeking solutions and wants to work together to find them.[10]

Meet Your Audiences Where They Are

Communications evolve continuously. As an environmental advocate, you will sometimes be initiating and sometimes responding to others in your communications. You and your allies will need to gain skills in media relations, tactics, and tools. You will learn how to organize events and create messaging that gets media and public attention. You will come to understand the biases and constraints of the media outlets and journalists you work with. You will use these skills and tools on an ongoing basis.

But no matter how you craft your messages and get them out, you will need to meet your audiences where they are—physically, online, and emotionally. To be effective, you'll need to understand how they go about their day, how they receive information, how they think, how they view the world, and what they are afraid of. You must get to know all these things in order to move your issue forward. If you do this successfully, you will move everyone toward a healthier, more equitable, and more compassionate world.

14

Epilogue:
Eight Reasons to Be
Optimistic in Troubled Times

Faith is the substance of things hoped for, the evidence of things not seen.

—HEB. 11:1

Will we make it?

This question is on many minds. We worry. We get anxious. A better question to ask is, "What do we want our future to be, and how do we get there?" I invite you to join me in envisioning the future we want, and then take steps to realize it.

VISION

All life on earth is respected, revered, and nurtured

- No race, class, gender, or any group of people is judged to be better or worse than any other.
- All people have access to fresh water, nutritious food, and safe housing.
- The earth's natural ecosystems are thriving. Farming, forestry, and fishing both harvest and replenish the earth's bounty.
- Every child has a healthy, loving, and safe home.
- All people have access to affordable, high-quality health care.
- All people have an opportunity to learn, in a wide variety of high-quality educational settings.
- All people have an opportunity to succeed in expressing their unique gifts in the world.
- Every woman can choose the number of children she has.
- Governments set reasonable rules based on what the majority wants, and enforcement of those rules emphasizes helping violators find a better path rather than punishing them.
- The world economy serves people equitably, is based on providing goods and services people need, and is not dominated by fear, lack, or greed.
- The world's unique peoples and cultures respect each other's differences and live in peace.

You may have additions to this list. And yes, you may call me a Pollyanna. But before you do, let me lay out the case for a big vision, and then provide evidence to support it. You see, when we *focus on the future we want*, the steps that could take us there begin to emerge from the fog. And when we act on those steps, as millions are doing, we feel energized and rewarded.

Here are eight reasons to be optimistic, despite the current difficulties. I offer these as a foundation for choosing the positive and working toward a future that works for everyone.

1. Creative and proactive people are everywhere.

I got chills when the town of Cranberry Isles, with just 140 year-round residents living on three islands off the coast of Maine, voted to borrow $2.1 million to build a state-of-the-art fiber broadband network to serve their community—a huge commitment. That was several years ago. Their network is now up and running. In working with communities, I'm continually inspired by the people I've met and the things they've accomplished.

In many rural and inner-city neighborhoods, addiction, unemployment, and hopelessness are real concerns. But people everywhere are stepping up to address these concerns. The constant flow of bad news in the media tends to drown out the good things that are happening. The COVID-19 pandemic put a dent in our communities by shuttering small businesses, isolating families, and disrupting schools and work. But human creativity is alive and well. Creative, proactive people are everywhere, pitching in to help. What are local citizens creating in your hometown or neighborhood? What might you create?

2. Young adults embrace diversity and economic equality.

The world is witnessing an extraordinary shift. The generations that grew up with the internet and lived through two recessions are the least prejudiced and most empathic of any generation in recent history. Sixty-two percent believe that "increasing racial and ethnic diversity is a good thing for our society."[1] They champion the rights of women, people of color, LGBTQ people, poor people, and people with disabilities.

A report commissioned by the Career Advisory Board found that among young adults in their twenties and thirties, "doing work that is personally meaningful is just as important as earning a high salary," with 30% identifying meaningful work as "the single most important measure of a successful career."[2] The same study showed that 23% of American college students have studied abroad, and 73% favor liberal immigration policies.

According to futurist Jeremy Rifkin, these generations measure freedom as "having access to a diversity of experiences, rather than by owning property."[3] This shift away from ownership and toward a sharing economy will continue to have a profound effect on the economy, our culture, and the environment. Young adults are leading the world toward a more equitable society where respect for others will dominate.

3. Advocates can build on existing models.

In the 1960s and 1970s, Denmark was a small, poor country, reliant on imported oil, and located far from markets, with an aging, almost all-White population. So what did the Danes do? They invested in people and they worked together. They made a commitment to equality and a fair economy. They made their schools the best in the world. They crafted and implemented aggressive sustainability goals. Norway, Sweden, Finland, and Iceland followed suit. These countries are now in the top ten most prosperous countries in the world. They also lead the world in renewable energy and reduced carbon emissions.[4]

Scandinavians are good at working together. They've embraced cooperatives in manufacturing, banking, insurance, retail sales, wind, solar, biomass, housing, agriculture, and child care. Scandinavian countries are stable and prosperous, with more startup companies and entrepreneurs per capita than the United States.[5]

You may argue that these countries have high taxes. They do, but they also have higher wages. Minimum wages are double what they are in the United States, and health care is free. Among other things, their prison population is 75% smaller, mental illness and obesity rates are 66% lower, and trust in others is 75% higher than in the United States.[6] When you add up the costs and benefits, the balance is on their side. We can learn from the best practices of other countries and craft our own version of an economic model that supports equality and the earth that sustains us.

4. We have the tools for change.

Not only do we have models of what works; we have the tools to get there. As I reflect I can see many big changes that have taken place just during my lifetime. I remember the women's movement in the 1970s. At that time, there were women's consciousness-raising groups meeting in living rooms across the country. We learned to run campaigns and lobby for change. Women advanced in sports, politics, nonprofits, and business. More action for gender equality is needed, but we know how to do this!

Many environmental organizations are using the tools for change to organize, strategize, and act. They're addressing climate change, industrial pollution, and environmental injustice. Students, community members, activists, advocates, policy makers, and businesses are taking action globally. The bottom line is: we have the knowledge, tools, and skills to organize and effect change. We just need to increase our use of them.

5. New technologies will move us toward sustainability.

Technology can't solve environmental problems entirely. To do that, we have to stop harmful carbon emissions, toxic pollution, and damage to the earth's ecosystems. But innovative technologies will continue to provide products and services that move humanity toward sustainability.

Advances in software allow us to sense and track environmental changes, run cap-and-trade programs, develop carbon-offset markets, use energy more efficiently, and improve transportation and communications. Quantum computing and artificial intelligence promise to offer opportunities we've never had before. They will speed innovation in all areas—energy, materials, transportation, medicine, communications, buildings, and so on—and that will speed social change.

In 1977, it cost $77 to generate 1 watt of power from a solar panel. Today that same watt of power costs thirty cents to generate—a 250-fold price reduction.[7] Improvements in solar and wind technologies have made renewable energy competitive, and in some cases cheaper than fossil fuels. New technology will soon allow deep-water turbines to be installed on floating platforms, giving us access to tremendous offshore wind resources.

Innovation continues to provide new products and services that replace older, less efficient ones. For example, electric ferries built from carbon fiber materials are 40% lighter than steel and aluminum boats. These ferries are faster and use much less fuel than conventional ferries, and if they are charged by solar panels, they offer zero-emissions transportation. New technologies like this hold tremendous promise and will move us to a healthier future.

6. Conservative support for addressing climate change is growing.

Young conservatives who have seen climate change impacts firsthand are joining others in their generation in tackling climate change. The Pew Research Center found that Republicans ages eighteen to thirty-nine are significantly more likely to say that human activity "contributes a great deal to climate change, that climate change is impacting their local community, and that the federal government is doing too little to reduce the effects of climate change."[8] Some young adults are forming and leading evangelical Christian

"Creation Care" groups to address climate change. Both House and Senate Republicans have supported a package of climate-related measures. The emerging conservative support for addressing climate change provides an opening for bipartisan and market-based environmental policies, such as a carbon tax, to become law.

Conservatives' growing awareness of climate change also provides an opening for environmental advocates to introduce them to other important environmental issues, such as habitat destruction, wildlife extinction, toxic waste, and environmental racism. Environmental advocates are well positioned to build bridges on a variety of environmental issues and to persuade conservatives and moderates to support a broader spectrum of environmental policies.

7. Creating an economy based on sustaining life is within our reach.

Many companies have chosen to be good corporate citizens by considering multiple stakeholders—customers, suppliers, employees, owners, local communities, and the earth—in business policies and decision making. Many companies have demanded that the government address climate change, too. The Business Roundtable, an organization consisting of CEOs of leading US corporations, has defined the purpose of a corporation as putting the interests of employees, suppliers, and communities on par with shareholders. General Motors has pledged to stop making gasoline and diesel powered cars by 2035. These efforts are a start. Continued citizen advocacy and pressure from multiple stakeholder groups can make corporate social responsibility the norm.

On the recent fiftieth anniversary of the Friedman Doctrine—the philosophy stating that the sole mission of business is to generate ever-increasing shareholder profits—many said it was time to retire this doctrine and expand the mission of business to include much more. Many people and institutions are working to do this through socially responsible investing, green certification programs, and laws that facilitate businesses becoming socially and environmentally responsible in their operations. When these actions reach critical mass, the economy will be more life-affirming and the environment will be cleaner and healthier.

8. The current disruptions may be our best opportunity in years.

Positive social change usually emerges from periods of social disruption. The Great Depression of the 1930s, resulting from uncontrolled stock market speculation and inequality, brought down the economy. At the same time, the Ku Klux Klan was rising, as was a Nazi movement. From this disruption arose Franklin Roosevelt's New Deal, along with Social Security, the Banking Act, and other legislation passed to stabilize the economy and give relief to the poor and the working class.

In the 1960s and 1970s the United States saw the civil rights movement, anti–Vietnam War protests, the women's movement, the Black Power movement, Students for a Democratic Society, the Weather Underground, and other movements. We also saw the first Earth Day and the revolt against massive environmental pollution. The outcomes of that tumultuous time include the Civil Rights Act, the Clean Air Act, the Clean Water Act, the Environmental Protection Agency, and many other landmark changes. In many places, the rivers run clean and the sky over our cities is blue again as a result of changes made during that time.

Over the past five years, our society has been disrupted by fear, polarized views, heightened awareness of economic inequality, racism, COVID-19, economic recession, excessive corporate power, and climate devastation. This creates tension like a rubber band stretched to its limit. We are caught between the reality of living in a world we don't want and the vision of a world we do want.

Can the current disruptions lead to major changes in how we live, relate to each other, and work? Can they lead to a smoothly functioning government in which there is agreement on the value of democracy and the kind of leadership needed to sustain it? Will we respond to climate change and industrial pollution by working together to create a healthy environment for the next generations? Can we respond to the wealth gap by creating a fair and equitable economy? The answers are up to us. Let's not miss what may be our best opportunity in years to create a country, an economy, and a world that works for everyone.

And If We Act Together ...

I began my advocacy work because I wanted to change the world for the better. Rather than try to quantify the difference I may have made, I find it more rewarding to relish the process. Do you get up in the morning energized by the possibilities of a new day? If you do, I applaud you. If you don't, I invite you to find one thing you can do to make the world a better place today. By taking positive action, no matter how small, you will have changed the direction of the world, and you can feel good about doing that. If most of us on the planet do this, we will reap the rewards of many small accomplishments, and we will be collectively happier.

But we can do even better. If we act together in campaigns and movements that affirm and support life on earth, we can achieve the larger vision and create a world that is compassionate, fair, safe, and healthy for all.

Sample Legislative Testimonies

(Note: below are three testimonies on the same bill. They show the range of testimonies that can be given, from personal stories to expert analysis. Each testimony follows a format, and they all were presented both orally and in writing.)

Sample Testimony #1

LD 1646 TESTIMONY
STACI COOMER, ROCKPORT, ME
MAINE CLIMATE ACTION SUPPORT FOR LD 1646
MAY 14, 2019

Senator Lawrence, Representative Berry, and distinguished committee members:

I am here to lend support for LD 1646 on behalf of Maine Climate Action, a statewide coalition supporting bold action on climate and energy issues, including A Climate to Thrive, 350 Maine, Maine Youth for Climate Justice, Sierra Club-Maine Chapter, Center for an Ecology-Based Economy, and Maine Youth Action Network. Today, I am representing A Climate to Thrive, 350 Maine, and Maine Youth for Climate Justice for today's testimony.

Our coalition organized the April 23 Day of Action here at the State House, which brought four hundred young Mainers and allies to the Capitol to advocate for urgent climate action. The UN Intergovernmental Panel on Climate Change has explicitly given the world eleven years in which to make dramatic changes in order to ensure our survival or stem catastrophic climate change. Steps such as this bill are crucial to Mainers ability to take charge.

This bill that creates the Maine Power Delivery Authority as a consumer-owned utility for the state has the potential to change the framework for our energy future. Not only will this lead to lower electricity costs for consumers; a ratepayer-owned utility has greater potential to generate power from a smarter, greener grid. Maine residents, not foreign investors, will set the priorities. Greater investment in renewables and efficiency, a more rapid adoption of electrification of heating, cooling, and transportation, and support for progressive policies on energy and climate issues would be possible.

Maine people need a utility we can afford, a utility we can depend on, a utility willing to work with distributed energy generators rather than trying to block them, and a utility that supports rather than opposes meaningful and bold climate policies. Maine Climate Action supports this bill and believes that a consumer-owned utility will serve as a foundation for a green energy future. Thank you.

Sample Testimony #2

TESTIMONY OF SETH YENTES

(Note: this testimony appeared in chapter 1 as an example of a personal story used effectively in advocacy.)

Senators and Representatives of the Energy, Utilities, and Technology Committee:

My name is Seth Yentes and I am here in strong support of LD 1646, An Act to Restore Local Ownership and Control of Maine's Power Delivery Systems.

I live in Monroe, a small, rural town in Waldo County, with fewer than nine hundred residents. I am a farmer, volunteer firefighter, chair of the planning board, and a father.

With deep roots in my community, I see the hardships and successes of rural Maine. I have talked to many neighbors and friends that are completely fed up with CMP [the electric power company]. Their poor billing systems, losing power after storms, and lack of support for residential solar installation has made it clear that they don't care about Maine people. CMP is a foreign corporation that prioritizes its shareholders and profits.

As a small-business owner, I know the effects that losing electricity has. A couple years back we were in the midst of our busiest season on the farm. In late October, we lost power for three days. We were milking cows, trying to keep the water pump running, keeping our milk tank cool, digging nursery trees to bring to our wholesale buyers, and cleaning up fallen trees on the town roads. Our generator fried over five hundred dollars' worth of electric controls. Now, I know that there are always going to be power outages, but I believe that more could have been done. If we had a consumer-owned grid run by Mainers, we would know that all the money going to pay for electricity would be going back into our infrastructure. We would know that we were not paying some shareholder's dividends. We would know that Mainers come first.

This is a bipartisan issue. We all use electricity. We all want a reliable grid. This bill will save Maine people and businesses money and in turn strengthen our economy.

Thank you.

Sample Testimony #3

TESTIMONY BEFORE THE
JOINT STANDING COMMITTEE ON ENERGY,
UTILITIES, AND TECHNOLOGY

L.D. 1646–AN ACT TO RESTORE LOCAL
OWNERSHIP AND CONTROL OF MAINE'S POWER
DELIVERY SYSTEMS

MAY 14, 2019

Chair Lawrence, Chair Berry, and members of the committee:

My name is Jim Cohen of Verrill Dana LLP, and I am here today on behalf of Emera Maine to testify in opposition to LD 1646.

Executive summary. We understand there is anger, but that does not justify imposing the death penalty on CMP and Emera Maine and the hundreds of people who work there. If LD 1646 passes, the involuntary government taking of two companies that are not for sale and that operate the vast majority of Maine's electric system would represent one of the most significant and ill-advised acts of the Maine legislature in fifty years. Passage of this bill would mean the following:

- Years of costly litigation that will cost the state millions with no guarantee of success

- Tremendous uncertainty for the electric grid at a critical time when we need the grid to support new renewable energy investments

- Coming up with $7–$9 billion in bonds to acquire CMP and Emera Maine, if permitted by the courts

- Many people wish that government could function more like a business, but this bill goes the other way by placing control of our electric grid in the hands of partisan state government, which has

been unable to provide sufficient resources to maintain our roads
and highways.

- No guarantee of lower rates, and the risk of higher rates due to
the government takeover

- A state budget hole of $35–$40 million

- Reduction or elimination of property tax contributions from
Maine's two largest property taxpayers, by far

- Operational control of our electric grid will be placed in the
hands of a potentially revolving door of private contractors who
will be allowed to mark up their costs above what they are today.

- Tremendous uncertainty for hundreds of CMP and Emera Maine
employees and their families

In the end, Maine needs to ask itself, do we want to pass a bill that
will require years to implement, if at all; will cost us billions of dollars;
and will lead to short- and long-term grid uncertainty and employee
disruption, only to end up with an electric system that could potentially
be operated by one of the same utilities who operate the grid today?

Moreover, is it reasonable to pass such catastrophic legislation for a
bill that has been in print for less than three weeks, where the public was
given just five days of prior notice for the public hearing, at the tail end
of a legislative session, that deprives individuals of their property and
their livelihood without due process or adjudication of need, and that
only allows the targets of this legislation increments of three minutes to
defend themselves?

The obvious answer to these questions is "no," which is why we
strongly urge this committee to reject this unwarranted and unconstitutional government taking. Instead, let's put this kind of divisive and
destructive legislation behind us and focus on working together to
ensure an electric grid that is safe, reliable, affordable, and responsive to
the climate needs of our planet. We don't have a moment to waste.

Proponents bear a heavy burden of proof. Very simply, before Maine adopts without due process what effectively amounts to the death penalty for two longstanding Maine companies, this legislature must be sure beyond a reasonable doubt that such an extreme exercise of government power is justified. Anything less would be irresponsible for the workers and customers of these two Maine companies.

[The testimony goes on for many more pages here, with charts, maps, graphs, and other supporting data that are not presented in this excerpted sample.]

Conclusion. Overall, it is clear this bill is before us today based on substantial public anger related to one utility. However, we believe the proper way to address these public concerns is to let Maine's longstanding regulatory process work rather than pass a bill like LD 1646 that will throw Maine's entire electric grid—as well as the people who work there—into disarray for years. Under Maine's current regulatory process, the Maine PUC has the ability to perform independent management audits and issue substantial financial penalties that have been effective in obtaining compliance over the years. So, rather than trying to fix a current problem by passing legislation that will break it more, we encourage the committee to reject the heavy-handed approach of LD 1646 and focus instead on collaborative solutions that will move Maine forward.

Thank you, and we ask the committee to give LD 1646 an "ought not to pass" report.

B

Sample Communications Documents

1. Sample Press Release

(Note: in press releases, more important information appears first, and quotes and details follow later, following the "inverted pyramid" format.)

FOR IMMEDIATE RELEASE
Yarmouth's First Parish Church Goes Solar
3/27/2017

Yarmouth, ME—First Parish Congregational Church has recently installed 128 solar panels on their roof. This system will provide clean electricity for the next 40 or more years and will save the church thousands of dollars on electricity bills. The panels will provide 95% of the church's electrical needs, reducing the church's electricity costs and eliminating roughly 33,660 pounds of greenhouse gas emissions annually.

First Parish is purchasing their solar power through the help of a power purchase agreement (PPA) with ReVision Energy. Under the PPA, ReVision Energy will own and maintain the solar equipment, and First Parish will purchase the electricity generated by it. This allows ReVision to take advantage of federal solar tax credits and regional renewable energy credits, while allowing First Parish to reduce its dependence on fossil fuels with no upfront cost to the church. PPAs have been used to bring solar power to churches, schools, municipal buildings and other nonprofits.

Nick Sampson, solar PPA relationship manager at ReVision Energy, explained that "First Parish was incredibly helpful in moving this project forward, and we're excited to see them benefit from the sun's energy." Through the PPA, First Parish Church will receive a $0.01 discount for every kilowatt-hour of solar electricity that their system produces. With very low solar equipment costs, this is a great time for churches and other nonprofits to consider this clean energy technology.

Sustaining the historic character of the 1860s church building was of paramount importance to the congregation. "Because the solar panels are flush-mounted and the roof is steep, the visual impact from the ground is minimized," said Jim Highland, chair of the trustees at the church. The church congregation voted unanimously to approve the project, noting that it is in keeping with Jesus' teachings and the church mission to steward the earth and conserve the environment.

Every kilowatt of solar installed in Maine will save ratepayers $4,000 in electricity bills over the next 25 years. "Solar is an environmentally and economically responsible investment for any home or business and is less expensive than paying the utility for power over the long term," said Nate Bowie, solar experience manager at ReVision Energy. ReVision Energy has developed and installed more than 50 PPA projects in the northeast.

In a show of support for the First Parish community, ReVision has agreed to contribute $500 to First Parish Church for every member of the church who invests in a solar array from now through the end of the year. The funds will be used to support the church's purchase of the solar array in 2024.

RIBBON CUTTING AND PRESS EVENT

A ribbon cutting and press event for the solar project will be held Sunday, April 9, at 11:20 a.m. ReVision Energy and church solar project leaders will be on hand to answer questions about the project. Please join us.

ABOUT REVISION ENERGY

ReVision Energy began in 2003 with the mission to help people and businesses transition toward sustainable solar energy. Trusted as the industry leader in solar design, installation and service in northern New England, ReVision Energy provides a full range of services for homes, businesses, municipal buildings and nonprofits. To date, ReVision Energy has installed over 5,000 systems and has branches in Portland and Liberty, Maine, and Exeter and Concord, New Hampshire. For more information, please visit www.revisionenergy.com.

CONTACT INFORMATION

To learn more about commercial installations or ReVision Energy please contact:

Deborah Smith
142 Presumpscot Street
Portland, ME 04103
Office: (207) 221-6342
dsmith@revisionenergy.com
To learn more about the church's project please contact:
Sue Inches, trustee
(207) 618-5891
susan1@firstparishchurch.org

2. Sample Frequently Asked Questions (FAQs)

(Note: if you are posting these on the web, listing each question and then having a drop-down box for each answer is an efficient, space-saving way to convey this information. Having printed copies of your FAQs to hand out at events and to give to decision makers is also helpful.)

MAINE POWER DELIVERY AUTHORITY (MPDA) FREQUENTLY ASKED QUESTIONS
JUNE 2, 2020

1. **Has a conversion to a consumer-owned utility (COU) been done before?**

   Yes, and we can learn a great deal from the successes and challenges of others. For instance, Winter Park, Florida, converted from an investor-owned utility to a COU. They repaid their acquisition cost in ten years and dramatically increased reliability, even with bigger storm events in Florida.

   An act of the New York legislature created the Long Island Power Authority (LIPA). When LIPA took over the systems of the Long Island Lighting Company in 1998, rates for all customer-owners dropped by 20%. Today, LIPA rates remain lower than those of neighboring utility Con Ed.

2. **Are there any COUs in Maine?**

   Yes. Maine has a history of locally owned electric, water, and telephone utilities. Ninety-seven of Maine's 488 communities are currently served by these Maine COUs:

   - Kennebunk Light and Power
   - Madison Electric Works
   - Houlton Water Company

- Eastern Maine Electric Co-op
- Fox Islands Co-op
- Van Buren Light and Power
- Isle au Haut Electric Power

3. Are the rates of these COUs lower than the rates of investor-owned utilities in Maine?

Yes. For most, rates range from 2–4 cents per kilowatt-hour, or 20%–30% lower than CMP and Emera. Exceptions are Fox Islands and Eastern Maine, which are the same or slightly higher.

4. Will this impact our state budget?

No. Maine Power will not be funded with tax dollars. Utilities use rates, not taxes, to pay for investments and operations. If anything, by reducing our electric rates over time, it will help to attract and retain businesses in Maine, boosting incomes and increasing taxes collected.

5. How will this impact municipalities?

A COU will pay fees to towns in lieu of taxes. Towns will remain whole, and there will be no impact on town budgets—except lower electric rates over time.

6. What about the free market?

There is no free market for electricity delivery. Because multiple wires on each street would be inefficient and unsafe, the grid has to be a monopoly.

7. What about renewable energy?

A COU will invest in the things that consumers and businesses most need, like connecting local and regional renewable energy to the grid, energy storage, and time-of-use rates that allow more efficient use of energy (like charging electric vehicles at night).

Where Maine's investor-owned utilities have fought cost-effective energy programs and renewable energy policies, a COU will embrace the energy policies and needs of Maine ratepayers.

8. **What would Maine Power cost ratepayers?**

No more than we pay now in the short term, and far less than we'll otherwise pay in the long term. By owning and financing our future grid at lower interest rates, Maine Power will cost less.

9. **Are there any constitutional issues that would prevent establishing a COU in Maine?**

No. A recent study from the London Economics Group researched this question and found no constitutional issues in transitioning to a COU.

10. **What is the timeline and process for transitioning to a COU?**

LD 1646, which establishes the MPDA, lays out a specific timeline for acquiring the assets and transitioning to a COU. Although it is hard to predict exactly, it is expected that the process will be complete in three to four years.

11. **Fewer rate hikes and better reliability? Is this too good to be true?**

It's math. Maine Power would finance its infrastructure at 2%–5% interest using tax-exempt revenue bonds. CMP and Emera's equity investments cost us—its captive customers—between 9% and 13%.

Substantial new investment will be needed to strengthen the grid and achieve our state's climate goals. Financing these investments at lower interest rates will keep rates low while improving reliability, something only a COU can do.

Where can I find out more?

Go to: www.mainepower4mainepeople.org.

3. Sample Fact Sheet

(Note: this fact sheet presents just three main points, with supporting data. Fact sheets can be dressed up with visual images, which is especially good for attracting attention on the web.)

STRENGTHEN MAINE'S MUNICIPAL RECYCLING PROGRAMS

This bill will save taxpayer money by making recycling more effective, sustainable, and equitable.

Maine's recycling programs are struggling to survive.

- Mainers want to do the right thing for the environment by recycling but are increasingly frustrated by the lack of access and confusion about what is recyclable.

- Maine taxpayers must unfairly cover the full cost of recycling. With the taxpayer bill for packaging alone totaling an estimated $16 million to $17.5 million each year, many municipalities are scaling back or eliminating recycling programs due to cost.

- Big corporations that are flooding Maine with packaging pay nothing for the growing volume of waste they create, so they have no incentive to design less wasteful packaging or to ensure that packaging is recyclable and ultimately recycled.

Extended producer responsibility (EPR) for packaging is a proven solution to help Maine towns.

- EPR for packaging has been successfully implemented in forty-seven jurisdictions worldwide and has been in place in some areas for thirty years.

- Under EPR for packaging, large corporations like Amazon and Walmart pay their fair share by helping to finance recycling programs, and they have an incentive to produce less wasteful, more easily recyclable packaging.

- EPR for packaging will help Maine finally reach its long-established 50% recycling goal, which would reduce as much carbon pollution as taking 166,000 cars off the road.

Towns across Maine support this solution to save taxpayer money and make recycling more effective, sustainable, and equitable.

- EPR shifts the financial burden of recycling packaging from Maine taxpayers to producers, who would reimburse municipalities for the net costs of recycling the materials they create.

- Corporations that produce more recyclable packaging would pay less, creating an incentive for producers to create less wasteful packaging.

- Maine's cities and towns can easily and profitably manage less wasteful packaging, even when global recycling markets are unfavorable.

Product packaging (including plastic, cardboard, glass, and metal) makes up 30%–40% of the materials managed by Maine's municipal waste management programs.

Support recycling reform. Support extended producer responsibility for packaging. For more information contact: Susan Annise, sannise@conservation.org.

Maine Conservation Voters. 2020. www.maineconservation.org. Used with permission.

For Further Reading

Below is a list of books and news outlets that have shaped and informed my thinking. It's not a comprehensive bibliography, but it does provide more in-depth information on many of the topics discussed in this book. Happy reading!

Advocacy and Story

Ball, Rachel. *When I Tell My Story, I'm in Charge.* Melbourne, AU: Victoria Law Foundation, 2013. https://victorialawfoundation.org.au/sites/default /files/attachments/VLF%20-%20CLC%20final%20report%2012-13%20 _Final_web.pdf.

Rush, Elizabeth. *Rising: Dispatches from the New American Shore.* Minneapolis: Milkweed Editions, 2018.

Simmons, Annette. *The Story Factor: Influence, Inspiration, and Persuasion through Storytelling.* 3rd ed. New York: Basic Books, 2019.

Campaigns, Organizing, and Strategy

Gallagher, Nora, and Lisa Myers. *Tools for Grassroots Activists: Best Practices for Success in the Environmental Movement.* 3rd ed. Ventura, CA: Patagonia, 2016.

Gavin, Melissa. *The Art of Campaign Planning: How to Design a Successful Campaign and Win.* RE-AMP Network Organizing Hub. www.reamp.org/wp-content /uploads/2019/01/The-Art-of-Campaign-Planning-24.pdf.

Lakey, George. *How We Win.* Brooklyn: Melville House, 2018.

Licata, Nick. *Becoming a Citizen Activist: Stories, Strategies, and Advice for Changing Our World.* Seattle: Sasquatch Books, 2016.

Sierra Club. *The Sierra Club Movement Organizing Manual 2016.* Oakland, CA: Sierra Club, 2016. www.sierraclub.org/sites/www.sierraclub.org/files/program /documents/Movement-Organizing-Manual-2016.pdf.

Caring Economy, the Nordic Model, and Capitalism

Eisenstein, Charles. *Sacred Economics: Money, Gift, and Society in the Age of Transition.* Berkeley, CA: North Atlantic Books, 2011.

Eisler, Riane. *The Real Wealth of Nations: Creating a Caring Economics.* Oakland, CA: Berrett-Koehler, 2008.

Klein, Naomi. *This Changes Everything: Capitalism vs. the Climate.* New York: Simon and Schuster, 2014.

Lakey, George. *Viking Economics: How the Scandinavians Got It Right—and How We Can, Too.* New York: Melville House, 2016.

McKibben, Bill. *Deep Economy: The Wealth of Communities and the Durable Future.* New York: Holt Paperbacks, 2007.

O'Leary, Michael and Valdmanis, Warren. *Accountable: The Rise of Citizen Capitalism.* New York: Harper Collins, 2020.

Perkins, John. *New Confessions of an Economic Hit Man.* Oakland, CA: Berrett-Koehler, 2016.

Rifkin, Jeremy. *The Green New Deal: Why the Fossil Fuel Civilization Will Collapse by 2028 and the Bold Economic Plan to Save Life on Earth.* New York: St. Martin's Press, 2019.

Communications

Grimm, Kristen. *Mindful Messaging.* Washington, DC, and San Francisco: Spitfire Strategies, 2017. https://mindfulmessaging.spitfirestrategies.com/wp-content/uploads/2016/11/Mindful-Messaging-print2.pdf.

McKenzie-Mohr, Doug, and William Smith. *Fostering Sustainable Behavior: An Introduction to Community-Based Social Marketing.* Gabriola Island, BC: New Society Publishers, 2011.

Perez, Robert, and Amy Simon. *Heartwired: Human Behavior, Strategic Opinion Research, and the Audacious Pursuit of Social Change.* Los Altos, CA: Packard Foundation, 2017. www.packard.org/wp-content/uploads/2017/05/Heartwired-digital.pdf.

Earth Stories and Indigenous Wisdom

Eisenstein, Charles. *The More Beautiful World Our Hearts Know Is Possible.* Berkeley, CA: North Atlantic Books, 2013.

Francis. *Laudato Si' (On Care for Our Common Home).* Rome: Libreria Editrice Vaticana, 2015.

Kimmerer, Robin Wall. *Braiding Sweetgrass: Indigenous Wisdom, Scientific Knowledge, and the Teachings of Plants.* Minneapolis: Milkweed Editions, 2015.

Lushwala, Arkan. *Deer and Thunder: Indigenous Ways of Restoring the World*. Self-published, CreateSpace, 2017.

Mitchell, Sherri. *Sacred Instructions: Indigenous Wisdom for Living Spirit-Based Change*. Berkeley, CA: North Atlantic Books, 2018.

Perkins, John. *Touching the Jaguar: Transforming Fear into Action to Change Your Life and the World*. Oakland, CA: Berrett-Koehler, 2020.

Wollheben, Peter. *The Hidden Life of Trees: What They Feel, How They Communicate—Discoveries from a Secret World*. Vancouver, BC: Greystone Books, 2016.

Environmental Policy

Eisenstein, Charles. *Climate: A New Story*. Berkeley, CA: North Atlantic Books, 2018.

Hanna-Attisha, Mona. *What the Eyes Don't See: A Story of Crisis, Resistance, and Hope in an American City*. New York: One World, 2018.

Hawken, Paul. *Drawdown: The Most Comprehensive Plan Ever Proposed to Reverse Global Warming*. New York: Penguin, 2017.

Plante, Jake. *Uncle Sam and Mother Earth*. Self-published, CreateSpace, 2015.

Van Rossum, Maya. *The Green Amendment: Securing Our Right to a Healthy Environment*. Austin, TX: Disruption Books, 2017.

Facilitation and Training

Freshley, Craig. *The Wisdom of Group Decisions: 100 Principles and Practical Tips for Collaboration*. Brunswick, ME: Freshley, 2010. https://craigfreshley.com/book/.

Holman, Peggy, and Tom Devane. *The Change Handbook: The Definitive Resource on Today's Best Methods for Engaging Whole Systems*. Oakland, CA: Berrett-Koehler, 2007.

Lakey, George. *Facilitating Group Learning: Strategies for Success with Diverse Learners*. 2nd ed. Oakland, CA: PM Press, 2020.

Owen, Harrison. *Open Space Technology: A User's Guide*. Oakland, CA: Berrett-Koehler, 2008.

Straus, David. *How to Make Collaboration Work: Powerful Ways to Build Consensus, Solve Problems, and Make Decisions*. Oakland, CA: Berrett-Koehler, 2002.

News Outlets

E&E News. Online news journalism covering energy and environmental policy. Publishes seventy environmental news stories daily. www.eenews.net.

The Economist. Bimonthly magazine covering world news, politics, economics, business, and finance. In-depth global coverage from a British perspective. www .economist.com.

Grist News. Web news focusing on climate, sustainability, and social justice. www .grist.org.

The Guardian. British-owned newspaper and website, with a US edition. Well-researched feature articles and news. www.theguardian.com.

Inside Climate News. Independent professional journalism on a wide variety of environmental topics. Nonprofit and nonpartisan. Easy-to-find articles on a wide variety of environmental topics. www.insideclimatenews.org.

Medium. A web platform with a combination of professional and amateur people and publications. Readers can subscribe by topic, such as "environment." www .medium.com.

New York Times. Researched news, opinion, and feature stories. Online and in print. www.nytimes.com.

Orion. Quarterly environmental magazine with features, photo essays, and thought pieces. www.orionmagazine.org.

Sierra. Official bimonthly magazine of the Sierra Club. In-depth features and news about the environmental movement. Anyone can subscribe to the magazine, whether you're a Sierra Club member or not. www.sierraclub.org/sierra.

Sojourners. Monthly magazine focused on social and environmental justice from a progressive Christian perspective. www.sojo.net.

Stanford Social Innovation Review. Quarterly magazine and online newsletter covering news, features, and research on social change. Published by the Stanford Center on Philanthropy and Civil Society. www.ssir.org.

Waging Nonviolence. Online media platform with original reporting on social justice and activism. Allows social justice organizations to post stories. www .wagingnonviolence.org.

Washington Post. Researched news, feature stories, and opinion pieces. Online and in print. www.washingtonpost.com.

Yes! Quarterly magazine and website focused on building community and social change. www.yesmagazine.org.

Spiritual and Personal Growth

Hicks, Esther, and Jerry Hicks. *Getting into the Vortex: Guided Meditations and User Guide.* Carlsbad, CA: Hay House, 2010.

——. *The Vortex: Where the Law of Attraction Assembles All Cooperative Relationships.* Carlsbad, CA: Hay House, 2009.

Kane, Ariel, and Shya Kane. *Practical Enlightenment.* New York: ASK Productions and Waterfront Press, 2015.

Straub, Gail. *The Rhythm of Compassion: Caring for Self, Connecting with Society.* Boston: Tuttle Publishing, 2000.

Tadd, Ellen. *The Infinite View: A Guidebook for Life on Earth.* New York: Tarcher Perigee, 2017.

Tolle, Eckhardt. *A New Earth: Awakening to Your Life's Purpose.* New York: Penguin, 2008.

Vision, Power, and Social Change

Antal, Jim. *Climate Church, Climate World: How People of Faith Must Work for Change.* Lanham, MD: Rowman and Littlefield, 2018.

Crutchfield, Leslie. *How Change Happens: Why Some Social Movements Succeed While Others Don't.* Hoboken, NJ: Wiley, 2018.

Figueres, Christiana, and Tom Rivett-Carnac. *The Future We Choose: Surviving the Climate Crisis.* New York: Alfred A. Knopf, 2020.

Gates, Melinda. *The Moment of Lift: How Empowering Women Changes the World.* New York: FlatironBooks, 2019.

Gershon, David. *Social Change 2.0: A Blueprint for Reinventing Our World.* West Hurley, VT: Highpoint/Chelsea Green, 2009.

Klein, Naomi. *No Is Not Enough: Resisting Trump's Shock Politics and Winning the World We Need.* Chicago: Haymarket, 2017.

Liu, Eric. *You're More Powerful Than You Think: A Citizen's Guide to Making Change Happen.* New York: PublicAffairs, 2017.

Wilkinson, Richard G., and Kate Pickett. *The Spirit Level: Why Greater Equality Makes Societies Stronger.* New York: Bloomsbury Press, 2011.

Worldviews

Lakoff, George. *Don't Think of an Elephant! Know Your Values and Frame the Debate.* White River Junction, VT: Chelsea Green, 2014.

———. *Moral Politics: How Liberals and Conservatives Think.* Chicago: University of Chicago Press, 2016.

Acknowledgments

Writing a book is a journey—and a new and different one for me. As I researched material to take this book beyond my own advocacy experience, I felt gratitude and awe for the many, many people who have stepped forward with courage and advocated for the environment. A few examples are Dr. Mona Hanna-Attisha, who called for action to get rid of the lead in the drinking water in Flint, Michigan; Maya K. van Rossum, who established the constitutional right to a clean and healthy environment in Pennsylvania; Julia Olson, the chief legal counsel for Our Children's Trust, who is prosecuting the case to establish rights to a healthy environment under the US Constitution; Sharon Levine, who is standing up to oil and petrochemical companies that operate fossil fuel and petrochemical companies in Cancer Alley along the Mississippi River; and Dr. Dorceta Taylor, who wrote the first book-length history of environmental injustice in the United States.

I'm also awed by Arkan Lushwala, Sherri Mitchell, Kaye Lawrence, and the many other Indigenous leaders and shamans who, despite generations of abuse, continue to share wisdom and best practices for how to live in partnership with the earth. I am also inspired by Greta Thunberg, Isra Hirsi, Anna Siegel, and many other youth leaders who are speaking with clear-voiced passion for a clean, healthy, and safe future. Here in my home state of Maine, students, community leaders, activists, educators, business leaders, and politicians are stepping up and taking action for the environment. I thank them all for being the inspiration behind this book.

The idea for this book grew out of a college course I developed called Advocating for the Environment. I'm grateful to Professor Jane Costlow, recently retired from Bates College, and the staff of the Purposeful Work Program there, for offering me the opportunity to teach their students. Likewise, I have gratitude for Russell Johnson, associate provost and dean of the faculty at Colby College, and Phil Nyhus, chair of Colby's Environmental Studies program, for their support for my course being taught at the college. And of course I loved working with the students who took a leap and signed up for my course. Young people who are stepping up for the environment, you are my heroes!

The idea for this book began with my college teaching, but it launched for real on a summer day when I was enjoying morning coffee with author and activist George Lakey. George was on a book tour at the time and was staying at my home for the night. I asked George what he thought of the idea of turning my course into a book. "Absolutely," he said. "Do it!" Anyone who knows George will understand how supportive and enthusiastic he can be. As I worked on the book, I asked him questions and sent him chapters to read. He was responsive, generous with his time, and insightful in his comments—a true mentor, for which I am very grateful.

As I soon discovered, a book isn't written entirely by an individual. In this case, I had a wonderful group of people who read and commented on chapters where they could offer expertise and insight. These beta readers were: Cathy Lee, Jake Plante, Rick Peterson, Michael Belliveau, Marianne Hill, Janice Cooper, Jeanne Scudder, Jim Shaffer, Jason Gootman, Andy Burt, and George Lakey. Many thanks to you all! Your comments and ideas helped move this book beyond where I could have taken it alone.

The staff at North Atlantic Books were superlative, and I owe special thanks to my editor, Shayna Keyles, for recognizing my vision for the book and encouraging me with insightful edits and prompt answers to all my new-author questions. Thanks also to Trisha Peck, my production editor, and the design and copy editing team for making the book look polished and professional. It was a joy to work with you all!

Pauline McKeen, I thank you for being my research assistant, tracking down sources of information, and getting permissions to reprint pieces for the book. It was fun having you in Ecuador and me in Maine working together on this project.

I'm also grateful to several people who had excellent ideas and connections to help get this book into the hands of readers. Rich Kilmer, Becky Bartovics, Sara Hunter, and the staff at North Atlantic Books helped me make connections and understand better how book marketing works.

I have friends and family to thank, too, for they continued to encourage and support me throughout the process: Jay Reighley, who is always ready to give me a break from writing to go on outdoor adventures; my sister, Alison, who is an author herself; my brother, Rob; my cousin Andy; and my ninety-five-year-old Mom, who provided encouragement along the way, as did two wonderful groups of women—my Friday night beer club and my Books That Matter reading group. There are many others who answered questions and encouraged me. If you don't see your name here, please be assured that I appreciate your support.

Finally, my husband, Bob Sessums, was my bedrock of support, day in and day out. He discussed ideas, read and commented on much of the text, and made delicious home-cooked dinners, which we both truly enjoyed. His wonderful balance of patience, critiques, grocery shopping, and meals was an essential part of this project.

Notes

Introduction

1 Erica Chenowith and Maria Stephan, *Why Civil Resistance Works: The Strategic Logic of Nonviolent Conflict*, Columbia Studies in Terrorism and Irregular Warfare (New York: Columbia University Press, 2012).

2 Jer. 31:33–34.

1. What's Your Advocacy Story?

1 Sherri Mitchell, *Sacred Instructions: Indigenous Wisdom for Living Spirit-Based Change* (Berkeley, CA: North Atlantic Books, 2018).

2 West End Revitalization Association, accessed November 28, 2020, https://wera-nc.org.

2. What Advocates Do

1 Sam Levin, "Dakota Access Pipeline: The Who, What, and Why of the Standing Rock Protests," *The Guardian*, November 3, 2016, www.theguardian.com/us-news/2016/nov/03/north-dakota-access-oil-pipeline-protests-explainer.

2 Associated Press, "Judge Suspends Dakota Access Pipeline over Environmental Concerns," July 6, 2020, www.theguardian.com/us-news/2020/jul/06/dakota-access-pipeline-environment-oil.

3 Siham Zniber, "Members of Congress, Tribes, State Governments Formally Join Call to Shut Down Dakota Access Pipeline," *Earthjustice News*, September 23, 2020, www.earthjustice.org/news/press/2020/members-of-congress-tribes-state-governments-formally-join-call-to-shut-down-dakota-access-pipeline.

4 Earth Quaker Action Team, accessed November 28, 2020, www.eqat.org.

5 Jake Plante, *Uncle Sam and Mother Earth* (self-pub., CreateSpace, 2015).

6 Our Children's Trust, accessed November 28, 2020, www.ourchildrenstrust.org.

7 Maya K. van Rossum, *The Green Amendment: Securing Our Right to a Healthy Environment* (Austin, TX: Disruption Books, 2017).

8 Mont. Const. art. II, § 3, and art. IX, § 1.

9 Van Rossum, *Green Amendment.*

3. Earth Stories and Why They Matter

1 Gen. 1:28.

2 Francis, *Laudato Si' (On Care for Our Common Home)* (Vatican City: Libreria Editrice Vaticana, 2015).

3 Alicia Vanorman and Linda Jacobsen, "US Household Composition Shifts as the Population Grows Older; More Young Adults Live with Parents," Population Reference Bureau, February 12, 2020, www.prb.org/u-s -household-composition-shifts-as-the-population-grows-older-more -young-adults-live-with-parents/.

4 Elinor Polack, "New Cigna Study Reveals Loneliness at Epidemic Levels in America," May 2018, www.cigna.com/about-us/newsroom/news-and -views/press-releases/2018/new-cigna-study-reveals-loneliness-at-epidemic -levels-in-america.

5 Jeffrey M. Jones, "US Church Membership Down Sharply in the Past Two Decades," *Gallup News,* April 18, 2019, https://news.gallup.com/poll/248837 /church-membership-down-sharply-past-two-decades.aspx.

6 Pierre Ferrari, "Dear Humanitarians," *World Ark,* spring 2020, 11, https://media .heifer.org/world-ark/2020/pdf/2020_Spring_WA_Magazine-Digital_Final .pdf.

7 Maine Department of Marine Resources (2019 Atlantic cod landings, accessed December 23, 2020, www.maine.gov/dmr/commercial-fishing/landings /documents/cod.graph.pdf; 2019 American lobster landings, accessed December 23, 2020, www.maine.gov/dmr/commercial-fishing/landings/documents /lobster.graph.pdf).

8 Michael Pollan, *The Omnivore's Dilemma: A Natural History of Four Meals* (New York: Penguin, 2007).

9 US Department of Agriculture, *Acreage,* June 2020, https://downloads .usda.library.cornell.edu/usda-esmis/files/j098zb09z/vx022244t/8910kf38j /acrg0620.pdf.

10 James Cameron and Suzy Amis Cameron, "Animal Agriculture Is Choking the Earth and Making Us Sick. We Must Act Now," *The Guardian*, December 4, 2017, www.theguardian.com/commentisfree/2017/dec/04/animal-agriculture-choking-earth-making-sick-climate-food-environmental-impact-james-cameron-suzy-amis-cameron.

11 "US Arable Land 1961–2020," www.macrotrends.net/countries/USA/united-states/arable-land.

12 Richard Conniff, "Could Abandoned Agricultural Lands Help Save the Planet?" *Yale Environment 360*, December 10, 2019, https://e360.yale.edu/features/could-abandoned-agricultural-lands-help-save-the-planet.

13 Julian Brave NoiseCat, "The Western Idea of Private Property Is Flawed. Indigenous Peoples Have It Right," *The Guardian*, March 27, 2017, www.theguardian.com/commentisfree/2017/mar/27/western-idea-private-property-flawed-indigenous-peoples-have-it-right.

14 NoiseCat, "Western Idea."

15 Francis, *Laudato Si'*.

16 Arkan Lushwala, *Deer and Thunder: Indigenous Ways of Restoring the World* (self-pub., CreateSpace, 2017).

17 Kennedy Warne, "The Whanganui River in New Zealand Is a Legal Person. A Nearby Forest Is Too. Here's How It Happened and What It May Mean," *National Geographic*, April 2019, www.nationalgeographic.com/culture/2019/04/maori-river-in-new-zealand-is-a-legal-person/.

18 US Energy Information Administration, "In 2018, the United States Consumed More Energy Than Ever Before," April 16, 2019, www.eia.gov/todayinenergy.

19 Kevin Crowley and Akshat Rathi, "Exxon's Plan for Surging Carbon Emissions Revealed in Leaked Documents," *Bloomberg News*, October 5, 2020, www.bloomberg.com/news/articles/2020-10-05/exxon-carbon-emissions-and-climate-leaked-plans-reveal-rising-co2-output.

20 Paul Hawken, *Drawdown: The Most Comprehensive Plan Ever Proposed to Reverse Global Warming* (New York: Penguin, 2017).

21 Hawken, *Drawdown*.

22 Indigo Agriculture, "Indigo Launches the Terraton Initiative to Remove One Trillion Tons of Carbon Dioxide from the Atmosphere," June 12, 2019, www.indigoag.com/pages/news/indigo-launches-terraton-initiative.

4. Bridging the Left and the Right

1 Christine Mai-Duc, "The 1969 Santa Barbara Oil Spill That Changed Oil and Gas Exploration Forever," *Los Angeles Times*, May 20, 2015, www.latimes.com /local/lanow/la-me-ln-santa-barbara-oil-spill-1969-20150520-htmlstory.html.

2 Colin Dabkowski, "A History of the Love Canal Disaster, 1893 to 1998," *Buffalo News*, August 4, 2018, www.buffalonews.com/news/local/history/a -history-of-the-love-canal-disaster-1893-to-1998/article_5df93af9-e5fe-5ae4 -be74-efed7dbf43ed.html.

3 Hernaldo Turillo, "Towards the Caring Economy: Shifting from Numbers to People," IntelligentHQ, May 16, 2018, www.intelligenthq.com/towards -the-caring-economy-shifting-from-the-numbers-to-the-people.

4 US House of Representatives, "The Women's Rights Movement, 1848–1917," accessed December 23, 2020, https://history.house.gov/Exhibitions-and -Publications/WIC/Historical-Essays/No-Lady/Womens-Rights/.

5 Note that Asian American immigrants didn't gain the right to become naturalized citizens, and thus to vote, until 1943; and Native Americans weren't guaranteed the right to vote until 1965. Melissa Block, "Yes, Women Could Vote after the 19th Amendment—But Not All Women. Or Men," *NPR*, August 26, 2020, www.npr.org/2020/08/26/904730251/yes-women-could-vote-after-the -19th-amendment-but-not-all-women-or-men.

6 Olga Emelianova and Christina Milhomem, "Women on Boards: 2019 Progress Report," MSCI, December 2019, www.msci.com.

7 Courtney Connley, "The Number of Women Running Fortune 500 Companies Is at a Record High," *CNBC*, May 16, 2019, www.cnbc.com/2019/05/16/the -number-of-women-running-fortune-500-companies-is-at-a-record-high.html.

8 Oxfam International, *The Tsunami's Impact on Women* (Oxford, UK: Oxfam International, 2005), https://oxfamilibrary.openrepository.com/bitstream /handle/10546/115038/bn-tsunami-impact-on-women-250305-en .pdf?sequence=1&isAllowed=.

9 Women's UN Report Network, "Reaching Out to Women When Disaster Strikes," Soroptimist International of the Americas, 2011.

10 Mary Halton, "Climate Change Impacts Women More Than Men," *BBC News*, March 8, 2018, www.bbc.com/news/science-environment-43294221.

11 World Health Organization, *WHO Gender, Climate and Health Report*, 2014, www.who.int/globalchange/publications/reports/gender_climate_change/en/.

12 World Health Organization, *Family Planning/Contraception Methods,* June 22, 2020, www.who.int/news-room/fact-sheets/detail/family-planning -contraception.

13 Paul Hawken, *Drawdown: The Most Comprehensive Plan Ever Proposed to Reverse Global Warming* (New York: Penguin, 2017).

14 United Nations, *Sustainable Development Goals,* accessed November 28, 2020, www.un.org/sustainabledevelopment/sustainable-development-goals.

15 World Population Balance, "Population and Energy Consumption," accessed December 23, 2020, www.worldpopulationbalance.org/population_energy.

16 BBC News, "How Many Roman Catholics Are There in the World?" March 14, 2013, www.bbc.com/news/world/21443313.

17 Dino Grandoni, "The Energy 202: Hunting and Fishing Groups Urge Congress to Work Together on Climate Change," *Washington Post,* July 28, 2020, www .washingtonpost.com/politics/2020/07/28/energy-202-hunting-fishing -groups-urge-congress-work-together-climate-change/.

18 Zoya Teirstein, "Meet the Conservative Answer to the Green New Deal," *Grist,* April 27, 2020, https://grist.org/politics/meet-the-conservative-answer -to-the-green-new-deal/.

19 American Climate Contract, accessed November 28, 2020, www .climatesolution.eco.

20 Sen. Lindsey Graham, "Senate and House Republicans Announce Formation of the Roosevelt Conservation Caucus," press release, July 10, 2019, www.lgraham .senate.gov/public/index.cfm/2019/7/senate-and-house-republicans -announce-formation-of-the-roosevelt-conservation-caucus.

21 Climate Solutions Caucus, accessed December 24, 2020, https://teddeutch .house.gov/climate/.

22 Juliet Eilperin and Steven Mufson, "In Rare Bipartisan Climate Agree-ments, Senators Forge Plan to Slash Use of Potent Greenhouse Gas," *Washington Post,* September 10, 2020, www.washingtonpost.com/climate -environment/2020/09/10/rare-bipartisan-climate-agreement-senators -forge-plan-slash-use-potent-greenhouse-gas/.

23 Valerie Volcovici, "In Rare Bipartisan Bill, US Senators Tackle Climate Change via Agriculture," Reuters, June 4, 2020, www.reuters.com/article/us-usa -climatechange-agriculture/in-rare-bipartisan-bill-u-s-senators-tackle -climate-change-via-agriculture-idUSKBN23B23J.

24 The Wildlife Society, "Recovering America's Wildlife Act: A 21st Century Model of Wildlife Conservation Funding," accessed December 24, 2020, https://wildlife.org/policy/recovering-americas-wildlife-act/.

25 Erica Chenowith, "The Success of Nonviolent Civil Resistance" (presentation, TEDxBoulder, 2013), https://tedxboulder.com/speakers/erica-chenoweth.

5. Developing Environmental Policy

1 Adapted from Moira O'Neil and Abigail Haydon, *Getting Stories to Stick: The Shape of Public Discourse on Oral Health* (Washington, DC: FrameWorks Institute, 2017), www.frameworksinstitute.org/wp-content/uploads/2020/06/dentaquest_mcffa_final_2017.pdf.

2 Sociology Index, "Friedman Doctrine," accessed December 24, 2020, www.sociologyindex.com/friedman_doctrine.htm.

3 Sherri Mitchell, *Sacred Instructions: Indigenous Wisdom for Living Spirit-Based Change* (Berkeley, CA: North Atlantic Books, 2018), 113–14.

4 Adapted from John Perkins, *Touching the Jaguar: Transforming Fear into Action to Change Your Life and the World* (Oakland, CA: Berrett-Koehler, 2020).

5 The term "caring economy" was coined by social scientist, lawyer, and activist Riane Eisler. Center for Partnership Studies, "What Is the Caring Economy?" accessed December 24, 2020, https://centerforpartnership.org/programs/caring-economy/.

6 Partnership Studies, "Caring Economy."

7 Conscious Capitalism, "Conscious Capitalist Credo," accessed December 24, 2020, www.consciouscapitalism.org/credo.

8 From a presentation by Steve Smith (CEO of L.L.Bean), Forest Society of Maine Annual Meeting, 2020, Freeport, Maine.

9 Christopher Marquis, "The B-Corp Movement Goes Big," *Stanford Social Innovation Review*, fall 2020, https://ssir.org/articles/entry/the_b_corp_movement_goes_big.

10 Anne Barnard, "New York's $226 Billion Pension Fund Is Dropping Fossil Fuel Stocks," *New York Times*, December 9, 2020, www.nytimes.com/2020/12/09/nyregion/new-york-pension-fossil-fuels.html.

11 Marianne Hill, "Taming the Corporate Beast," *Dollars and Sense*, July/August 2014, http://dollarsandsense.org/archives/2014/0714hill.

12 Nadja Popovich, "The Trump Administration Is Reversing 100 Environmental Rules. Here's the Full List," *New York Times*, November 10, 2020, www.nytimes .com/interactive/2020/climate/trump-environment-rollbacks.html.

13 Lisa Friedman, "Trump Weakens Major Conservation Law to Speed Construction Permits," *New York Times*, August 4, 2020, www.nytimes.com/2020/07/15 /climate/trump-environment-nepa.html.

14 Coral Davenport, "US to Announce Rollback of Auto Pollution Rules, a Key Effort to Fight Climate Change," *New York Times*, March 2020, www.nytimes .com/2020/03/30/climate/trump-fuel-economy.html.

15 Marianne Levelle, "Trump EPA's 'Secret Science' Rule Would Dismiss Studies That Could Hold Clues to Covid-19," *Inside Climate News*, April 8, 2020, https:// insideclimatenews.org/news/08042020/epa-secret-science-coronavirus-covid/.

16 Maine Climate Council Scientific and Technical Subcommittee, *Scientific Assessment of Climate Change and Its Effects in Maine*, August 2020, www .maine.gov/future/sites/maine.gov.future/files/inline-files/GOPIF_STS _REPORT_092320.pdf.

17 Center for Climate and Energy Solutions, "Regional Greenhouse Gas Initiative (RGGI)," accessed December 24, 2020, www.c2es.org/content/regional -greenhouse-gas-initiative-rggi/.

18 Kevin Miller, "Groups Pushing to Extend Timeline for Lawsuits over PFAS Pollution," *Portland Press Herald*, July 27, 2020, www.pressherald.com/2020/07 /27/groups-pushing-to-extend-timeline-for-lawsuits-over-pfas-pollution/.

6. Pulling Together Your Vision

1 Peter Senge, *The Fifth Discipline* (New York: Doubleday, 1990), 150.

2 Danone, "Our Vision," accessed December 24, 2020, www.danone.com/about -danone/sustainable-value-creation/our-vision.html.

3 City council of Oberlin, OH, *City of Oberlin Climate Action Plan 2019*, August 2019, www.cityofoberlin.com/wp-content/uploads/2019/09/2019-Climate -Action-Plan-Update.pdf.

4 US Climate Alliance, accessed November 28, 2020, www.usclimatealliance .org.

5 C40 Cities, accessed November 28, 2020, www.C40.org.

6 Used with permission. Vision for Vermont, "Second Draft: VISION FOR VERMONT Vision Statement," August 29, 2019, www.visionforvermont.org /vision-statement.

7 Sewing for Change, accessed November 28, 2020, www.sewingforchange.net.

8 Peggy Holman, *The Change Handbook* (Oakland, CA: Berrett-Koehler, 2007).

7. Using Power for Good

1 Robinson Meyer, "The Oil Industry Is Quietly Winning Local Climate Fights," *The Atlantic,* February 20, 2020, www.theatlantic.com/science/archive/2020/02 /oil-industry-fighting-climate-policy-states/606640/.

2 Adapted from: Sierra Club, *The Sierra Club Movement Organizing Manual 2016* (Oakland, CA: Sierra Club, 2016), 45–46, www.sierraclub.org/sites/www .sierraclub.org/files/program/documents/Movement-Organizing-Manual -2016.pdf.

3 Ellen Knickmeyer, "EPA Ends Regulation of Water Contaminant," *Boston Globe,* June 19, 2020.

4 Rachel Ramirez, "Wake Up Call," *Grist,* May 4, 2020, https://grist.org/justice /as-coronavirus-ravages-louisiana-cancer-alley-residents-havent-given-up-the -fight-against-polluters/.

5 Ramirez, "Wake Up Call."

6 Sabrina Canfield, "Cancer Alley Residents Decry Environmental Racism in Louisiana," *Court House News,* January 15, 2019, www.courthousenews.com /cancer-alley-residents-decry-environmental-racism-in-louisiana/; and Sabrina Canfield, "Scathing Report Calls 'Cancer Alley' Land Use Changes Deceitful," *Court House News,* June 13, 2019, www.courthousenews.com/scathing-report -calls-cancer-alley-land-use-changes-deceitful/.

7 Sabrina Canfield, "Louisiana OKs Permit for Plastics Plants in Cancer Alley," *Court House News,* February 4, 2019, www.courthousenews.com/louisiana -oks-permit-for-plastics-plant-in-cancer-alley/.

8 Ramirez, "Wake Up Call."

9 CBC Radio, "'Water Is Alive': Autumn Peltier Receives Water Warrior Award," March 29, 2019, in *Unreserved,* podcast, 6:00, www.cbc.ca/radio /unreserved/water-how-indigenous-people-are-turning-the-tide-1.5070498 /water-is-alive-autumn-peltier-receives-water-warrior-award-1.5075597.

10 Center for Courage & Renewal, "The Tragic Gap," podcast, 8:39, accessed January 4, 2021, www.couragerenewal.org/the-tragic-gap.

11 Doug McKenzie-Mohr and William Smith, *Fostering Sustainable Behavior: An Introduction to Community-Based Social Marketing* (Gabriola Island, BC: New Society Publishers, 2011).

12 Christiana Figueres and Tom Rivett-Carnac, *The Future We Choose: Solving the Climate Crisis* (New York: Alfred A. Knopf, 2020).

13 "Environmental Justice Case Study: Shintech PVC Plant in Convent, Louisiana," accessed December 24, 2020, http://umich.edu/~snre492/shin.html.

14 Canfield, "Cancer Alley Residents."

15 Gavin Musynske, "US Farmworkers Win Union on Farms of Campbell's Soup, 1978–1986," Global Nonviolent Action Database, October 10, 2009, https://nvdatabase.swarthmore.edu/content/us-farmworkers-win-union-farms-campbells-soup-1978-1986.

16 Corporate Campaign, "FLOC vs. The Campbell Soup Company: 1985–86," accessed December 24, 2020, www.corporatecampaign.org/history_floc_campbell_1985.php.

17 Associated Press, "Migrant Farm Workers End Dispute with Campbell Soup Co.," February 22, 1986, https://apnews.com/article/c3eb40fa19639297e7991c2a14af4cc6.

18 Musynske, "US Farmworkers."

19 BlackPast, "(1857) Frederick Douglass, 'If There Is No Struggle, There Is No Progress,'" January 25, 2007, www.blackpast.org/african-american-history/1857-frederick-douglass-if-there-no-struggle-there-no-progress/.

20 McKenzie-Mohr and Smith, *Fostering Sustainable Behavior*, 91–92.

21 Nelson D. Schwartz, "Pay Cuts Become a Tool for Some Companies to Avoid Layoffs," *New York Times*, May 29, 2020, www.nytimes.com/2020/05/24/business/economy/coronavirus-pay-cuts.html.

22 Libertina Brandt, "List of Business Leaders Giving Up Salaries during the Pandemic," *Business Insider*, April 1, 2020, www.businessinsider.com/list-of-business-leaders-giving-up-salaries-during-the-pandemic-2020-3.

23 APM Research Lab staff, "The Color of Coronavirus: COVID-19 Deaths by Race and Ethnicity in the U.S.," APM Research Lab, December 10, 2020, www.apmresearchlab.org/covid/deaths-by-race.

24 Daniel Raimi, "The Challenge of Diversity in the Environmental Movement, with Dorceta Taylor," in *Resources Radio,* podcast, 31:39, July 23, 2019, www.resourcesmag.org/resources-radio/challenge-diversity-environmental -movement-dorceta-taylor/.

25 Benjamin F. Chavis and Charles Lee, *Toxic Wastes and Race in the United States: A National Report on the Racial and Socio-Economic Characteristics of Communities with Hazardous Waste Sites* (New York: Commission for Racial Justice, United Church of Christ, 1987), www.nrc.gov/docs/ML1310/ML13109A339 .pdf.

26 Renee Skelton and Vernice Miller, "The Environmental Justice Movement," Natural Resources Defense Council, March 2016, www.nrdc.org/stories /environmental-justice-movement.

27 Dorceta E. Taylor, *The State of Diversity in Environmental Organizations* (Washington, DC: Green 2.0, 2014), https://orgs.law.harvard.edu/els/files/2014/02 /FullReport_Green2.0_FINALReducedSize.pdf.

28 Eric Liu, *You're More Powerful Than You Think: A Citizen's Guide to Making Change Happen* (New York: PublicAffairs, 2017), 26.

29 Camilo Maldonado, "Trump Tax Cuts Helped Billionaires Pay Less Taxes Than the Working Class in 2018," *Forbes,* October 30, 2019, www.forbes.com/sites /camilomaldonado/2019/10/10/trump-tax-cuts-helped-billionaires-pay-less -taxes-than-the-working-class-in-2018/?sh=22e25ac73128.

8. Creating a Winning Strategy

1 Women's March, "Women's Agenda," accessed December 24, 2020, www .womensmarch.com/agenda.

2 Jessa Crispin, "What Has the Women's March Accomplished, beyond Mere Visibility?" *The Guardian,* January 19, 2019, www.theguardian.com/commentisfree /2019/jan/19/womens-march-criticism-leaders-political-action-visibility.

3 Exploring Your Mind, "The Six Degrees of Separation Theory," April 23, 2019, www.exploringyourmind.com/the-six-degrees-of-separation-theory/.

4 Ecotrust, "Mission & Values," accessed December 24, 2020, www.ecotrust.org /about-us/mission/.

5 Sarah Rankin, "Energy Pipeline Companies Cancel Atlantic Coast Pipeline," *Portland Press Herald,* July 6, 2020, www.pressherald.com/2020/07/05/energy -companies-cancel-contested-atlantic-coast-pipeline/.

6 Groups working on this issue include the Environmental Working Group (www.ewg.org) and Defend Our Health (www.defendourhealth.org).

7 Jimmy Golen, "Student Climate Protests Delay Harvard-Yale Game," *Maine Sunday Telegram*, November 24, 2019, A11.

8 Emily Pontecorvo, "Harvard Activists' New Fossil Fuel Divestment Strategy: Make It an Inside Job," *Grist*, August 25, 2020, https://grist.org/climate /harvard-activists-new-fossil-fuel-divestment-strategy-make-it-an-inside-job/.

9. Building and Managing Your Campaign

1 Naomi Klein, *No Is Not Enough: Resisting Trump's Shock Politics and Winning the World We Need* (Chicago: Haymarket Books, 2017), 233.

2 America's Story from America's Library, "The Consequences of *Silent Spring*," Library of Congress, www.americaslibrary.gov/aa/carson/aa_carson_consequenc _1.html.

3 Emily Holden, "Revealed: How the Gas Industry Is Waging War against Climate Action," *The Guardian*, August 20, 2020, www.theguardian.com/environment /2020/aug/20/gas-industry-waging-war-against-climate-action.

4 Robinson Meyer, "The Oil Industry Is Quietly Winning Local Climate Fights," *The Atlantic*, February 20, 2020, www.theatlantic.com/science/archive/2020/02 /oil-industry-fighting-climate-policy-states/606640/.

5 Meyer, "Oil Industry."

6 Sandra Laville, "Top Oil Firms Spending Millions Lobbying to Block Climate Change Policies, Says Report," *The Guardian*, March 21, 2019, www .theguardian.com/business/2019/mar/22/top-oil-firms-spending-millions -lobbying-to-block-climate-change-policies-says-report.

7 Mona Hanna-Attisha, *What the Eyes Don't See: A Story of Crisis, Resistance, and Hope in an American City* (New York: One World, 2018).

8 Melissa Denchak, "Flint Water Crisis: Everything You Need to Know," Natural Resources Defense Council, November 8, 2018, www.nrdc.org/stories/flint -water-crisis-everything-you-need-know.

9 Karen Pinchin, "EPA Says Flint Water Is Safe—Scientists Aren't So Sure," *Frontline*, September 10, 2019, www.pbs.org/wgbh/frontline/article/epa-says -flints-water-is-safe-scientists-arent-so-sure/.

10 Hanna-Attisha, *What the Eyes Don't See.*

11 Amy McKeever, "How the Americans with Disabilities Act Transformed a Country," *National Geographic,* July 30, 2020, www.nationalgeographic.com /history/2020/07/americans-disabilities-act-transformed-united-states/.

12 Arlene Mayerson, "The History of the Americans with Disabilities Act: A Movement Perspective," Disability Rights Education and Defense Fund, 1992, https://dredf.org/about-us/publications/the-history-of-the-ada/.

13 *Crip Camp: A Disability Revolution,* written and directed by Nicole Newnham and Jim LeBrecht (Los Gatos, CA: Netflix, 2020), www.netflix.com/watch /81001496.

10. Working with Decision Makers

1 Hanna King, "US AIDS Coalition to Unleash Power (ACT-UP) Demands Access to Drugs, 1987–89," Global Nonviolent Action Database, accessed October 17, 2020, https://nvdatabase.swarthmore.edu/content/us-aids-coalition -unleash-power-act-demands-access-drugs-1987-89.

2 Michael Spector, "How Anthony Fauci Became America's Doctor," *New Yorker,* April 20, 2020, www.newyorker.com/magazine/2020/04/20/how-anthony -fauci-became-americas-doctor.

3 Spector, "Anthony Fauci."

4 Somini Sengupta and Lisa Friedman, "At UN Climate Summit, Few Commitments and US Silence," *New York Times,* September 23, 2019, www.nytimes .com/2019/09/23/climate/climate-summit-global-warming.html.

5 This is a paraphrase of Gandhi's words, which were: "We but mirror the world. All the tendencies present in the outer world are to be found in the world of our body. If we could change ourselves, the tendencies in the world would also change. As a man changes his own nature, so does that attitude of the world change towards him." Joseph Ranseth, "Gandhi Didn't Actually Ever Say 'Be the Change You Want to See in the World.' Here's the Real Quote ...," August 27, 2015, https://josephranseth .com/gandhi-didnt-say-be-the-change-you-want-to-see-in-the-world/.

6 Maine Stat. title 12, part 9, § 6072.

11. Framing Your Message

1 George Lakoff, *Don't Think of an Elephant! Know Your Values and Frame the Debate* (White River Junction, VT: Chelsea Green, 2004), xi.

2 Robert Perez and Amy Simon, *Heartwired: Human Behavior, Strategic Opinion Research, and the Audacious Pursuit of Social Change* (Los Altos, CA: Packard Foundation, 2017), www.packard.org/wp-content/uploads/2017/05/Heartwired-digital.pdf.

3 Lakoff, *Elephant.*

4 Lakoff, *Elephant,* xii.

5 Perez and Simon, *Heartwired.*

6 Maine Climate Table and Goodwin Simon Strategic Research, *Communicating with Mainers on Climate Change: A Toolkit* (Augusta: Maine Climate Table, 2017). Used with permission.

7 Perez and Simon, *Heartwired.*

8 Susan Nall Bales, Julie Sweetland, and Andrew Volmert, *How to Talk about Climate Change and the Ocean* (Washington, DC: FrameWorks Institute, 2015), www.frameworksinstitute.org/publication/how-to-talk-about-climate-change-and-the-ocean-prepared-for-the-national-network-for-ocean-and-climate-change-interpretation-with-support-from-the-national-science-foundation/. Used with permission.

9 Bales, Sweetland, and Volmert, *How to Talk.*

10 Bales, Sweetland, and Volmert, *How to Talk.*

11 Richard Wilkinson and Kate Pickett, *The Spirit Level: Why Greater Equality Makes Societies Stronger* (New York: Bloomsbury Publishing, 2011).

12 Wilkinson and Pickett, *Spirit Level.*

13 Wilkinson and Pickett, *Spirit Level.*

14 Wilkinson and Pickett, *Spirit Level.*

15 Wilkinson and Pickett, *Spirit Level.*

16 MICATS, "Breaking: Michigan and Indiana Activists Blockade Tar Sands Pipeline with Treesit," *Earth First! Journal,* September 16, 2013, https://earthfirstjournal.org/newswire/2013/09/16/breaking-michigan-activists-blockade-tar-sands-pipeline-with-treesit/.

12. Communicating with Impact

1 Doug McKenzie-Mohr and William Smith, *Fostering Sustainable Behavior: An Introduction to Community-Based Social Marketing* (Gabriola Island, BC: New Society Publishers, 2011).

2 McKenzie-Mohr and Smith, *Fostering Sustainable Behavior.*

3 Sunrise Movement, "About the Sunrise Movement," accessed December 24, 2020, www.sunrisemovement.org/about/?ms=AboutTheSunriseMovement.

4 Extinction Rebellion, "About Us," accessed November 29, 2020, https://rebellion.global/about-us/.

5 Extinction Rebellion, accessed November 29, 2020, https://rebellion.global.

6 Joel J. Davis, "The Effects of Message Framing on Response to Environmental Communications," *Journalism and Mass Communication Quarterly* 72, no. 2 (June 1, 1995): 285–99, https://journals.sagepub.com/doi/10.1177/107769909507200203.

7 Kit Smith, "53 Incredible Facebook Statistics and Facts," *Brandwatch,* June 1, 2019, www.brandwatch.com/blog/facebook-statistics/; David Carrington, "How Many Photos Will Be Taken in 2020?" Mylio, January 10, 2020, https://focus.mylio.com/tech-today/how-many-photos-will-be-taken-in-2020.

8 "From Photos to Video—10 Principles to Communicate Climate Change," Resource Media, May 14, 2019, www.resource-media.org/from-photos-to-video-10-principles-to-communicate-climate-change/. Used with permission.

9 Used with permission from Defend Our Health.

10 Rachel Ball, *When I Tell My Story, I'm in Charge* (Melbourne, AU: Victoria Law Foundation, 2013), https://victorialawfoundation.org.au/sites/default/files/attachments/VLF%20-%20CLC%20final%20report%2012-13%20_Final_web.pdf.

11 Used with permission from Defend Our Health.

13. Working with the Media and the Public

1 Beki Winchel, "Report: 83% of Journalists Use Twitter—but Most Still Want Email Pitches," *Ragan's PR Daily,* July 3, 2019, www.prdaily.com/report-83-of-journalists-use-twitter-but-most-still-want-email-pitches/.

2 Eli Rosenberg, "Trump Said Sinclair 'Is Far Superior to CNN': What We Know about the Conservative Media Giant," *Washington Post,* April 3, 2018, www.washingtonpost.com/news/style/wp/2018/04/02/get-to-know-sinclair-broadcast-group-the-conservative-local-news-giant-with-a-growing-reach/.

3 Journalism and media staff, "Video Length," Pew Research Center, July 16, 2012, www.journalism.org/2012/07/16/video-length/.

4 Wikipedia, s.v. "Inverted pyramid (journalism)," last modified October 2, 2020, 2:21, https://en.wikipedia.org/wiki/Inverted_pyramid_(journalism).

5 "Our Readers Write about ...," *The Working Waterfront*, December–January 2020, www.islandinstitute.org/working-waterfront-category/letters-to-the-editor/. Used with permission.

6 Ballotpedia, "Cities That Allow Direct Legislation Via Ballot Initiatives," accessed December 24, 2020, https://ballotpedia.org/Cities_that_allow_direct_legislation_via_ballot_initiatives.

7 City of Austin Office of the City Auditor, *Special Report on Citizen Initiatives*, October 2019, www.austintexas.gov/sites/default/files/files/Auditor/Audit_Reports/Citizen_Initiatives_AS19101_October_2019.pdf.

8 Nick Licata, *Becoming a Citizen Activist* (Seattle: Sasquatch Books, 2017).

9 Reid Wilson, "Initiative Spending Booms Past $1 Billion as Corporations Sponsor Their Own Proposals," *Washington Post*, November 8, 2013, www.washingtonpost.com/blogs/govbeat/wp/2013/11/08/initiative-spending-booms-past-1-billion-as-corporations-sponsor-their-own-proposals/.

10 For more information on self-organizing forums, see Harrison Owen, *Open Space Technology: A User's Guide* (Oakland, CA: Berrett-Koehler, 2008).

14. Epilogue: Eight Reasons to Be Optimistic in Troubled Times

1 Daniel LeDuc, "Who Is Generation Z," *Trust*, May 20, 2019, www.pewtrusts.org/en/trust/archive/spring-2019/who-is-generation-z.

2 Alexandra Levit with Dr. Sanja Licina, *How the Recession Shaped Millennial and Hiring Manager Attitudes about Millennials' Future Careers*, Career Advisory Board, 2011, www.careeradvisoryboard.org/content/dam/dvu/www_careeradvisoryboard_org/Future-of-Millennial-Careers-Report.pdf.

3 Art Kleiner and Juliette Powell, "Jeremy Rifkin on How to Manage a Future of Abundance," *Strategy + Business*, November 13, 2017, www.strategy-business.com/article/Jeremy-Rifkin-on-How-to-Manage-a-Future-of-Abundance?gko=5fad8.

4 Legatum Institute, *2016 Legatum Prosperity Index* (London: Legatum Institute, 2016), https://li.com/reports/2016-legatum-prosperity-index-10th-edition/.

5 Legatum Institute, *2016 Legatum Prosperity Index*.

6 Richard Wilkinson and Kate Pickett, *The Spirit Level: Why Greater Equality Makes Societies Stronger* (New York: Bloomsbury Publishing, 2011).

7 Peter Diamandis and Steven Kotler, *The Future Is Faster Than You Think* (New York: Simon and Schuster, 2020).

8 Cary Funk and Alec Tyson, "Millennial and Gen Z Republicans Stand Out from Their Elders on Climate and Energy Issues," Pew Research Center, June 2020, www.pewresearch.org/fact-tank/2020/06/24/millennial-and-gen-z-republicans-stand-out-from-their-elders-on-climate-and-energy-issues/.

Index

About the Author

Since childhood, Sue Inches has envisioned a world that is compassionate, inclusive, and environmentally aware. This vision guided her throughout her schooling and a twenty-five-year career in public policy. As deputy director of the Maine State Planning Office, Inches managed a portfolio of environmental issues on behalf of the governor. In this position, she directed research, designed and led public engagement processes, and lobbied in the legislature. Prior to this, she worked with the fishing industries as a director at the Maine Department of Marine Resources. Signature policy issues she has worked on include fisheries, land-use planning, smart growth, building and energy codes, renewable energy, energy efficiency, working waterfront access, community finance, and rural broadband.

In 2018, Inches developed a unique college course on environmental advocacy, which she now teaches at several private colleges. Few schools offer courses in advocacy skills, and students are eager to learn them. Demand for the course led her to write this book.

Inches now works as a speaker, educator, and advocate with a focus on the environment and climate change. She helps people find their power and provides them with the tools and guidance to address current environmental issues. She holds a BA in Human Ecology from College of the Atlantic, and an MBA from the University of New Hampshire.

About North Atlantic Books

North Atlantic Books (NAB) is a 501(c)(3) nonprofit publisher committed to a bold exploration of the relationships between mind, body, spirit, culture, and nature. Founded in 1974, NAB aims to nurture a holistic view of the arts, sciences, humanities, and healing. To make a donation or to learn more about our books, authors, events, and newsletter, please visit www.northatlanticbooks.com.